P9-DOF-938

The **Politically Incorrect Guide**™ to

THE SOUTH

(and Why It Will Rise Again)

The **Politically Incorrect Guide**™ to

THE SOUTH

(and Why It Will Rise Again)

Clint Johnson

Since 1947
REGNERY
PUBLISHING, INC.
An Eagle Publishing Company • Washington, DC
www.regnery.com

Copyright © 2006 by Clint Johnson

All rights reserved. No part of this publication may be reproduced or transmitted in any form or by any means electronic or mechanical, including photocopy, recording, or any information storage and retrieval system now known or to be invented, without permission in writing from the publisher, except by a reviewer who wishes to quote brief passages in connection with a review written for inclusion in a magazine, newspaper, or broadcast.

Cataloging-in-Publication data on file with the Library of Congress

ISBN 1-59698-500-3
ISBN 978-1-59698-500-1

Published in the United States by
Regnery Publishing, Inc.
One Massachusetts Avenue, NW
Washington, DC 20001
www.regnery.com

Manufactured in the United States of America

10 9 8 7 6

Books are available in quantity for promotional or premium use. Write to Director of Special Sales, Regnery Publishing, Inc., One Massachusetts Avenue NW, Washington, DC 20001, for information on discounts and terms or call (202) 216-0600.

This book is for
all the Southern soldiers in my family
and the women who loved them.

CONTENTS

Introduction: **Slamming the South**   1

Part I: WHY IT'S GREAT TO BE A SOUTHERNER   7

Chapter 1: **Southern by the Grace of God: What Other Regions Ain't Got but Sure Wish They Did**   9

Defining Southern culture

The Southern smile shines

Gentility and good manners are expected down South

Southerners always have a sense of place

Old-time religion is good enough for the South

Southerners love contact sports

Southerners carry guns

Southern culture in a nutshell: religious, funny good ol' boys and gals with a love of home and a smile for strangers

Chapter 2: **The South and Southerners We Love**   31

Southerners act different

Southerners talk different

Southerners eat different

Southerners are less race conscious than folks up North

Southerners aren't elitists

How to impress a Southerner: know cars, country music, racin', and Mayberry

True Southerners still have heroes

Chapter 3: **Things You Didn't Know about the South**   49

The South's anthem: "Dixie"

The best schools really are in the South

The South spawned rock and roll

The South was making movies when Hollywood was
    nowhere

Chapter 4:   **Places and Events That Explain the South**   59

Historic Southern locations

Historic Southern events

Historic Southern homes

Part II: AMERICAN HISTORY, SOUTHERN STYLE   75

Chapter 5:   **Southern Colonies Birth the New World**   77

The South once spoke Spanish

The South's lost colony

Jamestown and the arrival of black slavery

A Southern bouillabaisse of nationalities

Chapter 6:   **The South Starts and Wins the Revolution**   87

Protests of English taxes started in the South

Fighting for freedom started in the South

Southerners were more ready to fight than Northerners

Southerners win the Revolution

The South's redneck general was the best

Southerners were more patriotic

Chapter 7:   **Southerners Create America's Government**   101

Southerners bring order to chaos

Southerners drive the Constitutional Convention

Northerners argue that slaves are property

Northerners fight harder for federalism

Southerners fix the Constitution

Southerners select the nation's capital

Chapter 8:   **Southerners Expand the Nation**   111

Southerners create the modern-day Midwest

Southerners prove the Constitution works

Contents

Yankees threaten secession

How Southerners won the War of 1812

Slackers and fighters during the Black Hawk War

Southerners explore and acquire the American West

Chapter 9: **The Nation's "Mark of Cain"**   123

Northerners ran the slave trade

New York refused to abandon the slave trade

Not even war slowed the Yankee slave trade

Slavery was less cruel in the South

Southern slaves lived much like free blacks—and whites

The race of plantation owners may be surprising

Chapter 10: **Why the South Seceded**   135

There was no civil war

The South wanted its independence

Secession was an economic issue

When did abolition become a war aim?

The War wasn't about slavery; it was about states' rights

Chapter 11: **Total War versus Noble War**   149

Lincoln lied to everyone about Fort Sumter

Lincoln attacks early and often

The Union turns nasty

The South was kinder to its enemies

Defeat but not dishonor

The North threatens continued violence

Chapter 12: **The Secret History of the War**   169

An army of immigrants

War for cotton?

Cotton-producing states were targeted first

Lincoln planned to colonize freed slaves

Lincoln was no defender of civil rights

Davis ignored his critics

Why Lincoln's Emancipation Proclamation was a sham
Blacks get the "presidential" treatment
Andersonville and the horror of the prison camps
God recognized the Confederacy
Southern women were the backbone of the Confederacy

Chapter 13: **Reconstruction . . . or Deconstruction?**   **199**
Confederates were accused of treason, but never tried
Little "reconstruction" was done during Reconstruction
Reconstruction: the good
Reconstruction: the bad

Chapter 14: **The South Rises Again**   **209**
Wheeler praises his black soldiers
Bygones are finally bygones

Chapter 15: **The South Saves the World**   **217**
Southerners won World War II in the Pacific theater
Southerners won the European theater

Conclusion: **The Nation Should Thank God for the South**   231

Acknowledgments   241

Bibliography   243

Index   249

Introduction

SLAMMING THE SOUTH

The South is cultivated in collards and covered in kudzu. We eat collards with black-eyed peas and hog jowls on New Year's Day to bring good luck. Kudzu was once promoted for erosion control but now covers anything that doesn't get out of its way. Many of us are descended from Scottish settlers and African slaves—and we usually find that we have more in common with each other than with Northern urbanites.

The South is steeped in history and blood; home to the battlefields where the American Revolution was won by Southerners fighting Redcoats, and where the War for Southern Independence was lost by gray-coated Southerners fighting blue-coated Yankees.

The South is where folks ask you, "Who're your people?" in search of common ancestral ground.

New England has recognizable geographic boundaries, but I doubt that a fisherman in Portland, Maine, thinks he has much in common with a banker in Boston, Massachusetts. But a banker from Birmingham, Alabama, lost on a blue highway in the mountains of North Carolina can stop at a general store and feel right at home. That's because the big-city banker and the rural Tar Heel behind the counter can tell by each other's accents that they share a common ancestry. They are both Southerners; no matter how distant the relationship, they consider themselves kinfolk.

Guess what?

✖ The South has become *the* preeminent region of the nation, outstripping everywhere else in population and economic growth.

✖ There is an open, not-at-all-secret conspiracy to erase Dixie and all vestiges of the Old South from public memory.

✖ The South *is* different from every other region of the nation. And most of us don't want to change it.

Yankees might not be from around here, but most Southerners are tolerant folk, and we'll welcome them with open arms. I did. I married one from Wisconnnnnnnnnsin (the way it sounded and still sounds to my Florida-born ears). It was the first time anyone in my family had married outside our region in more than 350 years.

But even when trying to fit in with a Southern community, Northern transplants don't always understand what deep-rooted Dixie natives know intuitively: the South *is* different from every other region of the nation. We know it. We are proud of it. And most of us don't want to change it. Some of us will fight to keep it from changing.

It is different in the South because we lost a war here. More than 260,000 Southern lives and 360,000 Northern lives, the best of the generation born between 1830 and 1845, were lost. Aside from the deaths, virtually everything of value in the South—farmsteads, crops, livestock, cities, and cash money—was destroyed.

For the surviving Southerners, there was the pain of humiliation. For a decade after the war, the vanquished were given precise instructions by the victors as to what they could not do. The vanquished couldn't vote, couldn't protest the occupation, couldn't erect monuments to their war dead, couldn't even wear military-looking brass buttons on their civilian coats. Pride of service and pride of place were denied Southerners as a condition of losing the war.

When the decade called Reconstruction was over, the South underwent another hundred years of unofficial reconstructing. It wasn't until the 1970s that the South finally, shakily reemerged on the national scene as a region the rest of the country would have to reckon with.

Now, more than thirty years later, the South has become *the* preeminent region of the nation, outstripping everywhere else in population and economic growth as Northerners grow tired of big cities, big taxes, big weather, and big politicians. Even though chamber of commerce types have grafted Arizona, Nevada, and New Mexico onto our western border so they can dub the region the "Sun Belt," Southerners know what makes up the South, and areas west of Texas and north of Kentucky, Missouri, and Maryland ain't it.

We natives don't mind the increasing population in our region as much as we mind what is being done to the South to make everyone feel "included."

There is an open, not-at-all-secret conspiracy to erase Dixie and all vestiges of the Old South from public memory. The goal is to take away the South's distinctiveness, to make it a plain, homogenized version of most everywhere else in the nation with no interesting accents, no rebellious history, no cultural heritage. The South will end up covered with strip malls and fast-food joints, where the people meekly do what they are told by politicians and businesspeople who have no social, historical, or family ties to the people living here. If the leaders and followers of this movement succeed, the South will one day be no more a distinctive region than the amorphously named Midwest.

Southerners are religious, and honoring our ancestors, our sacred dead, is a duty. But today every single Confederate symbol—located in and out of the South—is under attack: battle flags, soldier statues, streets and public parks named after Confederate soldiers, even tunes like "Dixie." The most visible of these symbols, the Confederate battle flag, is already gone from public view. The next target will be memory itself. Even thinking fondly of the Confederacy has become suspect. The opening paragraph of a January 19, 2006, editorial in the *Dallas Morning News* declared that a state holiday designated as Confederate Heroes Day (January 19, Robert E. Lee's birthday) was "silly."

What is most troubling is that much of this "hate the South" movement is homegrown. That editorial could have appeared in any of the newspapers in any of the states that once made up the Confederacy. Virtually all of the South's newspaper editorial writers and the region's government officials favor erasing Southern history to salve the feelings of anyone who might be "offended"—and because they think it's good for the "business climate" because it removes "controversy."

But it also removes our history, our heritage, and a true understanding of what our history and heritage are, not only as Southerners, but as Americans.

The Politically Incorrect Guide™ to the South is here to even the score. It tells the truth about the South, its history, and what makes it great. This won't be a selective history—no defenses will be offered for slavery, segregation, or racial discrimination—but it will give the other side of the story too.

It's a side I know not only from study, but from personal experience. I was raised on a cattle and orange farm in pre-Disneyfied Florida in an unincorporated community called Fish Branch (named after a creek that feeds into the Peace River) in rural Hardee County. As a toddler, I rode on the laps of black farm workers, laughing as they sang to me, while my mother drove them back to town. As a boy I worked beside them in my father's fields.

I learned about my Confederate ancestors from my Georgia-born grandmother, and her stories took on new life in my imagination when I discovered *The Gray Ghost* television show in 1957. Each week, the upstanding, honest, brave Gray Ghost (Colonel John Singleton Mosby) would lead raids on the dastardly, lying, thieving Yankees. The next day I would put on my gray pants and a cheap felt cap with a Confederate battle flag on top, grab a long stick that looked to me like a musket, and run around the yard following the instructions of Stonewall Jackson to his troops at First Manassas to "yell like furies." What I didn't learn until much later was that Mosby was played by Tod Andrews, a native of New York State. Shocking, yes, but we Southerners are a forgiving lot. And in those days, Confederate heroes were still *American* heroes.

My fourth-grade teacher in Arcadia, Florida, Miss Frances Pooser, sealed my image of myself as a Confederate when she told the class the exciting story of how a militia force of old men and young boys repulsed a Union invasion at the Battle of Natural Bridge, near Tallahassee, in March 1865. A few weeks later, on a field trip to Thomas Edison's winter home in the small town of Fort Myers (named after Jewish Confederate colonel Abraham Myers), Miss Pooser told me to breathe deeply while standing next to a particularly fragrant flower. That flower was Confederate jasmine. I'm not much of a horticulturist, but I still like the sweet smell of that star-shaped white flower.

The South is all about memory, heritage, and pride of place. I refuse to go along with the expunging of that memory, heritage, and pride, and I hope the readers of this book, Northern and Southern, will rise up and join me in protesting those who are trying to do it. For all our sakes, it's time for the South to rise again.

Part I

WHY IT'S GREAT
TO BE A SOUTHERNER

Chapter 1

☆☆☆☆☆☆☆

SOUTHERN BY THE GRACE OF GOD

WHAT OTHER REGIONS AIN'T GOT BUT SURE WISH THEY DID

Novelist William Faulkner captured the uneasiness felt by non-natives when he wrote an exchange between a Yankee-born Harvard student questioning his Mississippi-born roommate in *Absalom, Absalom!*: "Tell about the South. What's it like there. What do they do there. Why do they live there. Why do they live at all."

Faulkner, a son of Mississippi himself, recognized that breathless Yankees speak so fast that they don't have time for question marks.

The appraisal of the region by people who ain't from around here hasn't changed much in sixty-five years. It is partly the fault of Southerners like North Carolinian W. J. Cash, who released his one and only book, *The Mind of the South,* in 1941. Cash described the South in some complimentary ways: "one of extravagant colors, of proliferating foliage and bloom, of floating yellow sunlight, and above all, perhaps of haze . . . a sort of cosmic conspiracy against reality in favor of romance," and "not exactly a nation within a nation but the closest thing to it."

While that was nice of him, Cash took the rest of the book to forever embed in some Northern minds that Southerners of all races and classes were lazy, violent, uneducated, and uneducatable. His assessment was popular in Northern circles. A 1941 *Time* magazine reporter wrote that anyone else describing the South would have to start where Cash left off. Even

Guess what?

- There has been an identifiable Southern culture since colonial days.
- Most native Southerners can trace their families back for generations in the Southland, and pride in one's Southern roots crosses racial boundaries.
- Southern women are prettier, Southern men are handier, and the South's climate is the best in the nation.

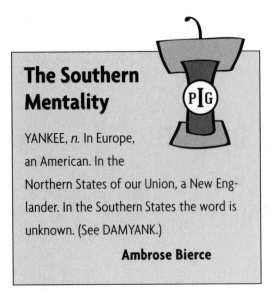

The Southern Mentality

YANKEE, *n*. In Europe, an American. In the Northern States of our Union, a New Englander. In the Southern States the word is unknown. (See DAMYANK.)

Ambrose Bierce

today, many Northerners still believe it is 1941 in the South. When a fiftieth anniversary edition of the book was reissued in 1991, the *New York Times* book reviewer wrote: "No one, among the multitudes who have written about the South, has been more penetrating or more persuasive than Mr. Cash."

Political writers seem most prone to—and enthusiastic about—perpetuating the image of a dark and dangerous Dixie. In 1976 *Newsweek* published an entire issue explaining the South to its sophisticated Northern readers who were shocked and puzzled at how a peanut farmer from Georgia captured the Democratic presidential nomination. The scene was replayed in 1992 when an Arkansan was elected president, and again in 2004 when North Carolina senator John Edwards ran for president. The Northern press was fascinated that Edwards, the son of a Southern textile mill manager, had gone to law school. The political accomplishments of Northeasterner John Kerry were only what was expected of him, but Edwards was treated as an anomaly, someone who had succeeded despite being Southern. At least the Democratic Party knows it can't win a national election without a Southerner on the ticket.

Defining Southern culture

There has been an identifiable Southern culture since colonial days, when Southerners and Northerners clashed over all types of issues—including how to govern the new nation, how to pay off American Revolutionary War debts, industrialization versus agrarianism, the need for a national bank, westward expansion, and the future admittance of territories as states. Two hundred and fifty years ago, Southerners thought of Northerners as crass, commercial, mannerless opportunists who often had no religion. Northerners thought of Southerners as uneducated, lazy, violent, bigoted rednecks and aristocrats (planters).

Today, Southerners have by and large softened their views on their distant neighbors, but curiously, the reverse has not happened. The Northeasterners and Left Coasters still seem to think of the South as a bigoted, backward, violent place. But guess what? The first state to elect a black governor was a Southern one—Virginia elected Doug Wilder in 1989, and he took office in the former Confederate capital. If the South is racist, why did a 2003 Census Bureau report find that hundreds of thousands of blacks are abandoning the North and moving South? The Northeast is the only region losing population in every single minority group. The South is the only region to show a gain in every single minority group.

According to the 2000 Census, the South had a net increase of nearly two million new residents, while the liberal Northeast had a net population decrease of more than one million. The South is now the nation's

★ ★ ★ ★ ★ ★ ★ ★ ★ ★ ★ ★ ★

Southerners Dig Deeper

The 2005 Generosity Index, released by the Catalogue for Philanthropy, shows Southern states in the top and Yankee states in the bottom when it comes to charitable giving. This index (based on 2003 tax returns) compared each state's per capita giving with income and found that of the top twenty states, *ten* are Southern. More astonishing is that the top two states, Mississippi (1) and Arkansas (2), are ranked as fiftieth and forty-sixth respectively in the "Having Rank" of well-to-do states. The top three stingiest states are New Hampshire (Having Rank: 8), Massachusetts (Having Rank: 3), and New Jersey (Having Rank: 2). Southerners are definitely the nation's most generous citizens. They'll even give you their last bottom dollar.

biggest region, with 36 percent of the nation's population despite the big cities of the Northeast and the West Coast.

What makes the South so attractive, so popular that people are flocking to it in huge numbers? The weather's nice, of course, but mainly it must be Southern culture, the way people of all races in the South have always lived their lives. While "culture" can be as hard to nail down as molasses, it can be defined in the South.

The Southern smile shines

Southerners visiting any Northern city are always struck by who and what they see on the sidewalks: blank-faced or frowning people walking with their heads and eyes down, their ears shielded from unwelcome sounds by plastic plugs blaring some kind of music. No one in the North looks at or speaks to each other as they rush toward another day in a big office tower. Personal contact with strangers on the street is virtually unheard of and socially discouraged. Perhaps that's a deep-seated psychological holdover from the Puritans who settled New England. Or maybe it's a defense mechanism adopted by big-city dwellers who see too many people every day to make friends with all of them.

Maybe the simpler explanation is that Yankees (defined by Southerners as anyone who lives or was born north of the Mason-Dixon Line between Maryland and Pennsylvania) are just plain unfriendly to each other.

Southerners *are* friendlier than Northerners, and they love to demonstrate it when visiting those strange lands to the north and west. Southerners in New York City and Los Angeles, those self-appointed trend-setting centers of style and human behavior, get a kick out of walking down the street, riding the bus or subway and smiling at strangers, maybe throwing in a "Hey!" or "Howdy!" just for good measure. The Yankees on the receiving end invariably wonder and worry about the unsolicited smile and the audacity of a stranger speaking to them.

Conversely, there is no shock to getting unsolicited looks and smiles in Southern big cities. Throwing grins and greetings to strangers in New Orleans, Birmingham, Dallas, and Charlotte only gets the same in return. That is because Southerners enjoy greeting one another whether they know each other or not. It may be as simple as the finger nod of a pickup truck driver to the gentle wave of elderly folks sitting on their front porches.

The Southern Mentality

"A southerner talks music."

Mark Twain

How did this tradition of friendliness catch hold in the South? It likely dates back to the days when the South was more rural. Farmers often depended on each other to borrow tools, help put in and harvest crops, and work livestock. With the exception of Charleston, South Carolina, which was a major colonial city along with Boston, Philadelphia, and New York, the South's big cities were really small towns compared to the metropolises of the North. Everyone of all races and classes knew each other, and even one's competitors deserved a greeting. It was silly and impolite to do otherwise.

Gentility and good manners are expected down South

Hand in hand with friendliness among folks comes manners and gentility, two other Dixie traits that puzzle Northerners who believe that brusqueness trumps thoughtfulness. Such thinking is considered rude among native Southerners.

One of the first books published in Virginia in the seventeenth century was *The Whole Duty of Man*, which outlined gentlemanly conduct. William Byrd II, owner of the largest private library in seventeenth-century Virginia and the founder of Richmond, wrote in his diaries that men displaying good manners received power and respect from their peers. By the time Baltimore native Emily Post published *Etiquette: In Society, in Business, in Politics, and at Home* in 1922, the South was well known as a region where good manners reigned supreme, and were expected from rich and poor Southerners alike. Here's a little primer:

★ ★ ★ ★ ★ ★ ★ ★ ★ ★ ★ ★ ★ ★

Want to know the South? Then know *Gone with the Wind*

Don't fall for what New England literary spinsters tell you when they say *Gone with the Wind* is just romantic trash. You know they read it by flashlight under the covers at night, wishing they were worthy of being wooed by Rhett Butler. And you know, don't you, that *Gone with the Wind* won the Pulitzer Prize for Literature in 1937?

Gone with the Wind is more than a darn good story. Author Margaret Mitchell did her homework, and the history in it is as accurate as can be. In fact, as a book of historical fiction, it is more history than fiction. She refers to real people, and she gets the history right, the battles right, and Southern thinking right.

And while most Southerners weren't wealthy planters, Margaret Mitchell had enough respect for historical accuracy to portray them as they really were, and not as politically incorrect propagandists would have you believe. *Gone with the Wind* is full of Southern archetypes, people you'll still find leading lives south of the Mason-Dixon Line:

Rhett Butler: Southern men are famous for being dangerous in the moonlight—and they still are.

Ashley Wilkes: Doomed Southern aristocrats? They may be doomed, but you'll still find them here and there, doing good works and asking nothing in return. And they're often married to **Melanie**s, long-suffering Southern women who do the right thing regardless of what it costs them and stand by their man, no matter what. Melanie's story is tragic, but Southern women have a tradition of feeling that society is happier when men are happy, and so women make it their business to keep men happy. That's how it was in the Old South, and today you'll find this attitude far more

- Don't flaunt your advantages: You might have an Ivy League college degree—a lot of Southerners went to Princeton too (Virginian Woodrow Wilson went from heading that university to becoming president of the United States)—but you won't win any points at the general store by telling everyone.

common in the South than anywhere else in the country. This might be one big reason why Southerners are lot more contented than anyone else in the country, and why our sense of family and good manners is a lot more pronounced. It's also why Southern men still think it's important to treat women like ladies. It's plain old mutual respect rather than damn Yankee competition.

Ellen O'Hara felt the *noblesse oblige* to look after those less fortunate than herself. She considered it her Christian duty to care for the sick, even to the point of sacrificing her own life. No one in the Old South looked to the state for help—they looked to their own family or relied on the sense of personal, Christian responsibility of well-to-do Southerners like Ellen O'Hara. Melanie and Ellen represent the Southern tradition of the Great Lady who "hated the sin and... loved the sinner/and... saw that gentlemen [got] their dinner," to paraphrase Stephen Vincent Benet.

Hot-headed Irish Southerner **Gerald O'Hara,** keen on fast horses, lives on in Southerners who nowadays have turned in their fast horses for faster cars. There's a deep daredevil streak that's been the death of more than one good ol' boy with a Scots-Irish heritage.

Scarlett: The Steel Magnolia is familiar to everyone.

Southerners love—and don't shun—their eccentrics, and **Aunt Pittypat** and **Prissy** show that this love knows no racial boundaries.

And **Mammy** shows that Southerners knew no color bar when it came to considering house slaves as members of the family.

Trying to understand a Southerner? Read *Gone with the Wind*. It's the how-to manual for understanding a lot about who we are.

- Everyone deserves respect until they demonstrate they don't deserve it. In the South children are taught to listen to their elders. Donald Trump may preach that power and money are all that matter in life, but Southerners know better. They know that everyone is made in God's image and deserves consideration and respect.
- Titles are still important in the South too. Southern boys still call their elders "sir" or "ma'am." You refer to a man as Mr. (last name) or Miss/Ms. (last name) until you're given permission to use a first name. And we like to use our military titles, even if we're only Kentucky colonels.
- Everyone else matters before you do in the South. Don't ever impulsively reach for the last biscuit in the basket. Southerners insist that guests take that last biscuit even if there are more in the oven. Don't ever head out the door without holding it open for the next person. Don't ever rush an elevator. It is simple politeness to think of others before yourself in the South.
- Be helpful. See cows out on the road? Stop at the nearest farmhouse and offer to help herd them back behind the fence. See a lady standing on the side of the road staring at her flat tire? Stop and change it—even if you are in a suit on your way to a meeting. Southerners always understand the necessity of good manners.
- Be friendly. Nothing's more Southern than a sunny smile and an offer of friendly conversation or help.
- Ask, don't demand. In the South, if you're pushy, you're written off as a Yankee. People in the South have long depended on neighbors. So asking favors is natural if it's done politely. But if you're rude and aggressive, it'll backfire.

- Use the right words: "Please," "Thank you," "Yes, ma'am," "Yes, sir." Most Southerners still end telephone conversations with customer service representatives with a friendly "Thank you, ma'am. I appreciate it." Customer service representatives in India might be baffled, but Southerners won't change their ways to accommodate a little thing like globalization.

Ignoring the South's history of gentility and good manners sometimes proves disastrous. When US Air (based in Pittsburgh) bought Piedmont Airlines (based in Winston-Salem) in 1987 the chairman of US Air said, "Warm Southern hospitality is going to be replaced with cool Northern efficiency." A Piedmont employee was quoted in the newspaper saying, "When that statement was made, we knew we were in trouble."

Formerly loyal Piedmont passengers were outraged at the change in tone and manner and quit flying Piedmont. US Air's "Northern efficiency" led to a bankruptcy filing within twenty years. But former Piedmont employees—who remember the good ol' days—proudly display twenty-year-old Piedmont Airlines license plates on the fronts of their cars.

Southerners always have a sense of place

Most native Southerners can trace their families back for generations in the Southland. There is a difference between being born into 350 years of Southern history and 80 years of Northern existence. Southerners are immensely proud that they have been Americans longer than most of their detractors. It is common throughout the South for men and women to readily and simply acknowledge that their land, china, books, you name it, have been in their families for hundreds of years. Some people can say, "I am the sixth generation to raise cattle on this land. Down by the creek is where my ancestors mustered to go fight the British."

You don't see many Chicagoans or New Yorkers claiming, "My sub-leased brownstone is on the same ground where my ancestor formed an investment bank. Down by the express elevator is where he fought off that hostile takeover."

Pride in one's Southern roots crosses racial boundaries. Booker T. Washington was one of the most important proponents of black education in the late nineteenth and early twentieth century. Washington could have abandoned his goal of educating blacks in a segregated South and taken a cushy job with one of the white Northerners who supported his efforts. But Washington said, "I was born in the South. I have lived and labored in the South. I wish to be buried in the South." He is buried on the campus of the Tuskegee Institute, an Alabama college he helped bring to national prominence.

First in war, first in peace, first in the hearts of their countrymen

At no time was the sense of place stronger in the South than in the spring of 1861. Seven Deep South states had already organized the Confederacy in the early winter, but four states, Virginia, Arkansas, North Carolina, and Tennessee, remained in the Union as of April 1861. It was not until President Lincoln demanded regiments from those states to put down the "rebellion" in the South after the bloodless firing on Fort Sumter that those states decided to leave the Union.

Dozens of Southern officers, the cream of the U.S. Army, decided to cast their lot with their home states rather than answer to a central government.

Colonel Robert E. Lee, who had spent more than thirty years as an officer in the United States Army, almost came to blows with hotheaded secessionists in Texas who saw him in his U.S. Army uniform in January

1861. In April, Lee declined a promotion to general and an army command of 75,000 men to invade the South. "Though opposed to secession and deprecating war, I could take no part in an invasion of the Southern states," Lee told an emissary for President Lincoln who had authorized the offer of command.

Albert Sidney Johnston and Edward Porter Alexander, both U.S. Army officers destined to become Confederate generals, brushed aside Northern friends' entreaties to stay in service in faraway California. Instead, they trekked home 4,000 miles to share the fate of their families.

Professor Thomas J. Jackson, out of uniform for nearly ten years, was such a devoted Unionist that he almost came to blows with a man in Lexington, Virginia, when the rabble-rouser pulled an American flag down from the county courthouse in early April. In July Jackson would acquire the nickname of Stonewall.

★ ★ ★ ★ ★ ★ ★ ★ ★ ★ ★ ★ ★ ★ ★

No Yankees Allowed

"Mississippi gets more than their fair share back in federal money, but who the hell wants to live in Mississippi?"

Charles Rangel, New York congressman, 2006

Congressman Chip Pickering of Mississippi responded:

"From the Coast to the Delta to the Pinebelt to the Hills and across Mississippi, there is beauty in every city, charity in every heart, love in every church, and majesty in every countryside. When I travel this state I see it in the resolute handshakes, the hospitable smiles, and the sincere prayers of our neighbors: we love Mississippi and we are proud and happy to live here."

Southerners living in the North also felt the pull to head south to defend their homeland. Colonel George Washington Rains of Augusta, Georgia, had married the boss's daughter and had managed an iron works in Newburgh, New York, for more than ten years when the war started. Without hesitation he joined the Confederacy and built the Confederate Powder Works in Augusta, where he manufactured more than 2.75 million pounds of black powder. After the war was over, Rains returned to running the iron works in Newburgh, where he is buried today.

Southern defeat meant a person's first loyalty could no longer be to his state rather than the central government. But it did not erase Southerners' sense of place. Ask a Northerner where he's from and he'll probably answer with just the name of his city: "Chicago," "Los Angeles," "New York City." Ask a Southerner the same question and he will almost always answer with both the city and the state, even if the city is large and well known: "Charlotte, North Carolina," "Birmingham, Alabama," "Nashville, Tennessee."

Southerners are still proud of their region and their state and want to be sure people know they are from the South.

Old-time religion is good enough for the South

Southerners tend to be more religious, believe what they read in the Bible, and believe that correct moral paths in life can be found by faith in God. If that makes newcomers to the region uneasy, then so be it. The South is a place where people believe in God. Those who wish to make it different should return to the region whence they came. Southerners believe that God can be vengeful—and they're willing to fight on His behalf.

Every religion is welcome in the South, though Southern Baptists and various other break-away Baptists dominate. The old Southern aristocracy, especially in Virginia, and especially among Southerners whose roots are English, tends to be Episcopalian. More middle-class Southerners tend toward the Methodists or the Baptists. And the Scots-Irish who stayed loyal to the kirk are mostly Presbyterian, although some can be found among the Baptists and Methodists. And, of course, Evangelicals of all stripes are welcome in the South. Southerners have a reputation for being clannish—and with our devotion to family, to kin, to place, and to church, that's true. But the gamut of Judeo-Christianity in the South is wide.

Of all the Christian faiths, Catholics are probably the least represented in the South, yet the Irish Catholic O'Hara family of the novel and movie *Gone with the Wind* is the most recognizable of any literary Southern family, and there are large concentrations of Catholics along the Gulf Coast, in Texas, in northern Virginia, and in Maryland (a Catholic colony).

While Northerners tend to think of Jews as living in enclaves of New York and New York South (Miami Beach), that faith was readily welcomed—and been prominent—in many Southern cities. Likewise, you'll find Quakers, Mennonites, Amish, and a variety of smaller sects and believers scattered across the South. Quakers, in fact, played a leading role in running the Underground Railroad in the South, and in providing safe haven for men who did not wish to serve in the Confederate Army. The culture of acceptance practiced by Southerners allowed these Quakers to co-exist with other religions that supported the war effort.

There are religious differences in the South that are rarely seen in the North. Prayer meetings in the South, midweek Sunday services for people

★ ★ ★ ★ ★ ★ ★ ★ ★ ★

South vs. North

"When you go apartment-hunting in the South, you encounter little old ladies who ask you if you use strong drink. In New York you encounter paranoids who wonder if you will commit suicide—not that they care; what they worry about is blood on their fresh paint, a dubious smell in the hallway, or a hole in the awning as you pass through on your way to the sidewalk. The Southerner who moves to any part of the country has problems, but the culture shock that attacks the Southerner who moves North is almost indescribable."

Florence King,
*Southern Ladies and
Gentlemen*

who can't wait until Sunday to hear a little more preaching, come on Wednesday nights. There's also "homecoming" at churches. People who have moved away from their home church come back to picnic and renew acquaintances. Every family brings a covered dish to share. Once blankets are spread on the ground, everyone eats and talks. Expect a lot of deviled eggs. Tent revivals last a week and are held in—what else?—a large tent set up in an empty field. The word "revival" refers to Christians' chances to renew their faith with the help of a traveling preacher who does not know them personally.

When someone moves to a new town in the South, they're often invited to "come to preaching this Sunday." That might startle a newcomer, but Southerners view religion simply as part of the social fabric of life. Sharing religion and prayer is a way to welcome people into the community.

Southerners are supposed to be in church and Sunday school on Sunday morning and back to prayer meeting on Wednesday evenings. Regular church meetings have always been a way rural Southerners have kept track of their souls and socialized with their neighbors.

Southern religion even has its own language. Every Baptist church in Dixie has an "amen corner" up front, where old-timers shout "Amen!" when the preacher has made a particularly good point in a sermon. A "Back-Sliding Baptist" is a man who belongs to the church but who may go fishing on Sunday morning instead of sitting in a pew. "Witnessing" makes even some Southerners uncomfortable because it often involves sharing your religious convictions publicly with others who may be of another faith or no faith at all. A "Bible Thumper" or a "Holy Roller" is someone who gets a little carried away with his religious enthusiasm.

But when liberal social activists and politicians start demanding "separation of church and state," the ears of religious Southerners perk up. When they hear that phrase, they know they are under attack. The term stems from a letter written by Virginian Thomas Jefferson in 1802 to some

Connecticut Baptists, in which he reiterates the idea that the government should not establish a national religion. Southern religious folks definitely do not want that. But they do want the freedom to practice religion without fear that the government will outlaw it, and they want the freedom to elect people of religious and moral standing into public office who will uphold laws that reflect America's Judeo-Christian heritage. Southerners don't take kindly to liberal activists misappropriating Jefferson's words.

With a strong tradition of active Protestants, Catholics, and Jewish communities, the South remains more religious than any other region in the nation. During and after the War, Southerners clung to religion as their spiritual salvation. Southerners have always admired the last line in *Gone with the Wind*: "After all, tomorrow is another day," and given it a religious significance. No matter how bad things are today, with prayer, we trust we can move mountains. Southerners are a "faith-based" people.

Southerners love contact sports

For decades the owners of professional teams in baseball, football, and basketball ignored the South's growing population. It was not until 1965 that the first Southern professional team, the Atlanta Falcons, debuted.

That didn't matter to Southerners. They barely paid any attention, in fact. That was because the South has always favored college teams. Northerners root for the schools they attended, but Southerners love college sports even if they did not go to college at all. Southerners pick college teams based on their regional identification. And college game day is a regional event, with folks waving school banners on their car windows. Rivalries between states and within states (like the "Iron Bowl" pitting Alabama versus Auburn) are fierce and are the stuff of yearlong bragging rights. If Sunday is for church, Saturday, in autumn, is for college football. And when it comes spring and summer, look for Southern teams to make it to the College World Series—which Southern teams have won fifteen of the last twenty-five years.

Even though Atlanta, Tampa, Miami, Charlotte, Raleigh (home of the Carolina Hurricanes, the 2006 National Hockey League Stanley Cup champions), New Orleans, Houston, Dallas, and Nashville have professional sports, Southerners still prefer college teams. Big pro contests don't impress us. But local boys who play hard for our schools sure do.

There is one contact sport that is purely Southern, although its owners are desperately trying to make it an international sport. That is stock car racing.

Stock car racing started as a way for young Southern men to test themselves and their mechanical skills against each other. A handful of them did run moonshine on the side, but not as many as NASCAR (the National Association for Stock Car Auto Racing) would have fans believe. Starting in the late 1940s the men would carve dirt tracks out of the Carolina hills and compete in the same passenger cars they drove to the field. Promoters like Bill France began to stage races on the hard-packed sand beaches south of Daytona.

As more fans showed up to watch the dirt track racing in the 1950s, the Frances and others started building permanent, paved tracks, including Daytona International Speedway. By the 1960s, stock car racing was established as a Southern sport ready to go nationwide. By the late twentieth century, it was a sport the Frances believed was ready for sophisticated audiences. Small Southern tracks were abandoned in favor of larger tracks closer to major metro areas in California, Illinois, Arizona, and Kansas.

Southerners are not as enthusiastic about stock car racing as they once were. Ticket, hotel, and food prices have jumped too high and media-trained, sponsor-spouting young men have taken over from axle-grease stained good ol' boys who worked on their own cars. Southerners who used to travel from Florida to the Carolinas to Tennessee to Virginia to follow the circuit are watching more on television, if they are watching at all.

Southern Women Are Prettier...

From Georgia peaches to Mississippi belles, there's no doubt about it: Southern women really are prettier. Since the first Miss America pageant in 1921, one-third of the winners have been Southern.

Year	Miss America	From
1921	Margaret Gorman	Washington, D.C.
1926	Norma Smallwood	Tulsa, Oklahoma
1942	Jo-Carroll Dennison	Tyler, Texas
1944	Venus Ramey	Washington, D.C.
1947	Barbara Walker	Memphis, Tennessee
1951	Yolande Betbeze	Mobile, Alabama
1953	Neva Jane Langley	Macon, Georgia
1957	Marian McKnight	Manning, South Carolina
1959	Mary Ann Mobley	Brandon, Mississippi
1960	Lynda Lee Mead	Natchez, Mississippi
1962	Maria Fletcher	Asheville, North Carolina
1964	Donna Axum	El Dorado, Arkansas
1971	Phyllis Ann George	Denton, Texas
1975	Shirley Cothran	Fort Worth, Texas
1979	Kylene Barker	Galax, Virginia
1980	Cheryl Prewitt	Ackerman, Mississippi
1982	Elizabeth Ward	Russellville, Arkansas
1986	Susan Akin	Meridian, Mississippi
1987	Kellye Cash	Memphis, Tennessee
1990	Debbye Turner	Mexico, Missouri
1993	Leanza Cornett	Jacksonville, Florida
1994	Kimberly Clarice Aiken	Columbia, South Carolina
1995	Heather Whitestone	Birmingham, Alabama
1999	Nicole Johnson	Roanoke, Virginia
2000	Heather French	Augusta, Kentucky
2004	Ericka Dunlap	Orlando, Florida
2005	Deidre Downs	Birmingham, Alabama
2006	Jennifer Berry	Tulsa, Oklahoma

Many racing fans are upset that NASCAR has started erasing the Southern history of the sport, even trying to ban Confederate battle flags from its tracks, when the flag used to be a standard backdrop for photographs in the victory lane. How popular racin' will remain with notoriously fickle Yankee fans is still to be determined. But NASCAR would be wise to start courting its old Southern fan base.

Southerners carry guns

There is a great line of dialogue in the Sandra Bullock movie *Miss Congeniality*, in which Miss Bullock plays an uncover FBI agent tracking down a threat to the Miss USA pageant. She tackles an innocent man in the crowd, and when she tries to explain her mistake by saying she thought the man was carrying a concealed gun, Candice Bergen, the pageant director, exclaims, "This is Texas! My hairdresser carries a gun!"

Despite the best efforts of gun-control politicians and activists to convince the public that personal ownership of guns is dangerous—or (even worse) not fashionable—gun ownership remains high in the South. According to a 2001 Harris Poll, gun ownership was lowest in the East (34 percent) and highest in the South (43 percent). Another poll shows that fewer than one in seven people living in the Northeast owns a handgun, while more than 40 percent of Southerners own a pistol. The same poll shows that 60 percent of people in Northeastern big cities favor gun-control laws while 60 percent of those in the rural South say there is no need for any more gun-control laws.

Starting with the matchlock muskets carried by the soldiers at Jamestown, Virginia, firearms have been part of Southern history. Thanks to the private ownership of hunting rifles by the Overmountain Men of Tennessee and the Carolinas in 1781, the patriots won the Battle of Kings Mountain, South Carolina. And Southern soldiers did their part to force the British surrender at Yorktown, Virginia. After the Revolution, the South was shaped by frontiersmen like Daniel Boone and David Crockett (he never called himself Davy). Every man, woman, and child learned to use firearms. Back in Boston and Philadelphia, food was bought in the markets. In the South you had to kill your own. In the urban Northeast violence rarely extended beyond a barroom fight. On the Southern frontier, you might have to fight an Indian to save your family. Musket-toting private citizens from Texas, the Carolinas, and Tennessee avenged the Alamo and created the state of Texas. A far-seeing Mississippian, Jefferson Davis, bought rifled muskets that proved to be the winning edge for the Americans at the Battle of Buena Vista during the Mexican War. Secretary of War Davis later ordered the United States Army to modernize by buying more of the weapons he had selected for his Mississippi volunteers. (Davis would later regret modernizing the U.S. Army when he had to send a lesser-equipped Confederate army against the might of the force he had built.)

Relocating Yankees are sometimes pleased, sometimes puzzled, sometimes appalled at the enthusiastic embrace of weapons ownership among Southerners. It has been more than twenty years since the residents of Kennesaw, Georgia, passed a local ordinance *requiring* every homeowner to own at least one gun. The news media still talks about the measure, which has resulted in a surprisingly low crime rate compared to neighboring Atlanta. In rural counties, teachers and principals expect low school attendance around the opening weekend of hunting seasons for deer and turkeys.

Southerners learn how to use guns when they are children because guns are considered just another potentially dangerous tool, like chainsaws. A chainsaw sitting in its plastic case is not at all dangerous. But pull the rope and get that chainsaw running and it becomes very dangerous. Southerners think of firearms the same way. A loaded pistol sitting

★ ★ ★ ★

A Dixie Fact

The title of *Gone with the Wind* comes from the poem *Non Sum Qualis Eram Bonae sub Regno Cynarae* by Ernest Dowson: "I have forgot much, Cynara! Gone with the wind."

★ ★ ★ ★

in a nightstand drawer is not going to kill anyone. But if an intruder breaks into the house, Southerners feel confident they can protect themselves and their families.

Perhaps another distinctive aspect of being Southern is this: Gun-control advocates, based almost exclusively in the North, claim that people are inherently unpredictable and that banning weapons from everyone is the only way to keep everyone safe. Southerners believe that people are inherently unpredictable and that individuals keeping weapons is the only way to protect the innocent from evil individuals.

Southern culture in a nutshell: religious, funny good ol' boys and gals with a love of home and a smile for strangers

There is a town outside Raleigh, North Carolina, that is home to so many corporate transfers from the North that town wags insist there is an acronym that goes along with the official chartered name of Cary: Containment Area for Relocated Yankees.

The long-term residents of the Raleigh area, the people who can legitimately lay claim to the state's nickname of Tar Heels, have welcomed the newcomers, who work mainly in the Research Triangle Park, one of the nation's first research-oriented parks. In the 1960s it was the driving force for making North Carolina a center of technology today.

All around Cary is evidence of the Old South. Nearby is the tobacco farm where Washington Duke launched his fortune by getting Union soldiers hooked on his pipe tobacco. Not far way is Bennett Place, where in late April 1865 Confederate general Joseph E. Johnston surrendered the largest Confederate army still in the field to Union general William T. Sherman. Beyond that is Stagville Plantation, once one of the state's largest food plantations, where slave cabins still stand. These symbols of

Books Y'all Aren't Supposed to Read

Long Gray Lines by Rod Andrew, Jr.; Chapel Hill, NC: University of North Carolina Press, 2001.

Of the 115 military colleges founded in the decades before the War, 99 were in the South. Andrew writes that Southerners, then as now, equate military service, honor, and patriotism with civic duty and character development. That would explain why so many Southerners rose through the ranks in succeeding wars, and why the South today is considered more patriotic than the North.

Southern by the Grace of God by Lewis Grizzard; Athens, GA: Longstreet Press, 1996 (or anything else by him, for that matter).

1001 Things Everyone Should Know about the South by John Shelton Reed and Dale Volberg Reed; New York: Doubleday, 1996.

the Old South, built when agriculture was king, stand within easy driving distance of where the New South, with its high-tech future, thrives.

Friendly Southerners never force their culture on newcomers, but we hope our friendly manners and established ways will win Yankees over—and to look at America's migration statistics, we are.

It's probably no surprise that a place that's so exceptional and so family-friendly attracts a lot of people. A place where taxes are lower attracts a lot of people too. And not to mention that our women are prettier, our men are handier, and our climate is better. So if you're not here already, you're welcome to come on down—just don't try to turn it into the place you left.

Chapter 2

THE SOUTH AND SOUTHERNERS WE LOVE

How are Southerners different from other folks? Let me count the ways....

As I mentioned in the last chapter, most of us have been here a lot longer than folks up North. And our idea of extended family—"our people"—can get pretty extended, to the point that we all seem to be related to each other. (Talk about a brotherhood of men!)

But it goes beyond that. Here are some of our defining characteristics.

Southerners act different

Southerners will do just about anything on a dare from their buddies, but they will also do anything to save their friends from danger. They will also do anything for someone they respect, including walking into the jaws of death.

It is no accident that the Army of Northern Virginia fought against overwhelming odds in every battle, winning massive victories at Seven Days, Second Manassas, Fredericksburg, Chancellorsville, the Wilderness, and Cold Harbor. It is no wonder its men were willing to fight their way out of a surrounded position at Appomattox Court House in April 1865 if only their commander had given the word.

Guess what?

* The South's storied barbecue tradition goes back to pre-colonial times.

* Race relations today are much better in the South than in the North.

* Southerners might speak slowly, but they are usually impulsive in action.

31

It was no accident that Chuck Yeager of Hamlin, West Virginia, became the first person in the world to break the sound barrier. After high school graduation, before the start of World War II, Yeager joined the Army Air Corps. Forced first into a mechanic's role, he pushed to be allowed to fly. He became a flying ace and after the war he volunteered to see what would happen when an airplane went faster than the speed of sound. No one knew if the airplane would disintegrate from some unforeseen forces, or what would happen to the pilot who flew at such speeds. Yeager, the adventurous Southerner, volunteered to find out.

It was no accident that Audie Murphy, a teenager from Kingston, Texas, who had dropped out of school after the eighth grade, jumped at the chance to join the military after fulfilling his dying mother's last wish to ensure the care of his younger brothers and sisters. Rejected by several military recruiters because he was too young, too skinny, and too short, he was finally accepted by the U.S. Army. Murphy would become the most highly decorated soldier in World War II, winning a Bronze Star, two Silver Stars, and the Congressional Medal of Honor for fighting the Germans. He put himself into many tight spots because he wanted to save the men under his command.

It's true that we Southerners might speak slowly and always make time for good manners, but in action we are usually fast and impulsive. This trait is not always a good thing. Rather than wait for the Yankees to fire the first shot at Fort Sumter, which would have proved that they were the true aggressors in the war, an impatient Jefferson Davis ordered the firing of the first shot. It's also why the prototypical last words of a good ol' boy cut off in his prime are, "Y'all watch this!"

Southerners talk different

Southerners have a way with words, and there are many variations on the celebrated Southern drawl. Some phrases used by Southerners are famous and famously misused by Northerners. The contraction of "you all" to "y'all" is, as every Southerner knows, never used to refer to fewer than two people. A sure sign that someone is a native Yankee trying to talk Southern is when they ask something like "When will y'all come over?" of a single person.

Southerners also instinctively know time limits when expressed in words. When a Southerner explains that he is "fixin' to go to town," it is obvious that

> ## Darn Tootin'
>
> "In the South, as in no other American region, people use language as it was surely meant to be employed; a lush, personal, emphatic, treasure of coins to be spent slowly and for value."
>
> *Time* magazine, September 1976.

the actual act of going to town is still an undetermined length of time in the near, but not immediate future. On the other hand, when a Southerner says, "I'm going directly," that means passengers should yell "Shotgun!" and scramble for the door.

Southerners know distances can be expressed in simple words. "Over yonder" means a pretty fair piece, perhaps across the ridgeline. That is much farther away than "hollering distance," up to several hundred yards away, which is the distance that a big-throated holler could be heard. And Southerners know the difference between "holler" and "hollow" even though they are pronounced the same. Most Yankees have never used either word in a sentence like, "I hollered up the hollow for Jeb, but it was such a fair piece, he didn't hear me. I reckon he must have been way over yonder."

All of these are spoken with the famous Dixie Drawl. The Southern drawl has many variations, but all are authentic Dixie. Stretch out words, add pauses, drop an occasional "g" from "-ing," and sprinkle your speech with Southern phrases such as "Looks like something the cat drug in," "Like a chicken with its head cut off," "Like a bat out of hell," "Like a duck on a June bug," "As mean as a snake," or "As naked as a jaybird."

★ ★ ★ ★ ★ ★ ★ ★ ★ ★

We're Southern, Mon

On the sea islands east of Beaufort, South Carolina, visitors encounter the last vestiges of the Gullah culture and language, which sounds vaguely Jamaican to visitors' ears. In reality the singsong dialect is left over from the slaves who were brought to the region from Angola and the Congo to grow the highly prized sea island cotton. Until recently the sea islands were remote. Now Yankee-based developers are making the former plantations into resorts.

Soft drinks in the South are never, ever called "pop." They are known as Cokes (even Pepsis can be called Cokes), dopes, cold drinks, belly-washes, and soda waters. One time that a brand name is used is when an expatriate Southerner in some God-forsaken land like New York City develops a hankering for an "RC and a Moon Pie." An RC is a Royal Crown Cola. A Moon Pie is two round pieces of chocolate-coated graham cracker with a marshmallow filling.

Sometimes Southerners say things just to irritate any Yankees in hearing distance. Few things give a Southerner more pleasure than to politely step into the back of an elevator, then ask the Yankee by the buttons to "Mash the fourth floor, please."

Southerners eat different

An obvious difference between Northerners and Southerners is what they see fit to eat. And there is no more broad dividing line than grits and sweet tea.

It is a lucky Southerner who can find grits at all in a Northern restaurant, and an even luckier one if the restaurant knows how to make them from scratch rather than dumping a packet of instant grits into a bowl. Southerners have always found it puzzling and disgusting that Northerners, if faced with grits, will inevitably put sugar on them. Every Southerner knows that the thing to be done with a mound of grits is to form a depression in the center of the mound, drop in two pats of butter so the heat of the grits melts them, liberally add salt and pepper, and then mix in the butter. Southerners also know that cheese and grits is a match made in Southern heaven.

Sweet tea is another aggravation for Southern visitors to the North. For reasons that are unfathomable, Northerners just do not seem to know how to brew tea. It is not difficult to boil water and drop in tea bags and sugar, but that skill eludes most Yankee restaurateurs. Most Yankee tea is instant, that tinny-tasting concoction that was almost certainly invented by someone north of the Mason-Dixon Line. Making good sweet tea (often expressed as one word, "sweettea") is just not that difficult an art form that it cannot be mastered by Northerners. They should work on it as a gesture of goodwill to their neighbors in the South.

It is impossible to find boiled peanuts in the North, and impossible not to drive more than ten miles on a rural road in the South without encountering a roadside stand with a big pot of them steaming away. There are tricks to boiling peanuts; the water has to have just the right amount of salt and the peanuts have to stay in the water just long enough so the nut can be sucked from the open shell with little effort.

Southerners like to fry stuff. There is nothing to rival the taste of a thin steak coated with a little flour then pan-fried in a black skillet that has been frying stuff for years. Likewise, pan-fried cornbread (with tiny chips of onions and red pepper inside) made in that same skillet tastes better than anything a fancy Northern restaurant could dress up and put on a plate. As for deep-frying, if it can be coated in batter, Southerners will eat it. That is why some places in the South offer alligator and rattlesnake. No one knows how to sauté those Southern natives, but a goodly number of good ol' boys will tell you how to deep fry them and that they taste like chicken.

"If God made a finer meal than this, then He must have kept it for Himself."

The late Georgia humorist Lewis Grizzard hit Southerners' love of barbecue right on the head with that one. Note that I said "love *of* barbecue"

★   ★   ★   ★

Grits in New York?

The effects of immigration north and south can be seen in the sales of some foods. According to one source, more grits are sold in New York City to descendants of blacks who moved north during the Depression than are sold in Atlanta to the transplanted Yankees who are still frightened to taste them.

★   ★   ★   ★

★ ★ ★ ★ ★ ★ ★ ★ ★ ★ ★ ★ ★ ★

A Barbecue Primer

Here's the quick lowdown on Southern regional barbecue styles:

Alabama: There are more barbecue joints in Bama than in any other state. Dreamland Bar-Be-Que in Tuscaloosa serves up what people have called the world's best ribs. And you'll find only ribs—no sides, utensils, or plates, just ribs, bread, and spicy tomato-based sauce.

Georgia: Georgians like their barbecue slow-cooked over oak and/or hickory chips, and their preferred sauce is a mix of ketchup, molasses, bourbon, garlic, and cayenne pepper. As in North Carolina, the farther east you go, the more vinegary the sauce gets. Brunswick stew, a thick concoction of corn, lima beans, tomatoes, and onions named for the town of Brunswick, almost always accompanies the meat.

Kentucky: Kentucky differs from the rest of the South in that mutton is often used in barbecue, especially in the western part of the state. The sauce is vinegar- and tomato-based, and is not always used in the cooking process.

Tennessee: Memphis-style barbecue is the most common in Tennessee. This features ribs two ways: wet ribs with a mild, sweet sauce basted during the smoking, and dry-rub ribs. Tennesseans also love their pork, served with tomato-based sauce.

Mississippi: Pork is king in Mississippi. Most barbecue joints serve only pulled pork, with a purely vinegar sauce—many places actually pride themselves on the complete absence of tomatoes in their sauces.

North Carolina: North Carolina barbecue varies within the state. Eastern dwellers like their sauce thin, spicy, and vinegary while those in the west (around Lexington, a barbecue hub), like theirs thick and sweet. Both sides use oak and hickory chips to smoke the meat before pulling it off the bone.

South Carolina: South Carolinians are unique among Southerners in that they have *four* types of barbecue to call their own. While it's all pork, the sauces vary from vinegar-pepper (Pee Dee and the Low Country) to mustard (Midlands and Columbia) to fruit juice (Orangeberg) to tomato (Rock Hill).

Texas: True to their heritage, Texans like to do barbecue their own way. Brisket is seen as often as pork, and chopped beef is also often on the menu. Whatever the meat, it often stands alone, without sauce—Texans believe that sauce masks the quality and flavor of the well-prepared barbecue. Texas barbecue often has a pink tinge caused by the meat's reaction to the smoke. Oak, mesquite, and pecan are all used in Texas.

rather than "love *to* barbecue." Because most everyone outside the South thinks of barbecue as a verb—what you do *to* your food, not what it *is*. This is not just an issue of semantics. When Southerners talk about barbecue, they're talking about a tradition going back to pre-colonial times; the word *barbecue* is thought to be derived from *barabicu*, which was used by the Taino people of the Bahamas and Hispaniola to mean "sacred fire pit." The word and the technique of slow-cooking an animal carcass over a hole in the ground migrated to America with the European explorers. Over time, different groups throughout the South developed distinctly different styles of barbecue, which remain today as some of the best indicators of where in the heck you are. Any Southerner worth his sauce knows that East Carolina style is thin but full of pepper and vinegar, and that the closer you get to the Appalachians, the sweeter and thicker it gets. And, of course, there's the famous Brunswick stew, which no Georgia hostess would be caught dead without.

Before the War of Northern Aggression, Southerners ate around five pounds of pork for every one pound of beef they consumed, and today most barbecue is still made from pork. But you can find Southern devotees of other meats. Texans sure love their beef brisket and Kentuckians have perfected the art of the mutton barbecue.

Southerners are less race conscious than folks up North

Southerners do not like being asked, "Is the Klan still active around here?" The appropriate answer is "Klan? What Klan?" The Klan in the South has been dead for at least thirty years, and it had been in decline for the hundred years before that, after its initial postwar founding. The only people who ever think about the Ku Klux Klan in the twenty-first century are a handful of race hustlers who dangle the Klan in front of the public whenever they want to boost their donations. Every once in a while the letters KKK will appear on a wall somewhere and the local

★ ★ ★ ★ ★ ★ ★ ★ ★ ★

Southern Food We Love

Southern fried chicken, cornbread, buttermilk biscuits, pecan pie, sweet potato pie, iced tea, okra, Tabasco, Texas Pete, pepper sauce, grits, Smithfield ham, fried green tomatoes, red beans and rice, barbecue, jambalaya, po-boys, chicory coffee, beignets, shrimp remoulade, gumbo, crawfish étouffée, she-crab soup, shrimp and grits, Low Country boil, Brunswick stew, fried catfish, Vidalia onions, Moon Pies, GooGoo Clusters, Elmer's candy, beef jerky, Coca-Cola, RC Cola, Barq's Root Beer, boiled peanuts

media will do a story on it. Police will invariably discover that the graffiti was written by bored teenagers hoping to see their work on television. In the late 1990s, the local head of the KKK in one North Carolina county called up the sheriff and turned in his robes. He was the only member of his "klavern." He said it seemed stupid to belong to a club of one.

For most Southerners, the postwar Klan might have had a purpose—to redress the wrongs of Reconstruction. But after that short period, the Klan was the South's dirty laundry. The only people who don't know the Klan and its history are the news media and transplanted Yankees who fear straw men.

A corollary to the Klan question that angers Southerners is the equally ridiculous "How are your race relations in today's South?" Southerners who are not too shocked to reply might say, "Much better than you have up North." While segregation after Reconstruction was an ugly chapter in Southern history, it does not exist today and has not for at least forty years. And because previous Southern history was of blacks and whites living together, of black nannies considered members of the family, and black children being considered suitable playmates for whites, such "segregation" as exists is no worse than—in fact, it seems better than—what you'll find in New York City and Hollywood.

Here's an example of how Southerners treat race, family, and history compared to the North. Dotting the Southern landscape are former slave graveyards. Many are surrounded by white picket fences and tended by the usually white owners of the private property in which they rest.

Contrast such reverential treatment with the African Burial Ground just east of New York City's city hall in lower Manhattan. A tiny plot of earth has been maintained of the remnant of a graveyard that once contained the bodies of upwards of 25,000 slaves who were literally worked to death in the eighteenth century. The vast majority of the slave dead are not in the cemetery; they're under high-rise buildings. Old times—and old family—may be tread on and forgotten in New York, but they are not forgotten in Dixie.

Southerners aren't elitists

If Yankees' stupid questions don't rile Southerners, superior attitudes will. Southerners have no pretenses about themselves. Southerners don't "put on airs" and don't "get above our raisings."

Restaurants are a good place for expatriate Yankees to experience this equality among natives. A shack that sells barbecue sandwiches dripping with sauce and grease handed out the back door by a man in an even greasier apron will attract bankers and lawyers eating side by side with bricklayers and ditch diggers. The attraction of the Southern restaurant is the barbecue, not the ambiance, the wine list, or the chance to be seen in this month's trendy bar.

The whole issue of moonshine and the South is instructive. Making moon in the South is a cultural tradition dating back to

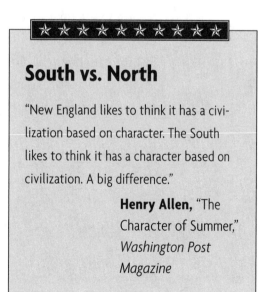

South vs. North

"New England likes to think it has a civilization based on character. The South likes to think it has a character based on civilization. A big difference."

Henry Allen, "The Character of Summer," *Washington Post Magazine*

when the first Scots brought whiskey-making to the mountains in the early eighteenth century. It was perfectly acceptable to transform low-profit corn into high-profit corn whiskey, until the federal government realized that Southern entrepreneurs were not paying taxes.

That was—and is—the primary issue of moonshiners versus the feds. The feds never really cared much about the occasional moonshiner who made bad batches of shine that blinded people. The issue was always the unpaid taxes on the sale of the liquor. Southerners have never paid too much attention to laws that they don't like—such as banning a man from transforming his stock of corn and sugar into corn squeezins'. While making moonshine is a dying art, true-blue Southerners are unlikely to turn in their neighbors when they smell that sour mash in the air on the ridgeline.

How to impress a Southerner: know cars, country music, racin', and Mayberry

There are many ways for non-native Southerners to impress each other.

Knowing how to tear down and put back together a pre–emission controls engine will win any newcomer friends. Not many Manhattan and Chicago natives can do this. But good ol' boys have a passion for automotive machinery. Another tip—always have some cold bottled beer on hand when working on the engine. It lubricates the friendships that develop over passing around greasy rags.

A Book Y'all Aren't Supposed to Read

The Politically Incorrect Guide™ to English and American Literature by Elizabeth Kantor; Washington, DC: Regnery, 2006.

If you're too old to slide under a car, then learn yourself some country music history. A Yankee who knows Kitty Wells's "It Wasn't God Who Made Honky Tonk Angels" will be off to a good start. Same is true if you know June Carter Cash was part of the Carter Family singers before she met Johnny. You don't need to know who was eliminated from *American*

The Southern Mentality

"Emerson said that the 'scholar is man thinking.' Had Southerners of that era taken seriously the famous lecture entitled 'The American Scholar,' they might have replied by saying that the gentleman is man talking. The accomplished Christian gentleman of the old South was the shadow, attenuated by evangelical Calvinism, of his Renaissance spiritual ancestor, who had been the creation of the rhetorical tradition, out of Aristotle through Cicero distilled finally by Castiglione. By contrast, the New England sage, embodied in Ralph Waldo Emerson, took seriously what has come to be known since the Industrial Revolution as the life of the mind: an activity a little apart from life, and perhaps leading to the fashionable alienation of the 'intellectual' of our time."

Allen Tate, "A Southern Mode of the Imagination"

Idol. But tune your radio dial to a country music station and listen to the oldies from Merle Haggard, Charlie Daniels, and (farther back) Ferlin Husky or the new stuff from Aaron Tippin, Alan Jackson, Toby Keith, and Trace Adkins. And no, the Dixie Chicks don't count. But gospel does.

Likewise, knowing the difference between the "old" NASCAR and "new" NASCAR and debating the merits of both is a sure way for immigrants to the region to wheedle their way into the conversation of native Southerners. Even knowing what NASCAR stands for is a good start. Even though the sanctioning body has been around for more than fifty years, many Northern newspapers still spell it "Nascar"—either not knowing or not caring that it's an acronym.

The "old" NASCAR began in 1949 and ended about 2000. Its drivers were men like Junior Johnson, Curtis Turner, the Flock brothers, Joe Weatherly, the Allison brothers (and their protégés the Alabama Gang), Leroy Yarbrough, Cale Yarborough, Darrell Waltrip, David Pearson, Bobby Isaac, and "The King," Richard Petty. The "old" NASCAR drivers usually did not have a college degree. Some, like Bobby Isaac, never even finished

What a Southerner Said

"Whenever I'm asked why Southern writers particularly have a penchant for writing about freaks, I say it is because we are still able to recognize one. To be able to recognize a freak, you have to have some conception of the whole man, and in the South the general conception of man is still, in the main, theological."

Flannery O'Connor

junior high; Isaac dropped out to work in a textile mill. Others, like Junior Johnson (immortalized as "The Last American Hero" in an *Esquire* magazine article by Tom Wolfe) ran a little moonshine on the side to make ends meet in the days before racing started paying bigger money. These were men's men—rough and tumble good ol' boys who would sometimes duke it out in the pits or on the track when someone got wrecked. They pulled their own racecars to the track and did their own mechanical work, and still managed to find time to talk to fans.

The "new" NASCAR came along at the beginning of the twenty-first century when corporate sponsors virtually took command of the sport. Stock car racing was no longer a sport as much as it was a vehicle for advertising and endorsements. Small tracks like North Wilkesboro and Rockingham in North Carolina were shut down completely, and venerable old tracks like Darlington in South Carolina were cut back to one event. Shifting the racing from the South's old tracks to newer tracks in Northern states like New Hampshire and Illinois made NASCAR a national experience.

Out went the older Southern drivers who had learned to race by banging around on small dirt tracks scattered throughout the region. In came the kids from California, Wisconsin, Indiana, and other Northern states who had spent a few years racing go-karts. Out went the slow-talking, Southern-accented drivers over thirty with the mustaches and barbershop haircuts who wanted to talk about racin'. In came the smooth-faced kids under twenty-five with their razor-cut hairstyles, who would only talk racin' after thanking a long list of sponsors once they climbed out of the car on cue from a television producer. Out went the old drivers who sometimes posed with a Confederate flag in the victory lane. In came the young drivers who posed with rap singers in their recording studios.

The "old" NASCAR, with its colorful drivers doing colorful things, is gone forever. How long the "new" NASCAR will remain popular with its Southern base is debatable. The grumbling is growing louder that the cars already look so much alike that brand loyalty no longer means anything, the racing is too boring, and the drivers look, sound, and act too much alike. Founded as a sport where the racecars looked exactly the way street cars looked, NASCAR is now promoting the idea of creating cars that will look so much alike that there will be no physical difference between makes.

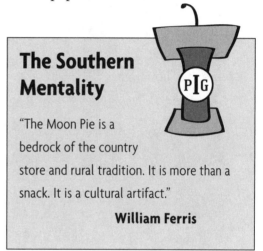

The Southern Mentality

"The Moon Pie is a bedrock of the country store and rural tradition. It is more than a snack. It is a cultural artifact."

William Ferris

Aside from cars and music, if Southern newcomers want a primer on how to act Southern, all they need to do is watch reruns of the *Andy Griffith Show*, which took place in the fictional town of Mayberry, North Carolina, based on Griffith's real hometown of Mt. Airy, North Carolina. The 249 episodes run continually on television stations in the South, and are even found on some Northern stations desperate to find some kind of family entertainment. True Southerners can usually recognize the plot of each episode within the first two scenes, and can repeat whole sections of dialogue between multiple characters. Mayberry was the South as it is and used to be; kind, in no hurry, family-oriented, and a desirable place to live.

Southerners have grown up with Andy's admonition to "Act like somebody!" and have followed Barney's advice to "Nip it in the bud!" And we all know how to react when someone goes, "Say 'Hey!' to Gomer." (The proper reply is, "Gomer says 'Hey!'")

How to Cook Southern

The Lee Bros. Southern Cookbook: Stories and Recipes for Southerners and Would-Be Southerners by Matt Lee and Ted Lee. These Charleston-born brothers "roll up their sleeves and get elbow-deep in Southern cooking in all its sugary, fried goodness."

The Lady & Sons Savannah Country Cookbook by Paula Deen. The "mythically Southern" Ms. Deen shares her favorite down-home recipes.

The All-New Ultimate Southern Living Cookbook. The venerable *Southern Living* magazine presents authentic, time-tested, family-pleasing recipes dear to Southern hearts.

Being Dead Is No Excuse: The Official Southern Ladies' Guide to Hosting the Perfect Funeral by Gayden Metcalfe and Charlotte Hays. These two ladies wouldn't be caught dead without tomato aspic, stuffed eggs, and congealed Jello-O salad.

Church Suppers: 722 Favorite Recipes from Our Church Communities. A charming collection of real good recipes from real churchgoing Southern families.

Southern Junior League cookbooks document regional cooking. One of the classics is *River Road Recipes: The Textbook of Louisiana Cuisine* by the Junior League of Baton Rouge. Originally published in 1959, it's in its seventy-fourth printing as of 2006. Another standout is *Charleston Receipts* by the Junior League of Charleston, South Carolina. For a compilation, try *The Southern Junior League Cookbook* by Ann Seranne.

True Southerners still have heroes

Southerners still love their heroes with unabashed passion. Boys are still named Robert Edward, Thomas Jonathan, and Jeb in honor of the triumvirate of Lee, Jackson, and Stuart. Prints depicting these three generals are guaranteed sell-outs for artists specializing in the War for Southern Independence. Lemons are still left on the grave of Jackson, who died in May 1863. Apples are still left on the grave of Traveller, Lee's horse, buried a few yards from his old master's tomb. Drivers still seek out the suburban

Richmond neighborhood to find the marble monument marking the spot where Stuart was mortally wounded in May 1864. They then drive to Richmond's Hollywood Cemetery to see his grave, sometimes playing him a tune on the banjo, an instrument he didn't know how to play but that he loved to listen to at headquarters parties.

Robert Edward Lee's potential as a wartime leader was so expected by General Winfield Scott that Scott persuaded incoming president Abraham Lincoln to offer Lee the job as commander of the United States Army in early April 1861. Lee paced all night in his bedroom pondering his duty. Was his loyalty to the United States Army, which he had served his whole adult life? Or was his loyalty to his home state of Virginia, his birthplace, and the birthplace and home of his wife, his children, and his ancestors? Was he willing to make war on his family's homeland?

He was not. He tendered his resignation from the U.S. Army, as was his right as an officer, once he knew Virginia had seceded from the United States. Finally given the chance to command a major force in June 1862, Lee blossomed into the leader Scott knew he was. On the battlefield, Lee proved to be bold, decisive, imaginative, and skilled in managing a force that was always outnumbered. No general on the other side, including Grant, ever matched him in tactical prowess.

They're That Good

"It was not a Southern watermelon that Eve took: we know it because she repented."

Mark Twain

After the war, Lee was asked if the war had been worth the personal losses he had suffered. Included among these were the loss of his wife's ancestral home, from which many priceless artifacts of President George Washington were stolen by occupying Union troops. Lee said, "I did only what my duty demanded. I could have taken no other course without dishonour. And if it were all to be done over again, I should act in precisely the same manner."

Duty to God, family, state, and personal integrity drove Lee to make virtually every decision. One of his beliefs was "There is a true glory and a true honor; the glory of duty done—the honor of integrity of principle."

Lieutenant General Thomas J. "Stonewall" Jackson was bold, decisive, tenacious, and instinctive. A former U.S. Army lieutenant with only five years of military experience, he had been out of uniform for ten years when the war began. Jackson's willingness to hit his enemy hard even when outnumbered and attack where he was not expected, as well as his desire to win against overwhelming odds, captured the old Scots-Irish spirit of combat. He drove his men hard. Not all of them loved him, but they respected him. He wanted to win the war. They understood that.

★ ★ ★ ★ ★ ★ ★ ★ ★ ★ ★

Maybe It Makes Sense to Yankees

At Harvard University's Memorial Hall there is a wall of honor for graduates who died in the nation's wars. Included among the names are one Nazi, but none of the 164 Harvard alumni who died in combat for the Confederacy.

Major General James Ewell Brown (J. E. B.) Stuart was more than the commander of the cavalry for the Army of Northern Virginia. He was its heart, displaying a sense of humor and fun mixed with piety that naturally made his men smile and pledge to do whatever he wanted them to do. He was the image of the dashing cavalryman, with a plumed hat, a cape, a big bushy beard, and an even bigger grin of white teeth. He was brash, boastful, and brave. He was reckless, endangering his own life to stay close to his men. He flirted with every woman he saw, but remained faithful to the only woman he ever loved, the mother of his children.

Stuart's major fault was that he did not realize how much Lee trusted him, and only him, to gather intelligence on the Federals. In Stuart's mind, he was Lee's cavalry commander, independent of Lee's staff. In Lee's mind, Stuart was a vital part of his staff, a man whose opinion could be trusted above all others. When Stuart left the immediate vicinity of

Lee's army to lead his cavalry deep into Pennsylvania, rather than staying immediately on Lee's flank, he never realized his mistake until the Battle of Gettysburg was already two-thirds over. Stuart has been blamed for leaving Lee "blind," but in reality, the two men never realized how much they meant to each other until the battle was over.

Lee's devotion to duty, Jackson's brilliant tactics, and Stuart's sense of bold action are traits that still endear these heroes to Southerners. Their characters remain unassailable. They are the men we aspire to be.

Chapter 3

THINGS YOU DIDN'T KNOW ABOUT THE SOUTH

Here are a few reminders of things most people don't know about the South. Dan Emmett, the Ohio-born minstrel singer and composer credited with writing the song "Dixie," may have been just another thieving Yankee out to take advantage of the South in general, and a black family in particular.

"Dixie" was first performed by Emmett in New York City on April 4, 1859, nearly two years before the firing on Fort Sumter. He and the minstrel band he was playing in received a standing ovation. One eyewitness said the New Yorkers "became wild with delight and seven encores were demanded." The song's catchy, march-like tune (called a "walkaround" in its day) and rollicking lyrics soon spread around the nation, not just in the South. Had there been a Top 40 playlist in those days, "Dixie" would have shot like a bullet to the top of the charts.

When the war started, "Dixie" became the dominant patriotic tune Southerners liked to sing, followed closely by "The Bonnie Blue Flag," also known as "We Are a Band of Brothers," a song inspired by the St. Crispin's Day speech in Shakespeare's *Henry V*. New verses were written for "Dixie" throughout the war. Even Northerners who reworked the lyrics kept the tune. Lincoln asked Union bands to play it twice in the days just before his assassination, saying it was his favorite song and now that the Union had won the war, they could fairly claim it again. Emmett

Guess what?

- ✛ Abraham Lincoln counted "Dixie" among his favorite songs.

- ✛ The oldest women's college and the first public university were founded in the South.

- ✛ America's first movie-making "Hollywood" was in the South.

★ ★ ★ ★ ★ ★ ★ ★ ★ ★

"Dixie"

I wish I was in the land of cotton

Old times there are not forgotten

Look away, look away, look away,

　Dixie land.

In Dixie land where I was born in,

Early on one frosty mornin'

Look away, look away, look away,

　Dixie land.

I wish I was in Dixie, hooray! hooray!

In Dixie land I'll take my stand to live and

　die in Dixie,

Away, away, away down south in Dixie,

Away, away, away down south in Dixie!

has always been credited with writing "Dixie," but his authorship was disputed as early as 1872. Emmett claimed that the tune and words came to him in a moment of inspiration and he wrote them down hastily, but more than thirty other minstrel singers claimed that he had stolen it from them.

The song may actually have been written by Ben and Lou Snowden, two brothers born south of the Mason-Dixon Line in Maryland to slave parents. Emmett knew the Snowdens and on occasion played with them in shows. What is most often disputed is whether Emmett knew the Snowdens before the war. Descendants of the Snowdens believe "Dixie" was their family's composition. On the Snowden family tombstone is carved: "They taught Dan Emmett 'Dixie.'"

Once a staple of high school and college bands in the South, the song is rarely performed in public today out of fear that someone will charge that it is "insensitive to minorities." But there is not a racist line in the song, which affirms that "old times there are not forgotten" in a region that extols family and tradition. Here are the lyrics—memorize them now before the PC police delete every word of them.

The best schools really are in the South

People wrongly think of education as somehow foreign to the South. But we've had the best schools all along, as well as some of the oldest. The second-oldest girls' school in the nation was founded here. The oldest women's college in the nation was founded here. The first public university, allowing the sons of yeoman farmers as well as the wealthy to attend, was founded here.

Salem College in Winston-Salem, North Carolina, began as a Moravian girls' school called Salem Academy in 1772. Both Salem Academy and Salem College (which began granting college degrees in 1890) still cater to young women.

The first true women's college founded as a college, Wesleyan College in Macon, Georgia, was founded in 1836. Most of the women's colleges in the Northeast would be founded much later. For example, Radcliff was founded as a Harvard-like college for women in 1879, forty-three years after Wesleyan.

The University of North Carolina at Chapel Hill was the nation's first state-supported university, opening for classes in 1795. The nation's second public university was the University of Georgia, founded in 1801. (There is a friendly debate between these two schools over who can claim the distinction of first state university. The University of Georgia was chartered four years before North Carolina, in 1785. But the University of North Carolina opened its doors six years before the University of Georgia.) By contrast, the University of New York was not founded until 1841. The University of Massachusetts was not founded until 1867; the University of Connecticut, in 1881. And if you want to talk about private schools, Virginia chartered the University of Henrico in 1618, which became a small school for Indians. (It was later destroyed in an Indian raid.) And

What's a Tar Heel?

While there are several legends behind this North Carolina nickname, perhaps the strongest theory comes from a letter written by Major Joseph Engelhard in which he quotes Robert E. Lee as saying, "There they stand as if they have tar on their heels" in describing the North Carolina men holding their ground in battle while supporting troops retreated.

Virginia's William and Mary, founded in 1693, is second only to Harvard as the oldest continuously operating American college.

Moreover, after the War of Northern Aggression more than a hundred black schools and colleges were founded in the states of the former Confederacy. Only a handful, such as the nation's oldest private black college, Wilberforce, founded in 1856, were started up North, though a handful of blacks were admitted to some of the North's elite schools after the war. For most of the nineteenth century and the first part of the twen-

★ ★ ★ ★ ★ ★ ★ ★ ★ ★ ★ ★ ★ ★

Ivy League Who?

Fourteen of the nation's top 50 schools are in the South:

#8 Duke University—Durham, NC

#16 Johns Hopkins University—Baltimore, MD

#17 Rice University—Houston, TX

#18 Vanderbilt University—Nashville, TN

#19 Emory University—Atlanta, GA

#23 Georgetown University—Washington, DC

#24 University of Virginia—Charlottesville, VA

#27 University of North Carolina–Chapel Hill—Chapel Hill, NC

#30 Wake Forest University—Winston-Salem, NC

#31 College of William and Mary—Williamsburg, VA

#38 Georgia Institute of Technology—Atlanta, GA

#44 Tulane University—New Orleans, LA

#47 University of Texas–Austin—Austin, TX

#48 University of Florida—Gainesville, FL

U.S. News & World Report, Best Colleges 2007

tieth century, the vast majority of black college graduates came from schools founded in the South.

Now let's talk about what's really important in Southern education: football.

There are essentially two college conferences in the South that matter to most people: the Southeastern Conference (SEC) and the Atlantic Coast Conference (ACC). There are other smaller college conferences, of

He Wasn't Just Whistling "Dixie"

"It is one of the best tunes I have ever heard."

Abraham Lincoln
on "Dixie"

course, but the national championship contenders are going to come from one of these two. The SEC used to be *the* conference in the South, but then both Florida State University and the University of Miami, once independents, joined the ACC, which also boasts Florida State, Clemson, Duke, Georgia Tech, Maryland, North Carolina, North Carolina State, Virginia, Virginia Tech, and Wake Forest.

The SEC is the more storied of the two conferences with powerhouses like Georgia, Alabama, Auburn, LSU, Tennessee, and Florida, as well as Arkansas, Kentucky, Mississippi, Mississippi State, South Carolina, and Vanderbilt. The SEC was "discovered" by the rest of the nation in the 1960s and 1970s when national television learned that people in Alabama were not only smart enough to attend college, but thanks to Coach Paul "Bear" Bryant, they could really tear up the football field. Not only could these hicks from the sticks play college football, they could play pro ball too. Bryant took a Yankee boy from Beaver Falls, Pennsylvania, and turned him into Joe Willie Namath, the New York Jets quarterback of the 1969 Super Bowl.

Football may be a Saturday afternoon diversion at many colleges, but SEC and ACC teams take it seriously. As do all those great teams in Texas, including the University of Texas, Texas A & M, Texas Tech, Texas Christian, Southern Methodist University, and Baylor, among others. It's an event. Stadiums are sold out, students prepare for days, and alumni drive and fly in from all over the country. The women are dressed to the nines, and their dates don't look too bad either. A large part of the day is the

★ ★ ★ ★ ★ ★ ★ ★ ★ ★ ★ ★ ★ ★ ★

Southern *"All-American Colleges:"* Top Schools for Conservatives, Old-Fashioned Liberals, and People of Faith, as Reviewed by the Intercollegiate Studies Institute

1	Asbury College: Wilmore, KY
2	Austin College: Sherman, TX
3	Belmont Abbey College: Belmont, NC
4	Centre College: Danville, KY
5	Christendom College: Front Royal, VA
6	The Citadel: Charleston, SC
7	University of Dallas: Irving, TX
8	Eastern Mennonite University: Harrisonburg, VA
9	Emory and Henry College: Emory, VA
10	Lee University: Cleveland, TN
11	Rhodes College: Memphis, TN
12	St. John's College: Annapolis, MD
13	University of St. Thomas: Houston, TX
14	Samford University: Birmingham, AL
15	Southern Virginia University: Buena Vista, VA
16	University of the South: Sewanee, TN
17	Southwestern University: Georgetown, TX
18	Virginia Military Institute: Lexington, VA

party factor. Parking lots at stadiums start filling up the night before in preparation for some serious tailgating. The annual Georgia-Florida football game, held every October in (almost) neutral Jacksonville, Florida, has long been billed "The World's Largest Outdoor Cocktail Party."

Sadly, the forces of political correctness are invading the once sacred grounds of football. It has long been a tradition at Louisiana State

---

★ ★ ★ ★ ★ ★ ★ ★ ★ ★ ★ ★ ★ ★ ★ ★

Southern Colleges as Reviewed by the Intercollegiate Studies Institute Guide 2006: *Choosing the Right College*

1	Auburn University: Auburn, AL	16	New College of Florida: Sarasota, FL
2	Christendom College: Front Royal, VA	17	University of North Carolina: Chapel Hill, NC
3	Clemson University: Clemson, SC		
4	Davidson College: Davidson, NC	18	Oglethorpe University: Atlanta, GA
5	Duke University: Durham, NC	19	Rhodes College: Memphis, TN
6	Emory University: Atlanta, GA	20	University of the South: Sewanee, TN
7	University of Florida: Gainesville, FL	21	Spelman College: Atlanta, GA
8	Furman University: Greenville, SC	22	Tulane University: New Orleans, LA
9	George Mason University: Fairfax, VA	23	Vanderbilt University: Nashville, TN
10	University of Georgia: Athens, GA	24	University of Virginia: Charlottesville, VA
11	Georgia Institute of Technology: Atlanta, GA	25	Wake Forest University: Winston-Salem, NC
12	Hampden-Sydney College: Farmville, VA	26	Washington and Lee University: Lexington, VA
13	Louisiana State University: Baton Rouge, LA	27	College of William and Mary: Williamsburg, VA
14	University of Mississippi: Oxford, MS		
15	Morehouse College: Atlanta, GA	28	Wofford College: Spartanburg, SC

★ ★ ★ ★

A Dixie Fact

The word "Dixie" comes from currency issued by banks in Louisiana. The ten-dollar note was labeled "Dix," French for the number ten. The notes came to be known as "Dixies" by the English speakers, and the area around the French parts of Louisiana came to be known as "Dixieland."

★ ★ ★ ★

University for fans to fly a Confederate battle flag in the purple and gold colors of the school. When a few activists on campus complained, the president of the university asked the fans to stop flying the flag. Naturally, the flags became even more numerous at LSU home games. The activists demanded that the flag be banned from campus. A careful president tried to explain that banning flags was not what football was about.

Other long-cherished football symbols are also under attack. The Colonel, a caricature of a man in a white suit who serves as the mascot of Ole Miss, has been called racist because some think he is supposed to represent a plantation owner. It seems doubtful that many plantation owners would have walked through Mississippi Delta mud in white suits, but the charge remains.

The South spawned rock and roll

From the late 1940s through the early 1960s, music was music and the world was glad of it. Thank a cadre of Southerners for creating what the Beatles, the Rolling Stones, the Eagles, and scores of other follow-along bands would seek to emulate.

One is hard-pressed to name an early rock and roller who was not a Southerner. The movement blending black blues and white country music, first called rockabilly and then rock and roll, began at Sun Records in Memphis, Tennessee. Elvis Presley was from Tupelo, Mississippi. Jerry Lee Lewis was from Ferriday, Louisiana. Buddy Holly was from Lubbock, Texas. J. P. "The Big Bopper" Richardson was from Sabine Pass, Texas. Gene Vincent was from Norfolk, Virginia. Carl Perkins was from Tiptonville, Tennessee. Roy Orbison was from Vernon, Texas. Johnny Cash was from Dyess, Arkansas.

The black blues and jazz singers who helped make the turn from rockabilly to true rock and roll were also from the South. Chuck Berry was from St. Louis; Chubby Checker from Spring Gulley, South Carolina; and Little Richard from Macon, Georgia.

Only one pioneering singer from that period, Bill Haley, was not a Southerner. Haley and his Comets were from Michigan, but their first onstage costumes were cowboy hats and suits; they wanted to be Southerners.

The South was making movies when Hollywood was nowhere

While the first real entertainment movie, *The Great Train Robbery*, was made in 1903 in New Jersey, the first true center of movie making was established in Jacksonville, Florida. By 1915 Jacksonville was home to more than two dozen motion picture companies, including one founded by Thomas Edison. Two years later, more than one hundred companies were making movies in Jacksonville. One of the actors finding regular work in Jacksonville was a young man from Georgia named Babe Hardy. He would later move to California and team up with Stan Laurel to form the comedy team of Laurel and Hardy.

Two incidents killed the film industry in Jacksonville.

One was a mayoral election. In 1917 the citizens of Jacksonville were fed up with the movie companies shutting down streets, making noise, and generally causing problems for regular businesses. On top of the regular disruptions, the actors who came to town seemed to be lacking in morals. Most of them weren't Southerners—at least, they

South vs. North

"I have found that anything that comes out of the South is going to be called grotesque by the Northern reader, unless it is grotesque, in which case it is going to be called realistic."

Flannery O'Connor

didn't have Southern manners. They acted too much like, well, like Yankees. The pro-movie mayor was defeated and replaced by a man who promised to bring the movie companies and their actors into line so decent folks could enjoy their city again.

The second incident was the release of a California-made movie that proved to movie producers that the faraway land of California had the same long stretches of sun that Jacksonville had, and, perhaps more important to the moviemakers, Hollywood, California, was free of the staid Southern morals of Jacksonville, Florida.

The movie that made Hollywood the center of the moviemaking industry was (ironically, a movie about the War and Reconstruction) *The Birth of a Nation*, a 1915 production made almost entirely with Northern actors. It was directed by Kentucky–born D. W. Griffith, one of the giants of silent cinema, from a novel titled *The Clansman*. The movie was a big hit nationwide, though it was also banned in some parts of the country because it portrayed the Ku Klux Klan in a largely favorable light. Despite the controversy, which surprised Griffith, the movie's huge financial success proved to other producers that Hollywood was the place to make movies.

Chapter 4

✫ ✫ ✫ ✫ ✫ ✫ ✫

PLACES AND EVENTS THAT EXPLAIN THE SOUTH

ournalists from the North assigned to explain the South to their sheltered readers are easily spotted when visiting Dixie. They are jumpy, petrified of visiting a strange land populated with even stranger—and dangerous, gun-loving—people.

These funny-talking scribblers react with a start when someone looks them in the eye and says "Howdy!" or "Hey!" Yankees don't understand why pickup truck–driving Southerners nod index fingers at each other on rural roads. (It's a laid-back, Southern wave.) And they don't under-stand—but love to report on—the iconic image of a pickup truck with a gun rack hanging in the rear window, and a Confederate battle flag hang-ing from it too. Once he sees that, the writer knows he can leave: he's got his story—without talking to a single Southerner. But of course he gets it all wrong: the gun rack is hunting equipment; Southerners turn their guns on deer, wild turkeys, and ducks, not reporters. And that Confederate flag is a symbol of patriotism and pride, and, yep, even a hint of typical Southern independent-minded rebelliousness. But as the saying goes, it's definitely a matter of heritage, not hate. (Just talk to the good ol' boy driv-ing the pickup truck—he might even have a John Deere cap–wearing black buddy sitting next to him.)

Don't trust a single word written by a Northern journalist visiting the South. Most come with a fixed agenda. Actually, one can't even trust the

Guess what?

✖ The Confederate flag is a symbol of patriotism and pride—and shows off typical Southern independent-minded rebelliousness.

✖ The Confederacy has its own memorial at Arlington National Cemetery.

✖ The South has its own Mt. Rushmore— at Stone Mountain, Georgia.

South's own newspapers and magazines, most of which are owned by Northern conglomerates and staffed by Yankee transplants or typical liberal media Yankee wannabees. To get a real sense of the South, you're much better off doing things the Southern way—talkin' to real people at the barbecue shack, the barber shop, the NASCAR track, the ballgame, at church, at the garden club, or at the Junior League. Or you could just try visiting one of the many places and events that make the South what it is today.

Historic Southern Locations

Museum of the Confederacy

The Museum of the Confederacy in Richmond, Virginia, is the best place to start. Virtually surrounded by Virginia Commonwealth University Medical School (Dr. Hunter McGuire, Stonewall Jackson's personal surgeon, was a physician there), the museum may be hard for visitors to reach (they are considering a relocation), but it fairly and unflinchingly describes the Confederacy and the war. Among the artifacts are items belonging to Lee, Jackson, Stuart, and other soldiers. The most poignant display is the sketchbook belonging to Jackson's civil engineer, who was shot the same night Jackson was wounded in May 1863. The book has two holes where the Minié balls penetrated before killing him. Beside the museum is the Confederate White House, where Jefferson Davis and his family lived during the war. The chilling sight here is the railing from which four-year-old Joe Davis fell to his death.

Custis-Lee Mansion

The Custis-Lee Mansion, at the top of the hill overlooking the lower portion of Arlington National Cemetery, was built by George Washington Parke Custis, the adopted grandson of George Washington and the father of Mary

Anna Custis, the wife of Robert E. Lee. Custis had filled the house with Washington artifacts to honor the man who raised him. Once the Federals occupied the property in April 1861, those artifacts began disappearing, stolen and shipped home by Union troops—even officers. All the artifacts would have been lost had it not been for a Lee slave who marched into the office of the Union commander. The woman expressed admiration for the Lee family she had served and demanded that the general do

The Southern Mentality

"The past is never dead. It's not even past."

Gavin Stevens in *Requiem for a Nun* by William Faulkner

something about the thieving Yankees who were stealing the nation's history. The general was so embarrassed that he immediately put a guard on the house. He did not, however, order the stolen artifacts returned. The original pew nameplate and silver communion service of the Washington family were also stolen by Yankees from Christ Church in downtown Alexandria. Today the church has a history display panel asking Northern visitors to return the items if their ancestors were the thieves.

It was in the Custis-Lee Mansion, in the first floor parlor, that Robert E. Lee married Mary in 1831. In a top-floor bedroom is a desk where Lee wrote his letter of resignation from the U.S. Army. It is arguably the most important piece of furniture in Southern history. His family wrote about Lee pacing back and forth in that bedroom all night before making the painful decision to resign his commission of more than thirty years.

Confederate Memorial at Arlington National Cemetery

The Confederate Memorial, the tallest monument in Arlington National Cemetery, located about four hundred yards south of the Tomb of the Unknown Soldier, gives the allegorical defense of the South through the use of thirty-two bronze figures. On the memorial is a statement written by a minister who fought in the war, describing the motivation of the average Confederate:

> Not for fame or reward
> Not for place or for rank
> Not lured by ambition
> Or goaded by necessity
> But in simple
> Obedience to duty
> As they understood it
> These men suffered all
> Sacrificed all
> Dared all—and died

Mount Vernon

About ten miles south of Arlington is Mount Vernon, George Washington's home and the location of his tomb. Despite all his accomplishments and his devotion to his estate, Washington cared little for the trappings of wealth and power. Washington's house is made of wood planks while the wealthy and powerful in that era lived in costly brick homes. The plaster decorations inside the relatively simple main parlor depict Washington's real love—farming. A walk on the grounds shows the cabins in which Washington's slaves lived just yards from his house. Upon his death, Washington freed his slaves and provided them with a pension until they died—a practice that was common among slaveholders in the South but unheard of for factory owners in the North.

George Washington's birthplace

Washington's birthplace, about forty miles east of Fredericksburg, is rarely visited by tourists, as it is in rural country far from the interstate.

Washington's actual birth house burned down in his lifetime, but the National Park Service maintains two amazing Washington artifacts that are worth the trip to see. In a glass case is the dress sword Washington wore at his swearing-in ceremony as the nation's first president. Below it is the cutlass he wore during the American Revolution. While working around Mount Vernon, Washington decided he needed a pruning saw, so he took his cutlass to the blacksmith and had notches cut into it. The sword at the side of the man who won independence for the United States was made into a gardening tool. That says a lot about Washington's sense of humility.

Just five miles away is Stratford Hall Plantation, the birthplace of Robert E. Lee and one of the most beautiful colonial-era homes in the nation. Lee moved before he was four years old. He never returned, but he dreamed about one day buying back the house of his childhood.

Colonial Williamsburg

Colonial Williamsburg, perpetually frozen in the mid-1770s, is virtually all reconstructed rather than preserved as Mount Vernon is, but the costumed interpreters here give a good sense of what life was like for Virginians in the eighteenth century. More than one hundred colonial-era buildings are owned by the Colonial Williamsburg Foundation, and many of them are open for touring. In the 1930s John D. Rockefeller, Jr., a New Yorker (!) was persuaded by the rector of the Episcopal church in Williamsburg to finance the re-creation of the Williamsburg of the Founders' era.

Confederate Memorial Hall

Confederate Memorial Hall in New Orleans has the second-largest collection of Confederate artifacts after the Museum of the Confederacy in Richmond. Among the most precious items found at this church-like museum is the crown of thorns woven for Jefferson Davis by Pope Pius IX.

Though it has reopened since Hurricane Katrina damaged the city, the museum is keeping only weekend hours until the tourist trade picks up. Even before the hurricane, New Orleans tourism officials did little to promote this historical gem of a building filled with wonderful heirlooms just blocks from the bars and strip clubs of Bourbon Street. Like many Southern cities, New Orleans has given in to political correctness and is embarrassed by its Confederate heritage. Several years ago a neighboring art museum tried to claim the Confederate Memorial Hall building through an obscure legal maneuver. The Confederate displays would

What a Southerner Said

"For every Southern boy fourteen years old, not once but whenever he wants it, there is the instant when it's still not yet two o'clock on that July afternoon in 1863, the brigades are in position behind the rail fence, the guns are laid and ready in the woods and the furled flags are already loosened to break out and Pickett himself with his long oiled ringlets and his hat in one hand probably and his sword in the other looking up the hill waiting for Longstreet to give the word and it's all in the balance, it hasn't happened yet, it hasn't even begun yet, it not only hasn't begun yet but there is still time for it not to begin against that position and those circumstances which made more men than Garnett and Kemper and Armstead and Wilcox look grave yet it's going to begin, we all know that, we have come too far with too much at stake and that moment doesn't need even a fourteen-year-old boy to think *This time. Maybe this time* with all this much to lose and all this much to gain: Pennsylvania, Maryland, the world, the golden dome of Washington itself to crown with desperate and unbelievable victory the desperate gamble, the cast made two years ago."

William Faulkner, *Intruder in the Dust*

have probably been pulled from the walls had the museum prevailed, but, fortunately, it did not.

New Orleans jazz halls

Within a mile of Confederate Memorial Hall are several establishments where Dixieland jazz lives on. Jazz has always symbolized the city, as well as the South as a whole. It is different from what is heard in Chicago and most certainly different from the jazz clubs of New York City. Perhaps the most noted jazz hall is Preservation Hall. As of 2006 the PC police have not yet called elderly black musicians "racist" for playing music that incorporates the word "Dixie."

Mass graves in Shiloh

The mass graves of Confederate soldiers at Shiloh, Tennessee, are scattered around the battlefield. The burial trenches, surrounded by cannonballs, seem impossibly small to hold the remains of the thousands of men buried in them. That is because the Federals dug the trenches deep and stacked the bodies of the Confederates high. Resting and praying beside these graves today gives Southerners a chance to muse on the sacrifices their ancestors made in defense of their land.

Confederate Avenue in Gettysburg, Pennsylvania

Confederate Avenue, on Seminary Ridge inside Gettysburg National Military Park, is the road marking the spot where the Pettigrew-Pickett-Trimble Assault was launched at 1:00 PM on July 3, 1863. Long misnamed Pickett's Charge because 1863 Richmond newspaper editors tried to claim glory only for Pickett's division of Virginians, the charge also included men from North Carolina, Mississippi, Tennessee, Florida, Louisiana, and Alabama. Each state has a monument to its troops at the spot where they stepped off to march about a mile across an open field into cannon and musket fire. A least 12,000 men began the march. Fewer than half that number returned unhurt. The most striking monument on the field is the one representing North Carolina, designed by Gutzon Borglum, the man who carved Mount Rushmore. The faces of the men, looking toward the Union position at Cemetery Ridge, reflect fear of what waits them and confidence that they can overcome it. One man whispers encouragement in the ear of a hesitant comrade. The 26th and the 55th Regiments of North Carolina both made it inside Federal lines and went farther than any other Confederate troops that day. These monuments represent the high-water mark of the Confederacy.

Chancellorsville National Military Park

Chancellorsville National Military Park, five miles west of Fredericksburg, has preserved the dirt road Stonewall Jackson's 28,000-man Second Corps took on its famous march to reach the far right flank of the Union Army. Visitors can drive or walk the entire length of the road to get a sense of what it must have been like to participate in Lee's greatest victory. Just outside the visitors' center is the spot where Jackson was accidentally wounded by a regiment firing in the dark on what they thought was a Union attack. It was Jackson and his party returning from a scouting mission.

Elmira, New York

Although located in the North, Elmira, New York, must be included when discussing places that explain the South. The Woodlawn National Cemetery in Elmira is the closest anyone will ever get to what has been called "Hellmira," one of the worst prison camps in the history of the war. The camp itself has disappeared under urban development, but the cemetery remains. While Northern historians have made sure that Andersonville in Georgia has received the bulk of attention about mistreatment of prisoners during the war, the truth is that Elmira was just as bad, and perhaps worse. While the conditions at Andersonville were horrendous, they were made that way by the federal government's refusal to hold prisoner exchanges. Elmira's prison was run by a sadist who made it clear that his job was to dish out cruelty. Rather than buy blankets for the Confederates unused to the harsh winter of northern New York, he returned much of his budget to the United States Treasury. The camp doctor boasted that he had killed more Confederates in his hospital than any hard-fighting regiment in the Union Army. Thanks to a kindly black man who buried each Confederate who died at Hellmira, the location of each victim's grave is known. Each one is marked by an individual tombstone. A statue of a crying Confederate soldier, his eyes downcast and his hat off in respect, stands watch over his fellows.

A Book Y'all Aren't Supposed to Read

The Southern Tradition at Bay: A History of Postbellum Thought, by Richard Weaver; Washington, D.C.: Regnery (reissue edition), 1989.

Traces the conservative intellectual tradition of the South.

Edmund Pettus Bridge

The Edmund Pettus Bridge in Selma, Alabama, now a tourist attraction focusing on the civil rights movement, marks the spot where on March 7, 1965, the civil rights movement in the South gained national attention. Black marchers were attacked by white officers to keep them from leaving the city to march to the state capital of Montgomery. A few days later Judge Frank M. Johnson ordered that the march be allowed to continue. Johnson, who had earlier ruled in favor of Rosa Parks when she refused to give up her seat on a public bus, said, "It seems basic to our constitutional principles that the extent of the right to assemble, demonstrate and march peaceably along the highways and streets in an orderly manner should be commensurate with the enormity of the wrongs that are being protested and petitioned against. In this case, the wrongs are enormous. The extent of the right to demonstrate against these wrongs should be determined accordingly."

Inspired by Judge Johnson's rulings and comments on what had been seen as a local issue, President Lyndon B. Johnson pushed through the 1965 Voting Rights Act later that year. The black marchers, including their leader Martin Luther King, Jr., benefited from the strict interpretation of the U.S. Constitution by Judge Johnson, a grandson of Confederate soldiers. A handful of racists received the bulk of the media attention but the "silent majority" of Southerners agreed with Judge Johnson then and now.

Stone Mountain, Georgia

Carved into the world's largest piece of exposed granite, the images of Robert E. Lee, Stonewall Jackson, and Jefferson Davis on horseback on the eastern wall of Stone Mountain are breathtaking. The figures measure 90 feet by 190 feet and are recessed more than forty-two feet into the mountain. Gutzon Borglum, the same man who carved Mount Rushmore and who designed the North Carolina monument at Gettysburg, started the project in 1915 but funding problems kept the project from being completed until 1972. Unless they blast away the side of the mountain, the PC police will never be able to erase the images of the South's two favorite generals and the Confederate president.

The Bear Bryant Museum

Football coaches are human too—but in the South, Bear Bryant does not quite fit into the category of "human." In a region and a state where religion is important and there is but one God, most everyone accepts without question that Bear was the god of Southern football. There is a museum on the University of Alabama campus in Tuscaloosa that is even open on Sunday, when most good Southerners know they should be in church.

The Paul W. Bryant Museum tells the story of University of Alabama football, of course, but that history really didn't start until alumnus Bryant returned to coach. He would eventually win six national championships and 323 games.

Graceland

Graceland in Memphis, Tennessee, the last home and resting place of Elvis Presley is proudly, defiantly tacky. That is appropriate because so was Elvis. Many of us Southerners who do not care what is being designed in Los Angeles or New York fit that description. We like what we like and if Elvis liked carpet on the walls, then who are we to complain about his decorating taste?

The King still attracts crowds thirty years after his death. That is because he was the pioneer who led young people of the 1950s—today's aging Baby Boomers—into adulthood. He was the rebel of his generation, but also one who served in the Army, was proud to have his picture taken with Richard M. Nixon, and loved the South.

If you really want to see what it was like to live like Elvis, eat a banana and peanut butter sandwich. He did. It is not found in most Southern cookbooks, but if he liked it, it must be good.

> ## A Movie Y'all Aren't Supposed to See
>
> *The Outlaw Josey Wales*, 1976 (Great Clint Eastwood shoot-'em-up with Confederate heroes and Yankee villains).

The Grand Ole Opry

The Grand Ole Opry (a play on "opera") in Nashville has been around since the mid-1920s, when WSM radio began broadcasting country music. Still discovering new talent and giving older recording stars a place where their fans can see them, the Opry is a Southern tradition. Country music is something that Southerners accept as a part of life, because it reflects our lives.

※　　　※　　　※

Several cities have become ambassadors for the South. All of them are definite musts for anyone visiting the region for the first time.

Charleston, South Carolina

Charleston, South Carolina, is one of the nation's top tourist destinations for both amateur historians who want to see Fort Sumter—where the war started—and for those who love architecture and who want to see the beautiful homes in the historic district. Charleston is a great place to visit, but wealthy immigrants who want to move into one of the multi-million-dollar historic homes may find they are not as welcome. United States senator and former vice president John C. Calhoun discovered that when he died in 1850. Because Calhoun was not a Charleston native, he could not be buried in the main church yard next to his wife. Because he was born in upland South Carolina, Calhoun had to be buried in the plot across the street from the church.

Savannah, Georgia

Savannah, another great colonial settlement, has a different flavor from Charleston. Charleston is aristocratic, while Savannah was settled by common people recruited from the poorhouses of London. Savannah is built around more than two dozen squares that were part of the original layout of the community in the early 1700s. Almost all of the squares survive, giving the city a more open, public feel than Charleston. Savannah also has more development along its river than Charleston does. But both cities are "must" visits.

Lexington, Virginia

Lexington is a small town at the southern end of the Shenandoah Valley. It is home to two colleges, Washington and Lee University and the Virginia Military Institute, but its significance for Southerners is more important than that. It was where Stonewall Jackson lived in the ten years before the war and where Robert E. Lee lived for five years after the war. Both of them are buried here. Both men's memories are honored with museums containing priceless artifacts that they owned.

New Orleans, Louisiana

Aside from the aforementioned Confederate Memorial Hall, there is more to see to understand New Orleans as an example of the South. New Orleans has always been the South's New York City, a polyglot of mixed cultures, an important port, a place where music and having fun seem to take precedence over conducting more serious business. Famous for both Mardi Gras and Jazz Fest, it is a major tourist destination.

Look beyond the strip clubs to find the real New Orleans, where Dixieland jazz and blues are played. If you have time to sort it all out, visit the state museum on the edge of the French Quarter to try to get a handle on the complicated history of the city, which still has mixtures of French, Spanish, and Acadian influences. and make sure to book a table for some of the best food in the South.

Historic Southern Events

A NASCAR race

To understand racin' one has to go to at least one NASCAR Nextel Cup race, though do it at a real Southern race track, not one of those found in Kansas City or Chicago. Try Darlington in South Carolina, Martinsville in Virginia, or if you want a big track experience, try Charlotte or Daytona Beach.

The Southern Mentality

"Anyone who wants to get to know the South should get to know her women. They are tough, loving, frail and powerful. They hold so many of our best kept secrets."

James Dickey

First-timers will calmly watch the forty-two-car field heading toward them, then will react in shock at the huge, unseen wall of sound that hits them as the cars pass by at full throttle. There is no way to describe it other than a wall of sound. Listen to the first couple of passes and then put in the earplugs to save your hearing.

Non-fans who complain NASCAR is "just cars going in a circle" don't appreciate the strategy, the technology, and the skill it takes to wrestle these 3,200-pound cars around a track, whether it is a half-mile oval like Bristol, Tennessee, or a 2.66-mile giant track like Talladega, Alabama.

The Kentucky Derby

The race itself is over in a few minutes, but it is the spectacle of the huge crowd, the hats the women wear, and the taste of the varying recipes of mint juleps that make the Kentucky Derby a Southern tradition. Horse racing has been in Southern blood dating back to colonial days, when horse owners would bet the ownership of one horse against the other.

The Masters

If Mardi Gras is raucous, and the Kentucky Derby is aristocratic entertainment, the Masters in Augusta, Georgia, is the epitome of the sedate pageantry of golf. The greens are perfect, the flowers along the fairway are beautiful, and the crowds are respectful. At least most of the crowd is respectful. A tiny knot of feminists continue to protest the Masters because the golf club that hosts it, Augusta National, does not admit women. Women can play there as guests, but the private organization has chosen not to admit them as members. The feminists have attracted few sympathizers in their quest to wreck the Masters. Most folks just ignore them. As a general rule, Southerners pretty much ignore folks championing causes in which we have no interest.

Historic Southern Homes

Tourists to New York City, Los Angeles, Chicago, and all those other cities where "old" means "about to be torn down" don't expect to find many "historic homes" to visit. One can visit few towns in the South without finding at least one to visit.

In Asheville, North Carolina, there is the Biltmore Estate, a French-inspired palace built by the Vanderbilt family in the 1880s as a summer home. In Natchez and Vicksburg, Mississippi, several houses that escaped Union occupation and destruction are open for tours to give visitors a sense of what living in the 1860s would have been like in a thriving port town. In New Iberia, Louisiana, is Shadows-on-the-Teche, an 1830s sugar plantation. Near New Orleans is Houmas House, an 1840s house that was once a sugar plantation spanning 30,000 acres.

A Book Y'all Aren't Supposed to Read

Huckleberry Finn by Mark Twain, 1884.

In Charleston there is the Heyward-Washington House, home to a signer of the Declaration of Independence, and a home in which George Washington really did sleep. Just a few blocks away is the Edmonston-Alston House, where Robert E. Lee slept after the hotel where he had been staying almost went up in flames. Several miles away are Middleton Plantation and Drayton Hall, two surviving examples of homes in which the landed gentry lived in colonial South Carolina.

In Savannah, the birthplace of Juliette Gordon Lowe, the founder of the Girl Scouts, is open for touring, as is the Davenport House Museum. It was the threatened destruction of this house for a parking garage that launched the city's historic preservation movement.

But just about everywhere you look in the South, you'll find something beautiful, old, and valuable, because here, as the Mississippi novelist William Faulkner said, "The past is not dead. In fact, it's not even past."

Part II

AMERICAN HISTORY, SOUTHERN STYLE

Chapter 5

★ ★ ★ ★ ★ ★ ★

SOUTHERN COLONIES BIRTH THE NEW WORLD

There might never have been a United States, had the South not embraced unfettered free enterprise early on. That, and the legend that drinking Southern water made one feel like a teenager. The members of the Mayflower Society don't like to talk about it, but United States history really began in the South. Pilgrims and Puritans may have been important in anchoring an English presence in the northeast, but they were really Johnny-Come-Latelies in terms of colonization. The South was where things happened at the beginning of the colonial era, and at the end.

Florida can lay claim to being the first place Europeans visited in the New World (1513), followed by South Carolina (1514), where both the Spanish and later the French would build forts near Parris Island. The first real attempt to colonize the New World was on Roanoke Island in North Carolina in 1586 and 1587, though all the attempts failed. Virginia had the first successful settlement in 1607. North Carolina began to get hardier settlers in its northern reaches in the 1650s, due to men and women who left Virginia because it was getting "too crowded." Georgia would be the last and most immediately successful colony, founded in 1733, barely forty years before all the colonies would declare themselves free of England.

Guess what?

✴ The United States was truly a nation built by Southerners.

✴ One of the very first slaveholders in the colonies was a black man.

✴ The largest American colony was founded in Florida.

And what were the future settlers of New England doing while Southerners were trying to figure out how to survive in the New World? Staying at home in secure England. The tardy Pilgrims, who too many historically challenged people still think were the pioneers of the New World, would not land at Plymouth, Massachusetts, until 1620, thirteen years after Virginia and North Carolina were creating settlements.

The South once spoke Spanish

If legend is to be believed, Spanish explorer Juan Ponce de León must have pondered some sobering questions: What is the perfect age? How old is too old? How young is too young? Where is the gold?

Born to a noble family in Spain, Ponce de León chose to be a soldier and adventurer, and fought in Ferdinand and Isabella's 1492 war to evict the Moors from Granada. In 1493, he became a soldier for Christopher Columbus's second voyage to the New World.

For the next two decades, Ponce de León fought for Spain in what is today Haiti, the Dominican Republic, and Puerto Rico. After finding gold and then developing the Puerto Rican gold mines, Ponce was rewarded with the governorship of the island. That appointment angered Diego Columbus, son of the explorer, who believed the title was his birthright. Diego Columbus took the matter before the courts and won his claim. Ponce de León left his office and set out to find a new source of gold.

By 1513, Ponce de León was fifty-three years old—not old by modern standards, but surprisingly old for an explorer. He had long heard stories from natives about a stream that restored youth to those who drank from it. An observant conquistador might have noticed that these natives aged like everyone else, but Ponce did not.

Some say that a wily Ponce de León never believed the story himself, but told it to his sponsor, the sixty-one-year-old King Ferdinand, who needed a son to succeed him on the throne. Whether for gold or youth,

Ponce de León and Ferdinand agreed that the explorer could rule over new, unexplored lands on the condition that he outfit his expedition at his own expense. On March 27, 1513, Ponce de León landed on the east coast of Florida. As it was Easter, called the Feast of Flowers by the Spanish, Ponce de León named his discovery "Florida." No relics have been found to prove exactly where he landed, but historians believe from crew accounts that the landing was between what are now the cities of St. Augustine and Daytona Beach.

Though he sampled various springs, streams, and rivers, Ponce de León never found his fountain of youth. In the spring of 1521, on a second expedition to the west coast of Florida in what was probably Charlotte Harbor, he was hit in the thigh by an Indian arrow. The wound became infected and he died in July on the island of Cuba.

Other Florida explorers recognized the peninsula for what it was—not a gold mine or a fountain of youth but a perfect base from which to protect the gold fleets coming up from Mexico and South America. In 1565 Spanish soldiers founded St. Augustine, forty-two years before Jamestown, Virginia, and fifty-five years before Plymouth, Massachusetts. The South can claim the oldest continually occupied city in the United States.

Spain's greatest mistake in the New World was sticking to its policy of conquest rather than colonization. It could have created a New Spain decades before England created a New England. But Spain kept St. Augustine a military outpost rather than a self-sustaining colonial base with settlers and cash crops.

The South's lost colony

Spain's glittering successes in finding gold and silver in the New World encouraged Queen Elizabeth I of England to listen sympathetically to Sir Walter Raleigh. In 1584 Raleigh wanted the queen to finance a colony in the New World, pinpointing what is now part of the Outer Banks of North Carolina. As proof of the friendliness of the New World natives, Raleigh introduced the queen to Manteo and Wanchese, two adventurous Croatoan Indians from Roanoke Island, North Carolina, who had traveled back to England from an exploratory expedition led by allies of Raleigh.

A colonizing party departed for Roanoke Island in 1585, but the starving, disappointed colonists decamped six months later when privateer Sir Francis Drake stopped by to check on them. A supply ship soon arrived but missed meeting the colonists now on their way back to England. A group of fifteen sailors from this supply mission agreed to stay to hold England's place in the New World. Those men had disappeared by the time the first true set of colonists, 117 men, women, and children arrived in 1587. That colony, including Virginia Dare, the first white child born in the New World, would disappear too. When the colony's founder, John White, returned in 1590 after a three-year delay in bringing supplies from England (due to a war with Spain), all he found of the colony was the word "Croatoan" carved in a tree.

The Lost Colony, as it has forever been dubbed, may not have been lost at all. The Lumbee Indian tribe in Robeson County, about 270 miles southwest of Roanoke Island on the mainland of North Carolina, believe they are the descendants of the Roanoke colonists. According to their oral traditions, the native ancestors of the Lumbees were the Croatoan tribe, who lived on an island south of Roanoke. When the Englishmen began to starve, the desperate colonists sailed to the island to plead for help from the tribe that had sent Manteo and Wanchese to England. They were welcomed and soon began assimilating to the Croatoan way of life, eventually intermarrying with the natives. For some reason, probably because the island was in the path of hurricanes, the new civilization then moved inland to its present location.

As early as the 1700s researchers speculated that the Lumbees might be the descendants of the Lost Colony, observing that some of the Indians had surprisingly narrow noses. Some even had blue eyes and blond hair. Today's Lumbees accept the legend that the Lost Colony wasn't lost but became part of the Croatoan tribe.

Jamestown and the arrival of black slavery

A more successful colony was planted at Jamestown, Virginia, in 1607. And it is here that black slavery began in the South.

Anthony Johnson, one of Jamestown's early settlers, was very successful, ambitious, and wealthy. His first farm encompassed more than 250 acres at a time when most settlers were scratching a living from tiny plots. Johnson would eventually own more than a thousand acres of prime real estate. He must have been articulate and respected as well, because he won every court case he brought before the bar.

Anthony Johnson was black, but his historic contributions to Jamestown have never been—and likely never will be—the focus of a Black History Month feature, because he was a slaveholder, one of the first in America, and apparently a cruel one.

Johnson's story is fascinating. Africans began arriving in Jamestown in 1619, and were traded to the colonists for food by Dutch sailors. "Antonio, a Negro" (who later adopted the name "Anthony Johnson") arrived in Jamestown two years later, in 1621. Historians believe he was born in Angola, and records indicate that he married an African woman a year after he arrived in Virginia.

By 1621, the cross-pollination of South American and North American tobacco had brought Jamestown its first success. Labor was needed to cultivate the crops, and one solution to the labor shortage was importing indentured servants, both from England and from Africa. Johnson was not a slave but an indentured servant; his services were purchased by a Mr. Bennett, who owned a plantation along the James River outside the pallisaded settlement of Jamestown.

The term "slave" for Africans living in Jamestown was not yet common. In fact, most records during that time list black colonists as "servants," or "Negroes," from the word *negro*, which means "black" in both Spanish and Portuguese. African- and English-born indentured servants were under contract for three to seven years to work off the cost of their passage from England (or elsewhere) to Virginia.

Antonio was nothing if not lucky—or perhaps resourceful. On March 22, 1622, just one year after he arrived, the Powhatan Indians staged a massive one-day raid on the outlying plantations along the James River. More than three hundred colonists were killed. On the Bennett plantation, more than fifty colonists and servants were killed, but Antonio and Bennett survived.

Eventually Anthony, his wife, Mary, and two sons and two daughters moved from Jamestown to what is now the still remote Northampton County, a thin peninsula connected to Virginia today by the Chesapeake Bay Bridge/Tunnel from Virginia Beach. Anthony began accumulating land deeded to him from the colony, starting with 250 acres in exchange for purchasing the "head rights" of five white "redemptioners," or indentured servants. A head right was the colonial version of sponsoring immigrants' passage to the colony. Just as Anthony had repaid Bennett for his passage from Africa by working for him for a contracted period, Anthony paid the way for five white English people to come to his growing plantation. In exchange, they pledged to work for him for a specified time.

Johnson and his family were well respected in Northampton County. When a fire burned down his plantation buildings, the county granted him relief from paying his taxes. In another dispute with a powerful white landowner, the court ordered that a full investigation be undertaken to be sure that both sides were treated fairly.

In November 1653 Anthony Johnson made the fateful decision to prove in court that he owned another man from Africa.

When Johnson was chatting with a neighboring white farmer, a black man named John Castor threw himself at the white farmer's feet and begged to be taken away from Johnson. Castor claimed Johnson was keeping him against his will as a slave, long after his indentured servant contract had run out.

Johnson said that Castor was not an indentured servant, but that he had purchased him. In Johnson's undisputed words, Castor was his "Negro for life." Still, Johnson allowed Castor to leave with the white farmer. Three months later Johnson sued the farmer, a man named Parker, and demanded the return of his property—John Castor. The court considered the case for nearly one and a half years before rendering its decision.

A Book Y'all Aren't Supposed to Read

Don't Tread on Me: A 400-Year History of America at War from Indian Fighting to Terrorist Hunting, by H. W. Crocker III; New York: Crown Forum, 2006.

Patriotic—and controversial—American history that's not afraid to wave the rebel flag.

On March 8, 1655, the court ruled that John Castor was indeed the property of Anthony Johnson. Johnson had proven his case so completely that Parker was even ordered to pay court costs. Castor was returned to Johnson, and he remained with the Johnsons, as their property, when they moved to Somerset County, Maryland, in the 1660s.

The magnitude of what Anthony Johnson had done was not immediately noted in the colonies. While slavery had existed for at least two decades, the court's decision was the first in American history to rule that one human being could own another.

Anthony Johnson died in 1670. One of his sons honored his father by naming their combined Maryland plantation "Angola."

Details of the Johnson family disappear from the history books after the turn of the eighteenth century, when Anthony's grandson died without an heir.

Johnson's case promoted a slave trade that flourished for more than one hundred years. The man who had proclaimed he "owned a Negro for life" was dead before most of the 500,000 Africans brought to the colonies from 1620 to 1803 arrived. Nevertheless, by 1705, fifty years after the precedent-setting case, the Virginia House of Burgesses had written further laws codifying how African slaves—not indentured servants—should be treated in Virginia.

Was Johnson responsible for all those other Africans arriving in America as slaves? Yes and no.

Yes because until Johnson filed his Virginia lawsuit in 1653, no court in any colony had ruled on the legality of one man owning another—though in 1641 Massachusetts had been the first colony to legalize the slave trade. Once the Virginia court ruled in Johnson's favor, the precedent had been set and the courts ruled that slavery was legal.

But the blame for slavery in the South cannot be laid solely at the feet of one man winning one lawsuit. The economics of raising tobacco and the rising cost of sponsoring indentured servants had even more to do with the legalization of slavery. It made more economic sense for planters like Johnson to import Africans by the shipload to work the tobacco fields than it did to recruit and sponsor smaller numbers of white indentured servants to do the same task.

A Southern bouillabaisse of nationalities

By the mid-1760s, a peaceful, polyglot colony speaking half a dozen languages was being founded in the South.

In 1763 England traded Cuba, which it had captured the previous year, to Spain in exchange for Florida. In 1765, the new governor of Florida listened to an interesting proposal by a Scotsman named Andrew Turnbull. Turnbull proposed settling the eastern Florida coast with indentured servants from the Mediterranean (his wife was Turkish) who would bring diverse farming skills to the New World, and who would be likely to come because they had suffered through several years of poor crop yields. In exchange for their labor, each person would be granted fifty acres of land at the end of their indentured service, somewhat the same deal that had been offered the English colonists who settled in Massachusetts.

The colonists would be evenly split among Greeks, Italians, Corsicans, Sicilians, and Minorcans. Turnbull must have been a better salesman than logistician. When his ships sailed to the designated Mediterranean ports to pick up the prospective colonists, they found more than three times the expected number of people waiting for them. Instead of turning anyone down, Turnbull welcomed them aboard, mindful that he had planned to feed only four hundred people once arriving in Florida.

In June 1768, Turnbull's fleet, loaded down with 1,200 colonists, farming tools, and cuttings of grapes, mulberries, and olives, landed on the eastern shore of Florida south of present-day Daytona Beach. The landing instantly created the largest colony ever founded on the American continent (in terms of initial settlement). New Smyrna had four times the land mass and ten times the number of colonists who had landed at Jamestown, established more than 161 years earlier. It would take Plymouth, Massachusetts, more than seven years of immigration before it would total 1,500 people.

Life for the colonists was rough for the first several months. The readily available food, stockpiled for 400 rather than 1,200, was quickly depleted. The hot, humid, heavy air of the tropics was foreign to colonists who were more used to a mountain clime. More than half of the colonists died in the first year. Still, the surviving colonists stayed on.

Written accounts from New Smyrna indicate that the various national groups got along without any trouble. Indeed, by the third year, the collection of cultures had cooperated to export more than twenty tons of indigo. Less successful was the attempt to raise insects (imported from Mexico) that made a brilliant red dye when their bodies were crushed.

★ ★ ★ ★

A Dixie Fact

The South claims the oldest continually occupied city in the United States: Florida's St. Augustine.

★ ★ ★ ★

Despite its success with indigo, New Smyrna as an official colony failed after ten years, because Turnbull's English backers were distracted by the American Revolution. Promised investments from England were never delivered, and zealous on-site overseers mistreated the colonists to the point that they staged a small riot in the main square of the town. In 1777 many of the colonists abandoned New Smyrna, walking almost seventy miles to St. Augustine. New Smyrna survived, but never achieved the successful status of other colonial port towns like Savannah or Charleston.

Mismanagement might have doomed New Smyrna, but the colony was the most striking example that many diverse cultures were welcome in the South. None of the colonists who landed along the harsh, hot, sandy Florida beaches at the start of hurricane season returned home to the Mediterranean. They had found a new home, and their descendants remain today in a geographic band hugging the coastline stretching from New Smyrna Beach north to St. Augustine.

It was—and remains—a far different place from Puritan Massachusetts.

Chapter 6

★ ★ ★ ★ ★ ★ ★

THE SOUTH STARTS AND WINS THE REVOLUTION

Most history books leave readers thinking the American Revolution started in New England. Boston's Faneuil Hall is considered by some to be the cradle of liberty.

True, wealthy Boston merchants resisting Parliament's imposition of taxes on paper and tea did play a major role in irritating King George III. Sam Adams's Circular Letter of 1768 called for the colonies to unite to protest taxation without representation in Parliament. In 1770 a crowd attacked British sentries in front of a government building, resulting in the Boston Massacre. In 1773 another group of Bostonians, fueled by rum, dumped crates of tea into Boston harbor rather than pay taxes on it. The 1774 Coercive Acts, passed by Parliament to solidify control over the colonies, were redubbed the Intolerable Acts by wily Bostonians familiar with the politically correct power of playing the victim.

Southern resistance to English rule normally gets short shrift, other than the obligatory reference to a March 1775 speech Patrick Henry made in a Richmond church, when he proclaimed, "Give me liberty or give me death!"

Protests of English taxes started in the South

On March 22, 1765, the English Parliament passed the Stamp Act, imposing a variety of small taxes on fifty-four different varieties of paper and

Guess what?

✖ Even after blood had been shed, the Northern colonists hoped to reconcile with England.

✖ North Carolina's Regulator War of 1771 showed that Southern colonists were willing to fight against troops representing the Crown.

✖ Thomas Jefferson based the Declaration of Independence on several Virginia documents, including the Virginia Resolution and the Virginia Declaration of Rights.

parchment documents used in the colonies. Everything from a newspaper to a college diploma was liable to be taxed, and the money was paid to tax collectors who would transfer the money back to England rather than keep it in the colonies.

On May 30, just sixty-nine days later, almost as long as it took a ship to cross the Atlantic Ocean with the news, twenty-nine-year-old Patrick Henry rose in the House of Burgesses in Williamsburg, Virginia. Henry, a home-schooled, self-taught lawyer, proposed six statements in reply to the Stamp Act. Other older, more loyal Burgesses must have sighed when the young firebrand took the floor. Two years earlier Henry had linked the words "king" and "tyrant" but had been careful not to name George III specifically.

The first three resolves Henry proposed were relatively mild, stating that the colonists of Virginia had the same rights as Englishmen. Then came the fourth, which stated: "That the general assembly of the colony, together with His Majesty or his substitute have in their representative capacity the only exclusive right and power to levy taxes and impositions on the inhabitants of this colony and that every attempt to vest such a power in any person or persons whatsoever other than the general assembly aforesaid is illegal, unconstitutional, and unjust, and has a manifest tendency to destroy British, as well as American freedom." Henry had just stated that King George III of England had no right to levy a tax on the colonies. Henry ended his presentation of the resolves with the sentence: "If this be treason, make the most of it."

Four of the resolves were passed. Two were not. The fifth said that the residents of the colony were not bound to pay any taxes not imposed by the General Assembly. The sixth resolve said anyone who suggested by speech or written word that the colony could be taxed without permission of the General Assembly was "an enemy of His Majesty's Colony." That statement, of course, could apply to King George himself. Henry had just given a clearly treasonable speech. The texts of all six resolves were reprinted in Virginia newspapers.

Henry's quick protest of the Stamp Act and the Burgesses' official response to his resolves caught Samuel Adams and the other Boston-based protesters flat-footed. While Henry directly attacked the Stamp Act, resulting in calls of "treason" from more loyal Burgess members, Adams and his associates were not as bold as Henry and the Virginians.

Several years later, in 1768, Massachusetts merchants issued a Circular Letter. It proposed a convention of the colonies in New York to discuss how to react to the recent Revenue Act. The convention resulted in a letter to King George in October. Passages of the letter appear to be influenced by the Virginia Resolves.

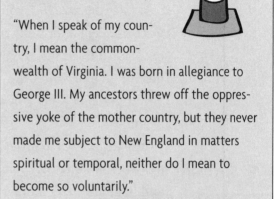

What a Southerner Said

"When I speak of my country, I mean the commonwealth of Virginia. I was born in allegiance to George III. My ancestors threw off the oppressive yoke of the mother country, but they never made me subject to New England in matters spiritual or temporal, neither do I mean to become so voluntarily."

John Randolph of Roanoke, 1773–1833

But while Boston revolutionaries were still organizing street protests, Virginians were leading official civil disobedience to the Crown.

Fighting for freedom started in the South

William Tryon, appointed by George III in 1765 as royal governor of the colony of North Carolina, was an efficient administrator, if a touch too blue-bloody for the yeoman farmers who made up most of the population.

In 1769 a loosely organized group of backwoods farmers, calling themselves Regulators, refused to pay the corrupt county tax collectors and sheriffs appointed by Tryon and his predecessor. In 1770 they beat one of

Tryon's personal friends, Edmund Fanning—a Yale-educated recorder of deeds whose rampant corruption was notorious—and drove him out of town. Tryon finally had to act.

In May 16, 1771, Tryon and his militia met a larger (but untrained) force of Regulators along Alamance Creek, close to present-day Burlington, North Carolina. Tryon called out one of the Regulator leaders to negotiate, and when the man turned his back to return to his lines, Tryon grabbed a musket and shot him. He then ordered the battle to begin.

The Regulators managed to kill just six militiamen while losing much more of their own. Tryon hanged one Regulator immediately at his camp and then marched another six to Hillsborough, the town his friend Fanning had to abandon. Those six were hanged in public as a warning to other rebels of the Crown's power. Many of the Regulators moved on to the wilds of Kentucky and Tennessee rather than wait for more retaliation from Tryon.

While the issues were really local taxation and corruption rather than national taxes, North Carolina's Regulator War of 1771 could be seen as the real start of the colonists' war against British taxation: it showed that Southern colonists would be willing to fight against troops representing the Crown.

Southerners were more ready to fight than Northerners

In September 1774 city leaders in Suffolk County, Massachusetts, issued the Suffolk Resolves. This mildly worded document urged other local governments to ignore royal control until the Intolerable Acts were repealed. The Suffolk Resolves are often represented as a document of rebellion, but their tone hints that the men of Massachusetts would be quite happy to remain under royal rule if the Crown backed away from its enforcement of collecting taxes. The first "resolve":

> That whereas his majesty, George the Third, is the rightful successor to the throne of Great-Britain, and justly entitled to the allegiance of the British realm, and agreeable to compact, of the English colonies in America—therefore, we, the heirs and successors of the first planters of this colony, do cheerfully acknowledge the said George the Third to be our rightful sovereign, and that said covenant is the tenure and claim on which are founded our allegiance and submission.

Even after blood had been shed at Lexington and Concord and the Provincial Congress of Massachusetts had ordered the mobilization of militias to surround Boston, the Northern colonists still hoped that England would back down on taxing the colonies. Led by a peace activist from Pennsylvania, John Dickinson, the Second Continental Congress issued first the Olive Branch Petition, to beg George III's attention to their grievances, and then the Declaration on the Causes and Necessity of Taking Up Arms in the event the king ignored the olive branch. No Northern colony stepped up to demand the Congress do something more concrete—such as declare independence from England. Down South, the sentiment among elected officials and average colonists was much less conciliatory. Just as the upper-class Virginians in the House of Burgesses were willing to poke George III in the eye when he proposed new taxes in 1765, so were the yeoman farmers of North Carolina when the British started a shooting war. On May 20, 1775, one day

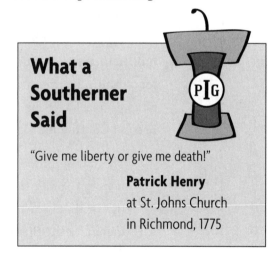

What a Southerner Said

"Give me liberty or give me death!"

Patrick Henry
at St. Johns Church
in Richmond, 1775

after word of the April 19 battles of Lexington and Concord had reached the wilderness outpost of Charlotte, North Carolina, a group of Mecklenburg County citizens passed a resolve stating:

> Resolved . . . That whosoever directly or indirectly abets, or in any way, form, or manner countenances the invasion of our rights, as attempted by the Parliament of Great Britain, is an enemy to his country, to America, and the rights of man.

The Mecklenburg Declaration, lost in a fire, has remained controversial. Even without an original copy of the declaration to demonstrate that average Southerners were ready for independence, there is still proof that Southern leaders were more interested in separating from England than were their Northern counterparts. The Halifax Resolves, issued on April 12, 1776, by North Carolina's Fourth Provincial Congress, were the first official call for separation from Great Britain. The Resolves further suggested that other colonies follow North Carolina's lead in declaring their independence. On June 7, 1776, Richard Henry Lee of Virginia (an ancestor of future Southern general Robert Edward Lee), acting on a vote taken a month earlier at the Virginia Delegation, presented a resolution to the Second Continental Congress in Philadelphia:

> That these united Colonies are, and ought to be, free and independent States, that they are absolved from all allegiance from the British crown, and that all political connection between them and the State of Great Britain is, and ought to be, totally dissolved.

The Congress appointed a delegation of five men (the "Committee of Five"), four Northerners and one Southerner, Thomas Jefferson, to consider Lee's resolution and write a formal declaration of independence. Jefferson later said that the other four unanimously insisted that he write the draft, based on Richard Henry Lee's Virginia Resolution. In an 1822 letter, John Adams wrote that he told Jefferson, "A Virginian should be at the head of this business" and that Jefferson should be the one to write the Declaration of Independence. Adams did not indicate what he meant by this comment, but he likely meant that since Virginia was the most populous colony, it should lead the way.

In starting his Declaration of Independence draft, Jefferson consulted the Virginia Declaration of Rights, written by George Mason and adopted by Virginia on June 12, 1776. When Jefferson presented his first draft to the Committee of Five, they approved most of it, including the following paragraph condemning slavery and its endorsement by King George III:

> He has waged cruel war against human nature itself, violating its most sacred rights of life and liberty in the persons of a distant people who never offended him, captivating and carrying them into slavery in another hemisphere, or to incur miserable death in their transportation thither.

After objections from slaveholding delegates, that paragraph, which went on to condemn the king for offering freedom to slaves who fought against the rebellion, was pulled. While Southern delegates have been blamed for pulling the language, slavery was legal in *all* colonies in 1776.

Several prominent delegates to the Congress did not sign the document, including New York's George Clinton and Robert R. Livingston, who were members of the Committee of Five, Pennsylvania's Thomas Willing, and John Dickinson of Delaware. Both Willing and Dickinson vehemently protested that the colonies were not ready for independence.

Southerners win the Revolution

The Second Continental Congress, composed of wealthy planters, merchants, and politicians from around the colonies, had few choices other than Virginian George Washington for commander of the still-to-be-formed

Continental Army. Washington's military experience, gained in the French and Indian War, far surpassed that of other leaders in the drive for independence. Politics also played a role. Virginia's population of more than 500,000 made it the largest colony, almost twice the size of Massachusetts. North Carolina's population was 200,000, about the same as New York's. South Carolina had 70,000 more settlers than New Jersey. Politically, the North needed a Southerner to lead its army.

But though Washington, who at age twenty-three had commanded Virginia's militia during the French and Indian War, he had never commanded more than a few hundred troops and on one occasion had been forced to surrender his army to the French. He had, by experience anyway, none of the logistical and organizational skills necessary to create an army. Still, in the eyes of the other delegates to the convention, he was what they needed—he was a Virginian who had led men into combat. After the June 17, 1775, Battle of Bunker Hill, Massachusetts, the war went into a lull until February 27, 1776. On that date, Patriot militia met and defeated British Loyalist militias in the fifteen-minute Battle of Moore's Creek Bridge, northwest of Wilmington, North Carolina. The battle was small, but the results were large. Though both militias were poorly trained, the word went through the colonies that a Patriot army had beaten a British-backed army. More important, the victory signaled to Loyalists in North Carolina that they could not openly back the king. For the rest of the war, most of North Carolina would be a Patriot stronghold.

A Movie Y'all Aren't Supposed to See

Ride with the Devil, 1999 (Pro-South movie that includes a black Confederate).

The British would occasionally stage successful forays into the hinterlands, such as the virtual destruction of Patriot general Horatio Gates's army at Camden, South Carolina, on August 16, 1780. Emboldened by this victory, Lord Charles Cornwallis started marching deeper into South and North Carolina with the goal of crushing any and all Patriots. British lieutenant colonel Patrick Ferguson, commanding one of the columns, was charged with recruiting more Loyalists to join his column, which was made up entirely of American colonists loyal to the crown.

Ferguson was heavy-handed in his recruitment. In one written statement he insulted the Tories who had not yet joined him by writing in a broadside poster: "If you choose to be pissed upon forever and ever by a set of mongrels [Patriots], say so at once and let your women turn their backs upon you, and look for real men to protect them."

Ferguson's mistake was sending a note to the Scots-Irish settlers in the mountains. These men had occasionally harassed the Loyalists but had yet to form an army to help the Patriot cause. Ferguson warned the mountaineers to steer clear of him, or he would "lay waste to their communities."

Southerners do not take kindly to threats from outsiders.

The Overmountain Men, as history dubbed this mountain militia of Scots-Irish farmers, caught Ferguson's column on top of King's Mountain, South Carolina, on October 7, 1780. The wily civilian hunters surrounded the base of the mountain and worked their way to the top, killing everyone they did not recognize. Nearly two hundred Loyalists were killed, compared to only twenty-eight Overmountain Men. Ferguson himself was shot multiple times by the Patriot hunters. They stripped his body and then fulfilled the prediction he made in his threat to the Loyalists.

The Overmountain men pissed on Ferguson's body.

The South's redneck general was the best

The best general the Patriots had during the war was Daniel Morgan, a rugged, down-to-earth farmer from Virginia. Morgan was technically not a native Southerner (he was born in either New Jersey or Pennsylvania), but as he had left home before age seventeen to move to the Shenandoah Valley, he had become a Southerner. Southerners always welcome newcomers willing to do things the Southern way. Morgan was.

Morgan had worked as a teamster during the French and Indian War. He developed a hatred of British officers when one sentenced him to five hundred lashes for being insolent. Southerners do not take kindly to being hit by foreigners—and Southerners hold grudges. Morgan's grudge lasted more than a decade, and it cost hundreds of English their lives.

When the Revolution came, the thirty-nine-year-old Morgan raised two rifle companies from the Shenandoah Valley. Morgan's good ol' boy, working-class rapport with his men shocked the privileged Northern officers in the army, but Morgan didn't care.

During the opening of the First Battle of Saratoga, in New York on September 19, 1777, Morgan's Virginia riflemen picked off every British officer with a single volley in the first British advance. In the Second Battle of Saratoga weeks later, one of Morgan's sharpshooters killed British general Simon Fraser, who had been successful in rallying his men.

Morgan should have been made a general after his performance at Saratoga, but the Continental Congress was embarrassed by the uneducated Southern redneck. On January 17, 1781, Morgan was moving in the open country of upland South Carolina when he heard that British lieutenant colonel Banastre Tarleton, a skilled British cavalryman who had built a reputation for hacking Patriot columns to pieces when they were in the open, was now after his force. Morgan stopped at a gathering point for cattle drives, called, simply enough, Cowpens.

Most of Morgan's men were barely trained farmers whose bravery was often called into question. Morgan realized he could use that reputation to his advantage. He walked among the men the night before the battle, asking them to promise that they would fire two volleys and then run as fast as they could to the rear. The next day, the militia did just that. The British broke ranks and chased them—right into the guns of the enlisted troops Morgan had stationed out of sight. Morgan then released his cavalry, who had also been hidden. Tarleton himself escaped, but the hourlong battle resulted in the death of a hundred men and the capture of nearly nine hundred, including more than two hundred wounded. Morgan lost only twelve killed and sixty wounded.

The October 1780 loss at King's Mountain had startled Cornwallis; the loss at Cowpens shocked him. Cornwallis had planned to use Tarleton's cavalry and light infantry to chase down and destroy Patriot general Nathanael Greene's army, then moving into North Carolina. Now, on top of losing Tarleton's force, Cornwallis feared that more Patriot militias would form and join Greene's army.

Cornwallis decided to chase Greene himself. He caught up with him at Guilford Courthouse, North Carolina, on March 15, 1781. It was a bloody battle, which ended when Cornwallis ordered his artillery to fire into a huge knot of troops that included his own men. The British technically won the battle, but with losses that so damaged his army that Cornwallis could do nothing but retreat again into South Carolina. Fewer than seven months later, he would surrender what was left of his army at Yorktown, Virginia. Though the bulk of the British forces were still free to roam at will in the Northern colonies, the loss of the largest army in the South led a discouraged Parliament to vote to end the war.

South vs. North

The Virginia Resolves: "Resolved, That his majesty's liege people, the inhabitants of this colony, are not bound to yield obedience to any law or ordinance whatsoever designed to impose any taxation whatsoever upon them, other than the laws and ordinances of the general assembly aforesaid."

The Massachusetts Circular Letter: "The House have humbly represented to the ministry, their own Sentiments that His Majesty's high Court of Parliament is the supreme legislative Power over the whole Empire."

Southerners were more patriotic

The British had started the Southern Campaign believing Southerners were more loyal to King George than their Northern brethren. This belief was based mostly on the fact that several hundred Scots had formed a militia early in the war that marched on Wilmington, North Carolina. The British forgot that those Scots had been defeated in February 1776 at Moore's Creek Bridge. They then leapt to the conclusion that the South was Loyalist because both Charleston and Savannah had been captured with no serious attempt by a Patriot army to retake them. That was true, but the British mistook the lack of major Patriot armies in the South for lack of Patriots.

There were plenty of Patriots in the South, men like Francis "the Swamp Fox" Marion, who led raids against British outposts. All throughout the Carolinas Patriot militia units fought Loyalist militia units. No British or Loyalist expedition was truly safe outside the major cities and towns because they would come under sniping fire from Patriots. In the South, the Revolution was a war of small skirmishes between Southerners loyal to the Crown and Southerners who considered themselves Patriots. It was not until late in the Revolution that larger battles such as Camden, Kings Mountain, and Cowpens would be fought in the South.

Up North, there were fewer skirmishes, more large battles, and more overt support for the British from the Loyalists. While Washington's troops were freezing in their tents at Valley Forge, the Tory merchants of Philadelphia kept the British warm and well fed. Two years later, while Washington's troops were starving at Morristown, New Jersey, during the severe winter of 1779–1780, farmers for miles around were selling their goods to the British in New Jersey and New York City—and refusing to sell to Washington's quartermasters. The Northern merchants and farmers were more interested in short-term profits than in any hopes for the future of a new nation. They banked on the occupying British winning the war, rather than Washington's raggedy forces.

Other evidence of support for the Revolution can be found in Tory evacuation figures. In 1783, nearly 30,000 Tories sailed from New York City to British-held lands. That represents, in one year, nearly one-third of the estimated 100,000 Tories who left the nation from 1775 through the end of the war. By contrast, Charleston, the largest Southern port, bade farewell to only 9,000 Tories by the end of 1782, when the city was evacuated by the British.

While Boston enjoys its claim as the cradle of the Revolution, it seems there were tens of thousands of Northerners willing to stay wrapped in the arms of Mother England. Southerners were the true revolutionaries, common folk and independent-minded planters tired of an imperial government. They were the ones who wore down the British army. Eighty years later their grandsons would try the same revolution against an imperial federal government, but the outcome would be very different.

Another name Southerners use for the War for Southern Independence is the Second American Revolution. The South saw the First American Revolution as throwing off the yoke of control imposed by England. It saw the Second American Revolution as throwing off the yoke of an intrusive, centralizing federal government by the North.

What a Southerner Said

"Caesar had his Brutus—Charles the First, his Cromwell—and George the Third—may profit by their example. If this be treason, make the most of it."

Patrick Henry

Chapter 7

SOUTHERNERS CREATE AMERICA'S GOVERNMENT

Popular history records that the American Revolution was won on October 19, 1781, when Lord Cornwallis's army surrendered at Yorktown, Virginia. Cornwallis was so embarrassed that he feigned sickness so he would not have to surrender to George Washington in person.

Real history is often different than popular history. In fact, all Cornwallis did was surrender his 8,000-man army. However, there were at least 20,000 British soldiers still under arms, including a 7,000-man army which turned around in Chesapeake Bay once it learned Cornwallis had already surrendered. Had those reinforcements from New York arrived earlier, they could have landed behind the Patriots and the outcome of the American Revolution might have been different.

But England's people and its Parliament were tired of hearing bad news, and when news of the disaster at Yorktown reached England, popular opinion was to let the Americans go their own way.

Skirmishing lasted another year and Washington would not officially resign as army commander until December 23, 1783. Congress ratified the Treaty of Paris on January 14, 1784, and then cleared the decks to answer a major question for the suddenly independent thirteen former colonies: what do we do now?

Guess what?

- Northerners considered slaves to be property, with no more rights than animals—while Southerners insisted slaves were human beings.

- Virginian George Mason refused to sign the Constitution because he thought it gave the federal government too much power.

- The Northern states wanted the new national government to take on Revolutionary War debts, but the Southern states had already paid most war debts on their own.

Southerners bring order to chaos

Long before Thomas Jefferson released his version of the Declaration of Independence, the Second Continental Congress was thinking how to govern the new nation that would come out of the Revolution. On November 15, 1777, Congress adopted the Articles of Confederation, a document based on a system of government suggested by Pennsylvanian Ben Franklin to a committee headed by fellow Pennsylvanian John Dickinson. A subcommittee made up of a New Yorker, a Bostonian, and a Virginian made further changes in the document before its final approval by Congress. It is important to note that three Northerners and one Southerner were the architects of the Articles.

The famous and only lasting effect of the Articles was the naming of the nation as the United States of America. Article II lays out in concrete terms what the Founding Fathers (thirty of the forty-eight representatives were Northerners) thought about the formation of the nation after the Revolution:

> Each state retains its sovereignty, freedom, and independence, and every power, jurisdiction, and right, which is not by this Confederation expressly delegated to the United States, in Congress assembled.

Article III bound the states to defend each other under under certain circumstances including "attacks made upon them, or any of them, on account of religion, sovereignty, trade, or any other pretence whatever."

Ninety years later the descendants of those same Northern politicians would declare that state sovereignty, at least Southern state sovereignty, meant nothing. Instead, the power of the federal government, as long as it was controlled by the Northern states, was omnipotent.

Within ten years of their adoption it was obvious to the Founding Fathers that the Articles of Confederation had not created a government that served a new and growing nation. The Articles were essentially government by committee of states. Under the Articles, there were no federal courts, no method of collecting taxes for federal use, and most important, no chief executive over the government. The only duty set down for the president was to preside over the Congress, which needed nine of the thirteen states to approve legislation.

The weakness of the Articles was demonstrated in August 1786 when a former Revolutionary War officer named Daniel Shays led a rebellion in protest of crushing taxes and debt. It took more than six weeks for Congress to authorize protection for the federal arsenal at Springfield, Massachusetts, threatened by Shays's Rebellion. But the rebellion was eventually crushed.

In September 1786 Virginia called for a conference in Annapolis to discuss ways to regulate interstate commerce, which was not provided by the Articles. Too few states attended the Annapolis Conference to do anything, but James Madison of Virginia suggested another conference be held to discuss the fundamental problems with the Articles.

Before the conference, Madison and the other Virginia delegates met to lay out their own ideas; among them was creating two legislative houses. The Virginia Plan was submitted to Congress as a framework four days after the convention began.

Southerners drive the Constitutional Convention

After officially convening on May 25, 1787, the Constitutional Convention quickly followed Madison's suggestions and shifted from modifying the Articles of Confederation into developing an entirely new form of government. Members of the convention proposed a number of alterations or substitutes to the Virginia Plan. A delegate from New Jersey suggested the chief executive of the government be elected by Congress. Delegate Alexander Hamilton from New York suggested the chief executive and members of the higher house of the legislature be appointed for life, and that the state governors be appointed by Congress. A plan from South Carolina called for a chief executive to be called the president, but he would be elected by the state legislatures.

For weeks the delegates debated the plans as they pieced together the Constitution. States like New Jersey, then a small state in population, demanded to be equal to large states like Virginia, while Virginia wanted the new legislative bodies to be represented by population. A compromise developed in which the states would be equal in the Senate while the House of Representatives would be proportional in population.

Other than Madison of Virginia, who laid out the first framework, and Charles Pinckney of South Carolina, who built on Madison's ideas, the third most important Constitutional founder was an expatriate foreigner, James Wilson, a Scottish-born lawyer from Pennsylvania. It was Wilson who insisted that the chief executive be one person, not a committee, and that this one person, the president of the United States, be elected by an electoral college, which would prevent large states from controlling national elections.

Northerners argue that slaves are property

When the issue of slavery came up, the room divided into two factions; Northerners considered slaves to be property with no more rights than oxen while Southerners insisted slaves were human beings.

The fear of Northern delegates was that the South's black and white population would perpetually overwhelm the North's ability to influence politics. The South had the opposite view; the North would overpower the South unless slaves were counted.

The debate rarely touched on the humanity (or inhumanity) of the slave trade or slave owning. Elbridge Gerry of Massachusetts put his opinion plainly if indelicately: "Blacks are property and are used to the southward as horses and cattle are to the northward and why should their representation be increased to the southward on account of the number of slaves, than horses and oxen to the north?"

Gerry was being disingenuous in his description of what sounded like a slave-free North. The law banning slavery in Massachusetts had not been passed until 1783, just four years earlier.

Oliver Ellsworth of Connecticut—a state that three times had rejected emancipating slaves in the preceding decade—said with regard to slavery: "Let every state import what it pleases. The morality or wisdom of slavery are considerations belonging to the states themselves." Connecticut would not get around to banning slavery until 1848.

James Wilson of Pennsylvania paired up with Charles Pinckney of South Carolina to propose that slaves be counted as three-fifths of a free white man both for representation in Congress and for taxation purposes. At several points during the debate, a Southern delegate would try to appeal for full representation of the slaves as human beings, but each time the suggestion was voted down.

Some Northerners fought the three-fifths rule right to the end. William Paterson of New Jersey said that he could see "slaves in no light but as property." He then erroneously said that the Southern states would use the three-fifths rule to encourage continuing the slave trade. The Southern states were actually more interested in finding ways to stop the trade, because at that time it appeared there were more slaves than could be usefully employed (this was before Eli Whitney's cotton gin, which was patented

Them Scaredy-Cat Yankees

Elbridge Gerry, delegate from Massachusetts to the Constitutional Convention, feared the admittance of western territories as states. He put forth a motion "to limit the number of new states to be admitted into the Union, in such a manner, that they should never be able to outnumber the Atlantic States." Rufus King of New York seconded the motion.

eight years later, in 1794). Slaveholders were worried that importing more slaves would devalue the ones they already owned.

Already there was a realization among some, though, North and South, that slavery was a stain on the new nation. Roger Sherman of Massachusetts did not even want to use the word "slave" in the Constitution at all, which explains why the phrases "other persons" and "persons held for service or labor" are used instead. But few Southerners saw a practical way to dispense with slavery entirely, even if they, like Washington and Jefferson, worried about the morality and its influence on the South's future.

Northerners fight harder for federalism

The United States Constitution, finally signed on September 17, 1787, looked nothing like what Virginian James Madison, sometimes called the "father of the Constitution," had in mind when he first proposed his vision of a strong national government. At one time or another Madison had imagined a higher legislative body (the Senate) that would be elected by the lower body. At one time he imagined one legislative body counting slaves for representatative purposes, and the other one not counting slaves. Madison was not the only person with odd ideas compared to what we know today. New Yorker Alexander Hamilton had proposed a government that was a virtual duplicate of England's. Hamilton even pushed the idea of a lifetime chief executive with the power to veto legislation without any recourse, and he saw no real need for any form of state government. Hamilton believed all government power should remain at the federal level.

While some delegates wanted an all-powerful federal government, others were not so sure about the new document. Of the fifty-five delegates who debated the Constitution, only thirty-nine signed it. Twenty-four of those came from Northern states and fifteen from Southern states. Of the sixteen delegates who objected to the Constitution, ten were from Southern states. Four of Virginia's seven delegates refused to sign, as did two of North Carolina's five delegates, two of Maryland's five delegates, and two of Georgia's four delegates. It was not a solid South. All four of South Carolina's delegates signed.

The most prominent man to refuse to sign the Constitution was George Mason of Virginia. Mason's two major objections were that there was no guaranteed "bill of rights for individuals," and that the Constitution allowed the slave trade to continue for twenty years. Mason, though a slaveholder himself, believed the Constitution should immediately ban the trade so the country could turn its attention to figuring out what to do with the slaves already in the country.

Interestingly, one of the strongest supporters of the Constitution was John Dickinson, the delegate from Delaware and author of the Articles of Confederation that had proven so inadequate in governing the country. Dickinson signed the Constitution and then wrote a series of letters under an assumed name to promote it. He was critical of the states that questioned the strong federal power granted the central government, because his alternative, the Articles of Confederation, had so obviously failed.

Southerners fix the Constitution

Southerners led the way again. It was they who set about enumerating and guaranteeing individual rights that were not specifically spelled out in the new Constitution. Only one Northerner, Elbridge Gerry of Massachusetts, joined the South in calling for a Bill of Rights.

Madison realized he had only a short time to address complaints about the Constitution, if it was going to be ratified. Already the country had split into warring political factions dubbed the Federalists (who were pro-Constitution, like Madison and Hamilton) and the Anti-Federalists (who were anti-Constitution, like Mason, Jefferson, and Patrick Henry).

Madison studied the constitutions of several of the new states and particularly looked back to Mason's Virginia Declaration of Rights, which Jefferson had read in preparation for writing the Declaration of Independence. Madison proposed twenty such rights, which were first whittled to twelve and then to the ten we know today. One curiosity is that the Virginia Declaration of Rights only mentions the people's right to organize into a trained militia in Article 13. Madison elevated it and wrote the Second Amendment with the clear intention of making the organization of militias secondary to the *individual* right of each person to bear arms.

With the promise that a Bill of Rights would be added to the Constitution, most states, including Virginia and New York, ratified the Constitution. The Bill of Rights was adopted in December 1791, nearly four years after the constitutional ratification process had begun.

Madison later wrote that "no government can be perfect and that which is the least imperfect is therefore the best government."

Southerners select the nation's capital

One of the early crises facing the first real Congress of the United States was what to do about the war debts accumulated by the states in fighting the British. The Northern states wanted the new national government to take on the debts since the Revolution had resulted in a new nation. The Southern states balked at that idea because they had already paid most war debts on their own and believed the "assumption plan" was simply a way to tax burgeoning imports and exports.

Alexander Hamilton of New York was the major proponent of the assumption plan because he saw it as a chance to create a true national economy and to prove that the national government could collect national taxes. Opposing him were both Madison and Jefferson, who believed Hamilton's plans, including creating a national bank, might have been unconstitutional.

But Madison and Jefferson, being politicians as well as Southerners, saw an opportunity. The government of the United States did not yet have a permanent capital. They made Hamilton an offer. They would support his "assumption plan" if he would support their "residency plan" to put the permanent national capital somewhere in the middle of the new United States, rather than in the North, where it had rotated for nearly twenty-five years.

Hamilton agreed to the Great Compromise of 1790. With the help of Southerners in the Congress, who reluctantly agreed to bail out the Northern states from their war debts, president and Virginian George Washington was given the task of finding the spot for a new capital. Washington chose a site within half a day's riding distance from his Mount Vernon home. The land chosen was carved out of Virginia and Maryland. By 1800 the District of Columbia had been forever designated as the home of the federal government.

As the nation entered the nineteenth century, the United States was largely a result of the work of Southern politicians like Patrick Henry, George Mason, Charles Pinckney, and John Marshall (fourth Chief Justice of the Supreme Court), among many others, not to mention that four of the first five presidents were Virginians (George Washington, Thomas Jefferson, James Madison, and James Monroe). The United States truly was a nation built by Southerners.

Movies Y'all Aren't Supposed to See

Want proof that good Northerners can cooperate with good Southerners? Then sit down and watch the John Wayne flick *The Undefeated* (or the John Ford-directed John Wayne classics about the U.S. cavalry: *Fort Apache*, *She Wore a Yellow Ribbon*, and *Rio Grande*) or the Sam Peckinpah epic, *Major Dundee*, starring Charlton Heston (a Union officer) and Richard Harris (a Confederate officer).

Chapter 8

★ ★ ★ ★ ★ ★ ★

SOUTHERNERS EXPAND THE NATION

Leaders in the powerful northeastern states of Massachusetts, New York, New Jersey, Pennsylvania, and Connecticut had little interest in expanding the new nation westward. They feared that the addition of new states would dilute their own political and economic power. But Southerners had different ideas and broader visions for the future.

Guess what?

- A brave Southerner doubled the size of the United States—and Congress didn't even thank him.
- New Englanders contemplated secession after the Louisiana Purchase and again during the War of 1812.
- All the states in the continental U.S. added after the original thirteen colonies were acquired while a Southerner was president.

Southerners create the modern-day Midwest

The 65 million people living in the Midwest have 175 Southerners (and French immigrants) from Virginia, Tennessee, and Kentucky to thank for the fact that they are Americans.

Before the American Revolution the region known as Kentucky was the American frontier. Settlers had migrated there from other Southern colonies, ignoring British edicts that made the Allegheny Mountains the western border of the American colonies (though British and Canadian claims extended farther).

Following the launch of the Revolution in 1775, violence on the frontier escalated when the British lieutenant governor of the region, based at Fort Detroit, began offering Indians cash for the scalps of American settlers. George Rogers Clark, a twenty-six-year-old native of Virginia living

in Kentucky, traveled to Williamsburg, Virginia, with a bold plan to present to Governor Patrick Henry. If Henry would finance the mission, Clark would recruit other Southerners to not only capture the English outposts beyond the Kentucky frontier, but also march on Fort Detroit to capture the British capital of the "Northwest Territories."

It was a bold plan to which Henry secretly agreed, not even telling Continental Army general George Washington what Clark had proposed. Henry authorized him to raise seven companies totaling 350 men, but it was difficult to recruit with battles raging in the east. He decided to press on with the mission with 175 men.

Clark boldly approached the Indian tribes who were loyal to Britain and laid out what he intended to do. He offered them two belts: a red one signifying never-ending war or a white one signifying peace. The Indian tribes were so impressed by Clark's bravery that they agreed not to hinder the mission.

In February 1779 Clark and his men started marching overland toward the British-held Fort Sackville in present-day Vincennes, Indiana. Conditions were terrible. The Wabash River and other streams had overflowed their banks. The march that would normally have taken five days took eleven, with the men often pushing their way through freezing, chest-deep water.

On February 23, Clark and his men arrived at Fort Sackville, where the British lieutenant governor was staying. After a three-day siege and battle, the British surrendered. Fort Sackville remained in American hands for the rest of the war. Clark never received the supplies and men he needed to attack Fort Detroit, as he had intended, but he had captured the leading British official in the region. The Northwest Territories, once British-held, were now de facto a vast region under control of the United States. Because the war was still centered on the coast, little attention from the Continental Congress was given to the tremendous victory Clark had achieved.

During the peace negotiations between the United States and England in 1783, American delegate Benjamin Franklin pointed out to the British that they had lost control of the Northwest Territories. To Franklin's surprise, England's representatives essentially agreed with him. Without much protest a clause was inserted into the treaty that ceded control of the region to the United States. In addition, the United States was granted free access to the Great Lakes.

While the Indians continued to raid frontier settlements for decades, the future of the Midwest was settled. More than 260,000 square miles would one day be carved into the states of Ohio, Indiana, Illinois, Michigan, Wisconsin, and part of Minnesota.

While Clark and his band of Southerners had virtually doubled the land under American control, the politicians in Congress were not happy with him. New England's representatives feared the political power the new states would wield once they were admitted into the union. To strike back at Clark, Congress refused to reimburse him for the personal debts he incurred while financing the war on the frontier. Congress's excuse was that Clark could not produce the original receipts for his expenses. No receipts—no payment.

Clark died in 1818, at the age of sixty-six, near Louisville, Kentucky. He had lived with his sister as creditors had taken all he owned. Years later a clerk found the receipts Clark had mailed east for reimbursement. A bureaucrat had put them in the wrong pile and had forgotten them. Clark's accounts tallied to the penny.

Today Midwesterners can stop by the George Rogers Clark National Memorial in the small town of Vincennes, Indiana, and

A Book Y'all Aren't Supposed to Read

Tobacco: A Cultural History of How an Exotic Plant Seduced Civilization by Ian Gately; New York: Grove Press, 2004.

Anti-smoking advocates would never admit it, but the United States likely would never have been founded had it not been for the whopping success of Virginia tobacco sold in England.

pay respect to Clark and his fellow Southerners, who had the vision and the bravery to make the Midwest American.

Southerners prove the Constitution works

The election of 1800 proved to the American people that their Constitution was not just a piece of paper. It was the foundation of freedom.

When John Adams of Massachusetts was elected president in 1796 after the two terms of Washington, the Federalists were firmly in control of the national government. They took advantage of their majority to pass laws such as the Alien and Sedition Acts, which controlled foreigners in the country. Worse, the Federalists threatened to jail anyone found criticizing the government, a flagrant violation of the First Amendment that Virginians James Madison and George Mason had insisted on in the Constitution.

The Anti-Federalist candidate in 1800 was Thomas Jefferson of the Democratic-Republican Party, who campaigned as the champion of small farmers and everyday citizens. It was a nasty campaign coordinated by Massachusetts politicians pushing for the reelection of home-state favorite Adams. His supporters spread stories that Jefferson was having an affair with black slave Sally Hemings. The Northeastern newspapers editorialized that if Jefferson were elected it would so empower the mob—the common people—that the nation would decline to the point that rape and incest would be acceptable. The *Connecticut Courant* newspaper editorialized that if Jefferson were elected president, "murder, robbery, rape, adultery, and incest will be openly taught and practiced, the air will be rent with the cries of the distressed, the soil will be soaked with blood, and the nation black with crimes."

In 1800 popular voting was not yet in effect. Electors were chosen by the states, and representatives voted for the candidates they wanted. Jefferson captured more state electors than Adams, but his vice presidential candidate, Aaron Burr, won the same number of electoral votes Jefferson did, making the presidential race, under the rules at the time, a tie between Jefferson and Burr. The House of Representatives finally elected Jefferson president on the thirty-sixth ballot.

Adams of Massachusetts left office. Virginian Jefferson took office. Despite the turmoil of the initial tie, there was no coup, no violation of the law. The government changed hands after an election just as the Constitution prescribed that it should. In world history, few governments have had such continuous peaceful political transitions as the United States. The governing documents of the United States, written by Southerners, worked and continue to work.

Yankees threaten secession

By 1800 Napoleon Bonaparte was on the march in Europe, and had designs on more fully developing French Louisiana, which he intended as a supply base for the French Caribbean. But France was unable to put down a slave insurrection on the Caribbean island of Hispaniola, Napoleon lost interest in America and offered to sell Louisiana to the United States for $15 million so he could pay his growing war debts. In 1803 President Jefferson was eager to agree, knowing that the acquisition of more than 800,000 square miles of uncharted territory would more than double the existing land area of the nation.

The Federalists, most centered in the Northeast, were horrified at the prospect of a growing nation. They were still reeling from absorbing the Northwest Territories in 1784. Now, not even twenty years later, Jefferson was doubling the nation again.

The wealthy merchants on the eastern coast feared losing their political power to the unwashed farmers and explorers who would be moving into new states like Ohio (admitted to the union in 1803), the remaining Northwest Territories, and now the territories that would come from the

Louisiana Purchase. Some Federalists, most notably former secretary of state Timothy Pickering of Massachusetts, even threatened to withdraw their states from the Union. Their idea was to form a separate New England republic that would not have to associate with Southerners and Westerners. The Federalists even tried to entice Vice President Aaron Burr to leave Jefferson's administration to head the new confederation of states.

The haughty New Englanders were serious about secession. In a letter to Rufus King, another Federalist from Massachusetts, Pickering wrote:

> Were New York detached [as under his plan it would be] from the Virginia influence, the whole Union should be benefited. Jefferson would then be forced to observe some caution and forbearance in his measures. And if a separation should be deemed proper, the five New England States, New York, and New Jersey would naturally be united. Among those seven states there is a sufficient congeniality of character to authorize the expectation of practicable harmony and a permanent union, New York the center. Without a separation, can those states ever rid themselves of Negro Presidents and Negro Congresses and regain their just weight in the political balance?

Jefferson essentially ignored his Federalist critics and pushed through the purchase. In 1804 he asked his personal secretary, Meriwether Lewis, a Virginian, to lead an expedition into the Louisiana Territory to see exactly what the nation had bought. Lewis asked Lieutenant William Clark, also a Virginian and the youngest brother of George Rogers Clark, to come along to act as security chief for the mission. Lewis and Clark were accompanied by some New Englanders—proof that New England secessionists did not represent everyone (or even the majority) in the Northeast. Also accompanying the mission was York, Clark's slave, born in Virginia, making him one of the first black explorers in the United States.

The two-year exploration of the Louisiana Territory was an astounding success, not only in mapping the land but also in discovering new plants and animals, making contacts with Indians, and finding routes that would guide future settlers. Remarkably, only one man died during the entire journey.

The Territory included what is today the states of Louisiana, Arkansas, Missouri, Iowa, the remaining part of Minnesota, North and South Dakota, Nebraska, New Mexico, northern Texas, Oklahoma, Kansas, and portions of Montana, Wyoming, and Colorado. By land mass, the area represents about 22 percent of the current United States.

In twenty years, two Southern leaders, Virginia governor Patrick Henry and President Thomas Jefferson, had more than quadrupled the size of the United States. In that same time span, three other Southern leaders, George Rogers Clark, his younger brother William, and Meriwether Lewis, commanding mostly Southerners, had either conquered or explored the huge land mass that would lead to the creation of twenty states. While selfish, elitist Northern politicians fought bitterly to deny America's growth and thus keep political power concentrated in New England, Southerners bravely expanded America.

A Dixie Fact

If you watch films from the golden era of Hollywood (and the golden era of television) you'll find plenty of sympathetic portrayals of Southerners and the Confederacy. Political correctness—and the virtual banning and sometimes actual banning of pro-South portrayals (like the disappearance of the classic Disney film *Song of the South*)—didn't happen until Hollywood decided to focus on bad language, brutal violence, pornography, and liberal preaching, roundabout the late 1960s, the same time liberals were burning their draft cards. So when it comes to movies and TV: stick to the classics.

How Southerners won the War of 1812

Most European leaders thought it was only a matter of time before the new nation of America would fall apart. The British still had forts in the Northwest, which by treaty should have been evacuated after the Revolutionary

War. An even bigger provocation was that American-flagged ships were being stopped and sailors impressed into the British navy.

Both nations entered the War of 1812 without any clear goals. So-called War Hawks in the Senate, including Kentucky's Henry Clay and South Carolina's John C. Calhoun, virtually forced President James Madison's hand in declaring war. Opposing the War Hawks were the New England Federalists, who once again talked of secession from the Union. The Federalists lifted their wealthy merchant noses into the air and sniffed that they wanted no part of "Mr. Madison's War." What the New England merchants did not openly talk about was that their main trading partner was England. If war came, they would be forced to stop trading with the enemy.

To their credit, most Northerners ignored the Federalists and did their part in fighting England once again in what some historians call the Second War for American Independence. The North's long seafaring history helped win the war, as men like Yankee Isaac Hull scored wins for the U.S. Navy on the high seas and on the nation's inland lakes. Hull commanded the USS *Constitution* (nicknamed Old Ironsides), made of hardy oak timbers cut from forests ranging from Georgia to Maine.

A Book Y'all Aren't Supposed to Read

American Legend: The Real-Life Adventures of David Crockett by Buddy Levy; New York: Putnam & Sons, 2005.

The South contributed the best land generals, including William Henry Harrison and Winfield Scott, both of Virginia, and Andrew Jackson of North Carolina (South Carolina and Tennessee also claim him as a favorite son).

New Englanders suffered another embarrassment in December 1814, when the war's end was virtually in sight. The Hartford Convention, called by the Federalists in Massachusetts, Connecticut, New Hampshire, and Vermont, met in secret to discuss the possibility of New England seceding from the United States. The New Englanders were still seething that the War of 1812 was interfering with trade with England. The delegates lacked the nerve to call publicly for secession, but settled on calling for seven different amendments to the Constitution. In the opening paragraphs of the Hartford Convention Report, the delegates, all New Englanders, came out strongly for states' rights.

One of the Hartford Convention's recommendations was amending the Constitution so that slaves would no longer be counted as people. Another amendment would have limited government-imposed trade embargoes to sixty days—an obvious reflection of the merchants' desire to trade with an enemy during time of war. Another would have prevented the election of the next president from the same state as the current president. At that time, Jefferson and Madison, both from Virginia, had served consecutive terms. The last president from New England had been John Adams of Massachusetts, and the Hartford Conventioneers wanted to ensure that New England got the presidency back.

When the Hartford Convention delegates arrived in Washington to present their final report, they were chagrined to discover that the war was over.

The Hartford Convention backfired on the Northeastern liberals who had led it. They were shocked that the rest of the nation did not embrace their elitist, antiwar, anti-growth, anti-Southern, anti–common man brand of politics. The only lasting impact of the Hartford Convention was to destroy the Federalist Party as a force in American politics.

Slackers and fighters during the Black Hawk War

During the 1830s Indians in Illinois under a chief named Black Hawk tried to reclaim land occupied by white settlers. The governor called out the militia and the United States Army to apprehend the Indian leader.

Among the militiamen called up for three consecutive thirty-day enlistments was a lanky lawyer named Abraham Lincoln. The Illinois militia carefully avoided any chance of actually meeting the Indians. The closest Lincoln came to combat was having his horse stolen—by a fellow militiaman. Lincoln used his ninety days in the militia to enhance his resume, claiming to be a combat veteran for the rest of his political career.

In contrast, a certain second lieutenant in the U.S. Army was involved in several real skirmishes with the Indians, including the one in which Black Hawk was captured. That lieutenant was given the responsibility of escorting Black Hawk to prison. The army lieutenant and the tribal chief came to respect each other's position on westward expansion into previously Indian lands. The soldier was Lieutenant Jefferson Davis, an 1828 graduate of West Point. In 1846, during the Mexican War, Davis resigned his seat in Congress in order to lead a volunteer regiment of his fellow Mississippians. Davis was cited for bravery and suffered a wound that plagued him for the rest of his life.

Lincoln, entering Congress in 1847, not only did not resign his seat to volunteer to serve his country, but was one of the leading antiwar activists in the House. Lincoln was defeated after a single term, while Davis was elected to the United States Senate and served as secretary of war. As secretary of war from 1852 to 1857, Davis aggressively led the effort to modernize the United States Army by developing new weapons and training methods. If any man can be given credit for the well-trained, if small, modern United States Army in 1860 it is Jefferson Davis.

Southerners explore and acquire the American West

The period between 1830 and 1850 saw such huge expansion in the United States that the nation adopted the term "manifest destiny," meaning it was God's will that the United States spread from one ocean to the other. Of the six presidents who served during the period, five were from the South. In fact, the history of this period is a series of Southern highlights.

In 1836 it was mostly Southerners (140 of them, compared to thirty-four Northerners and thirty Europeans) who fought Santa Anna's army and died at the Alamo in San Antonio, Texas.

In the mid-1840s Georgia-born John C. Fremont and Kentucky-born Kit Carson led explorations into the west, collecting specimens, mapping routes, and exploring land that would encourage settlers to make for California and Oregon.

The Mexican War (1846–1848) was led by Virginia-born generals Zachary Taylor and Winfield Scott. Their commander in chief was President James K. Polk from North Carolina and Tennessee (where he lived from age eleven). And just as they had during the War of 1812, Northerners protested the Mexican War, calling it "Mr. Polk's War," a war of opportunity to let slavery spread into the new territories that would be created once the war was over. Congressman Abraham Lincoln demanded to know the exact spot where American blood had been shed on American soil by Mexicans. Lincoln proclaimed that if that spot could not be shown to him, then the war was unjust. The voters of Illinois threw Lincoln out of office in the next election.

After the Mexican War, the sole remaining piece of land that would be acquired to complete the continental United Sates was bought in 1853. The Gadsden Purchase, orchestrated by South Carolinian James Gadsden, brought in portions of Arizona and New Mexico as part of Gadsden's dream of a cross-country railroad stretching from the South to California.

All the states in the continental United States that were added after the original thirteen colonies (including Vermont, which was carved from New Hampshire, and Maine, which was carved from Massachusetts) were acquired during the presidency of a Southerner, and only Oregon and Washington were not originally explored by Southerners.

Books Y'all Aren't Supposed to Read

Lanterns on the Levee: Recollections of a Planter's Son, by William Alexander Percy; Baton Rouge: Louisiana State University Press (reissue edition), 2006.

Destruction & Reconstruction: Personal Experiences of the Late War, by Richard Taylor; Chicago: J.S. Sanders & Co, 2003.

Richard Taylor was a Confederate general and the son of President Zachary Taylor.

Without Southerners brave enough to explore the uncharted lands, and aggressive enough to ignore New Englanders who wanted to limit the size of the Union, there never would have been a United States stretching from "sea to shining sea."

Chapter 9

THE NATION'S "MARK OF CAIN"

Slavery is the world's oldest, most despicable institution. The Egyptians used slaves to build the pyramids. Africans enslaved other Africans after tribal wars. It is possible that more ancient Greeks were slaves than free men and women. The Romans enslaved their conquests. Conquering Muslim armies spread a slave-based culture and economy, while medieval Europe abolished slavery within its own borders, but at least tolerated the slave trade during its first centuries of colonial expansion in the New World.

In America, slavery is widely considered to be exclusive to the South because it was introduced into Virginia, but slavery spread across all thirteen colonies. Judging by their own written records and by physical evidence, slaveholders in northern states like New York, Massachusetts, Connecticut, and Rhode Island were far crueler than Southern slaveholders, who tended to be more paternalistic. There were economic reasons for this differing treatment.

In the North, slaves were considered profitable imports to be sold to Southern plantations or disposable assets to be held on Northern farms until they literally wore out from hard work. In the South, the thinking was entirely different. Slaves were viewed as a permanent work force, laborers to be protected, nurtured, and developed.

Guess what?

- Northern slaveholders were much crueler to their slaves than Southerners were.

- New York City was the capital of the slave trade—even after it had been outlawed.

- The typical Southern slaveholder was more likely to be working in the field beside his slaves than sitting back and reaping the profits.

In the mid-1600s, when Virginians treated imported Africans as indentured servants, Massachusetts and Connecticut were legalizing slavery. In 1641 Massachusetts became the first colony to legalize the slave trade, followed by Connecticut in 1650. Virginia would not formally recognize the slave trade until 1661, twenty years after Massachusetts.

Northerners figured out how to make money on both ends of a slaving voyage. While tobacco planters in Virginia were importing black indentured servants from Africa, colony leaders in Massachusetts and Connecticut were capturing Pequot Indians and shipping them to Barbados, where they were traded for black slaves. The Northerners thus rid themselves of vengeful Indian warriors and received profitable slaves. So successful was this trade that Massachusetts's first governor, John Winthrop, was urged by his brother-in-law to expand the war on the Pequot in order to trade more Indians for blacks.

Many of the leading wealthy citizens of Massachusetts built fortunes on the slave trade. Cotton Mather, among other religious leaders in the colony, preached that slaves were the "miserable children of Adam and Noah," and that slavery was their fate.

A Book Y'all Aren't Supposed to Read

Myne Owne Ground: Race and Freedom on Virginia's Eastern Shore, 1640–1676 by T. H. Breen and Stephen Innes; New York: Oxford University Press, 1992.

This book tells the story of the nation's first wealthy black man and how he set the stage for the acceptance of slavery in the United States.

On at least two occasions slaves in New York City rebelled. In 1712 a slave revolt on Manhattan Island resulted in the deaths of six whites. In retaliation, New York City residents sentenced at least eighteen blacks to death. Records show most were hanged, some were broken into pieces, and some were slow-roasted over an open fire for eight hours.

Twenty-nine years later, in 1741, an even larger group of slaves was accused of trying to revolt. This time thirteen slaves were burned at the stake and seventeen were hanged. Another seventy were sold to Caribbean plantations. That fate may have been even crueler than being tortured in Manhattan, as the Caribbean plantations had a worse reputation for working slaves to death.

While there would be slave rebellions in the South (though not until twenty years after those in New York), there is little indication of the sadism, such as burning people alive or drawing and quartering people, that was dished out as punishment in the North. Rebelling Southern slaves were hanged—a routine sentence for many criminals in the South.

The reality of Northern cruelty to slaves was brought home to New Yorkers in 1991, when the General Services Administration started uncovering bones while digging the foundation for a new office building a few blocks west of New York City's city hall. Researchers discovered the area was the African Burial Ground—a place where eighteenth-century slaves buried fellow slaves. Howard University in Washington, D.C., studied the bones and found that most were young men and women in their twenties. Their arm and leg bones were misshapen, indicating that they had literally been worked to death.

Northerners ran the slave trade

Most of the 500,000 African slaves transported to Southern plantations came in Northern-owned ships—just like those sailing ships depicted in the state flags of New York, Pennsylvania, Delaware, and New Hampshire.

The state flag of Rhode Island features a ship's anchor, which is appropriate because Rhode Island, although the smallest colony, was the biggest slave trader. Records indicate that nearly 1,000 slaving missions were launched from Rhode Island ports and more than 100,000 slaves (20 percent of the slaves imported into America) arrived aboard those ships.

One Rhode Island family, the Browns, made so much money on the slave trade that they became major donors to Rhode Island College. A grateful administration renamed the college Brown College. Today, Brown University, a member of the Ivy League, does admit to its strong ties to slavery. In October 2006 the university issued a report detailing what its historians learned.

John Brown was not happy when the slave trade was abolished in 1808. In one letter he complains: "We might as well enjoy that trade as leave it wholly to others [meaning nations other than the United States]. It was the law of that country [Africa] to export those whom they held in slavery." Brown added that because of the abolition of the slave trade, "all of our distilleries and manufactures were lying idle for want of an extended commerce" in slaves.

Even when American-owned slaving ships called a Southern port home, they almost certainly originated in New England. According to records from 1803 in Charleston, ninety-one slave ships docking there were from England, eighty-eight ships were from Rhode Island, ten were from France, and thirteen were based in Charleston—but those thirteen ships belonged to businessmen who had moved to South Carolina from Newport, Rhode Island, to get closer to their market.

New York refused to abandon the slave trade

Even decades after importing slaves into the United States had been made illegal by Congress in 1808, one of the largest and most profitable industries in New York City was outfitting slave ships.

Others noticed Northern hypocrisy, even if New York City and state officials did not. The British consul reported in 1862 that of the 170 slave trading expeditions outfitted in New York City in the previous three years, at least seventy of them had sailed directly for Africa.

In 1859, just before the War for Southern Independence began, a New York newspaper called the *Continental Monthly* editorialized: "The number of persons engaged in the slave trade and the amount of capital embarked in it exceed our powers of calculation. The city of New York has been, until late, the principal port in the world for this infamous commerce; although the cities of Boston and Portland [Maine] are second to her."

Not even war slowed the Yankee slave trade

Even the impending threat of war between North and South did little to slow the slavers operating out of New York City.

In April 1861, off the coast of Africa, Lieutenant John Guthrie of the USS *Saratoga* boarded the *Nightingale*, a slave ship outfitted in New York City owned by three wealthy New Yorkers. Guthrie found 961 slaves in the hold, a cargo worth nearly $1 million in 1860 dollars—had all of them survived the Atlantic crossing. Guthrie returned the slaves to Liberia. When the *Saratoga* docked in America, Guthrie learned that his native Virginia had seceded from the Union. The man who had freed nearly a thousand slaves from the clutches of New York slave traders followed his conscience and joined the Confederate navy. Always a hero, Guthrie died in 1875 trying to save a shipwrecked crew off the coast of North Carolina.

The event that ended the illegal slave trade in New York was an execution. In the summer of 1860, Nathaniel Gordon, a Maine native living in New York City, left for his final slaving trip from the port of New York, captaining the *Erie*. The ship was stopped and boarded fifty miles off the mouth of the Congo River.

On board were 897 slaves ranging in age from six months to forty years. Significantly, Gordon's ship was half the size of the *Nightingale* yet carried about the same number of slaves. Gordon had stacked the slaves so precisely that the naval officers testified that one could not walk below decks without stepping on a human being.

A Book Y'all Aren't Supposed to Read

Narrative of the Life of Frederick Douglass, an American Slave by Frederick Douglass. This great work of abolitionist literature is Douglass's account of his life as a slave. It is a memorable and moving account by an exceptional man.

It was nearly two years before Gordon went to trial, thanks in part to threats from slick New York City lawyers to sue for slander anyone who tried to claim Gordon was the captain of the slave ship. Those threats were particularly directed at the poorly paid officers of the United States Navy who had witnessed the horrific conditions on the *Erie*. In addition, a petition carrying the signatures of at least 18,000 residents of Portland, Maine, was delivered to President Lincoln asking that Gordon's life be spared. (Only the president could pardon someone convicted of violating federal law.)

Lincoln, heavily lobbied by powerful people wanting to send a message to other slavers, refused to pardon Gordon. On February 21, 1862, Gordon became the only American ever executed for participating in the slave trade. Gordon's death did not, however, end the Yankees' dedication to continuing the trade. Within weeks of the execution U.S. marshal Robert Murray wrote to the secretary of the interior that the effect of Gordon's execution was minimal to the overall slave trade: "I am satisfied that the parties interested have removed their operations from New York to the ports of New London, New Bedford and Portland"—in Connecticut, Massachusetts, and Maine, respectively.

One year after the firing on Fort Sumter, not a single slave ship was operating in Southern waters, but there were scores sailing from New England ports carrying slaves to Cuba.

Slavery was less cruel in the South

The general public's perception of slavery in the South can be summed up in the famous photo of Gordon, a runaway slave from Mississippi whose shirtless back displayed a grotesque mass of criss-crossing scars, apparently the result of repeated whippings. According to the accompanying *Harper's Weekly* story published in 1863, Gordon escaped by rubbing his skin with onions to hide his scent from the dogs pursuing him.

Gordon made it to Union lines in occupied Baton Rouge, Louisiana, where Union men took the famous photograph. Gordon's back is a horrifying sight, evidence of an irrational, cruel, perhaps psychotic or sadistic owner who meted out a punishment that could have killed a man.

A Book Y'all Aren't Supposed to Read

Southern Tradition at Bay by Richard Weaver; New York: Arlington House, 1971.

The frequent appearance of Gordon's photo in books about slavery in the South actually raises more questions than it answers about Southern slavery: Where are the photographs of other badly whipped slaves? If whippings were common on Southern plantations there would likely be other photos of men and women like Gordon. So far, 140 years after the end of the war, Gordon's portrait is the only one regularly reproduced.

In the South, slaves were essential agricultural workers, and slaveholders had a vested interest in making sure their slaves lived long, productive lives. In the 1600s and 1700s, slaves helped grow and process tobacco, indigo, and rice. Indeed, many slaves were imported from certain regions in Africa because they already were skilled in growing rice. After Massachusetts native Eli Whitney patented the cotton engine in 1794 to separate cotton seeds from the raw cotton bolls picked from the plant, cotton became the largest and most important crop in the South. Slaves were needed to plant, cultivate, and then pick the cotton that would find its way to Northern and European mills.

Southern slaves lived much like free blacks—and whites

Many Southern slaveholders at the time truly believed they were doing Africans a favor by bringing them to America. One Presbyterian minister wrote a book in 1842 called *The Religious Instruction of Negroes*, in which he told his white readers that it was a "divinely imposed" obligation to take good care of their slaves. Another rice planter told his overseer that his first responsibility was "the care and well being of the negroes. The Proprietor is always ready to excuse such errors as may proceed from want of judgment; but he never can or will excuse any cruelty, severity, or want of care towards the negroes."

Pastors all over the South held the view that slavery was ordained in the Bible and that it was the Christian duty of slaveholders to take care of "their people." For the most part, they apparently did. The average height of a black slave, one measure of nutrition that can be gleaned from census records, was virtually identical to that of a white man. The average American slave was even one inch taller than the average British Royal Marine of the time. Also, according to census records, the mortality rate of slaves in the South was much lower than that of those living in the Caribbean.

Family life was important to both slaves and slaveholders, who wanted a docile work force. Contrary to claims by abolitionists, slaves were allowed to marry. Of the 3,225 recorded marriages performed by Episcopal churches in the South between 1841 and 1860, 52 percent were between slaves. Studies of slave sales in one of the largest slave markets, New Orleans, show that up to 80 percent of slave marriages were not broken up by selling one partner away from the other.

Slave labor has also been mischaracterized as lasting from "sun-up to sun-down." Research has found that cotton plantation slaves worked an average of fifty-eight hours per week compared to the seventy-two hours a week kept by British textile workers and sixty hours per week that Northern commercial farmers worked. Most slaves worked only half a day, if at all, on Saturday, and not at all on Sundays.

Not all slaves were field hands. Studies of census records show that at least one-quarter of Southern slaves were skilled workers: coopers, millers, carpenters, furniture makers, blacksmiths, and other tradesmen.

Southern slaves typically could move freely about the countryside, hunting with firearms, visiting neighboring farms, even hiring themselves out in their free time to make money on the side. Some slaves were so skilled they were able to buy their own freedom and go into business for themselves. Thomas Day of Milton, North Carolina, became such a renowned furniture maker that the governor bought his furniture for the governor's mansion. Day's waiting list was so long that he purchased fourteen slaves to expand his labor force. Original pieces of Thomas Day's furniture are among the most valuable antiques on the market today.

Enslaved black women also enjoyed a fair amount of freedom in the South. Elizabeth Keckley was a dressmaker who bought her freedom while living in St. Louis. She moved to Washington, D.C., where she found scores of fashion-conscious, wealthy women who wanted to wear the latest designs. Keckley became a nationally known dressmaker, delivering gowns to both Mary Lincoln and Varina Davis, the two First Ladies of the two nations in 1861. Mrs. Keckley delivered Mrs. Davis's dress in the summer of 1861, long after the war had begun, because, she explained, Mrs. Davis had contracted for it and Mrs. Keckley always kept her word.

Books Y'all Aren't Supposed to Read

Complicity: How the North Promoted, Prolonged, and Profited from Slavery by Anne Farrow, Joel Lang, and Jessica Frank; New York City: Ballantine, 2005.

New York Burning: Liberty, Slavery, and Conspiracy in Eighteenth-Century Manhattan by Jill Lepore; New York City: Alfred A. Knopf, 2005.

Hanging Captain Gordon: The Life and Trial of an American Slave Trader by Ron Soodalter; New York: Atria, 2006.

It was against the law in the South to teach slaves to read and write. But, like many laws, it was widely ignored. Nat Turner, the leader of the bloody 1830 revolt in Virginia in which more than one hundred white men, women, and children were killed in their beds, could read and write as well as any white man. His owners had taught him. In 1851 (a decade

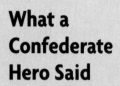

What a Confederate Hero Said

"In this enlightened age, there are few I believe, but what will acknowledge that slavery as an institution is a moral and political evil in any country."

Robert E. Lee

before he won the nickname "Stonewall"), Virginia Military Institute professor Thomas J. Jackson taught young slaves how to read the Bible. Though this was a clear violation of the law, no one in Lexington ever complained or admonished him, including Governor John Letcher, who had a home in Lexington and was a good friend of Jackson before the war.

Slaves and their masters lived side by side in the South. Slave cabins were often built just yards from the owner's house because the slaveholders were usually also the plantation doctors. The owner's wife often served much like a physician's assistant today, dispensing medicines to ill slaves and calling for a doctor if the illness progressed.

Frederick Law Olmsted, the Hartford, Connecticut–born landscape architect who designed New York City's beloved Central Park, toured the South and was surprised by the easy familiarity he saw between whites and blacks.

"I am struck with the close cohabitation and association of blacks and whites," he wrote. His diary mentions watching a black woman and daughter and a white woman and daughter on a train: "[They] talked and laughed together and the girls munched confectionary out of the same paper, *with a familiarity and closeness of intimacy that would have been noticed with astonishment, if not with manifest displeasure, in almost any chance company in the North.*" (emphasis added)

This familiarity among slaves and whites in the South is in sharp contrast to the earlier history of Northern-owned slaves, who were severely punished if found on the streets at night or tried to buy products in an open-air market. One Massachusetts law forbade slaves from owning pigs. Other laws prohibited female slaves from having sex, because pregnancy would make them less productive. These sorts of restrictions were absent from the development of Southern slavery.

The race of plantation owners may be surprising

The image of a huge Southern plantation with hardworking blacks watched from the verandah by lazy white masters is a myth. 1860 census records show that only about 25 percent of white Southerners owned any slaves; seven-tenths of 1 percent owned more than fifty slaves; and just one-tenth of 1 percent owned more than two hundred slaves. Moreover, only 2.5 percent of the 4 million slaves living in the South in 1860 actually worked and lived on large plantations.

What do all these statistics mean? They mean that the typical Southern slaveholder was more likely to be working in the field beside his slaves than sitting on the verandah sipping a mint julep.

It is true that there were some large slaveholders in the South. The third-largest slaveholder in South Carolina was a man named William Ellison. Ellison and his family were staunch supporters of the Confederate cause, and one of his sons left the plantation to join an artillery unit. Instead of raising profitable cotton during the war, the Ellisons switched their plantation's production to foodstuffs needed to feed the Confederate armies in the field.

One other thing about this wealthy slaveholding family—they were black, and William Ellison was a former slave.

Ellison was one of the richest men in South Carolina. By 1860, the eve of the war, he owned more than sixty slaves, putting him in the top 5 percent of slaveholders in South Carolina. His claimed wealth was more than $65,000, higher than 90 percent of his white neighbors. Some historians suspect he might have been even richer and was hiding some of his wealth to avoid taxes. All that disappeared after the war, because Ellison invested heavily in Confederate bonds that were worthless after the Confederacy's defeat.

Holding on to slavery beyond 1808—when the slave trade, but not slavery, was prohibited by federal law—was the greatest mistake in the South's history. It skewed political arguments within and without the South, stripped the South of the moral high ground when it argued in favor of states' rights, and left the South vulnerable to international criticism when the War for Southern Independence began in 1861.

★ ★ ★ ★ ★ ★ ★

Chapter 10

WHY THE SOUTH SECEDED

When historian Shelby Foote was asked why the Civil War seemed to be so important to Southerners even one hundred years afterward, Foote replied that Southerners were the only Americans to have lost a war on their own soil, and it still bothered them.

The Civil War, War of Northern Aggression, War for Southern Independence, War Between the States—whatever anyone prefers to call it—had been building for at least thirty years before it finally broke out in 1861. Tensions had been mounting since the 1830s when South Carolina broached the idea of seceding over high federal tariffs. Fellow Southerner but ardent nationalist President Andrew Jackson threatened to invade South Carolina if it tried to defy national laws.

Over the next thirty years tariffs kept edging higher. The North was growing fast in population and more powerful in industrial might. The South, used to running things in the era of Washington and Jefferson, began to fear it would be forever forced into second-class status by the North. Then Abraham Lincoln was elected president without the support of a single Southern state.

Something had to give.

The two biggest myths about the War are that it was a civil war and that it was simply about slavery. The popular image presented is that a peaceful nation exploded, splintering a large family into two warring parties,

Guess what?

✖ The War was not about slavery.

✖ Virginia, Arkansas, Tennessee, and North Carolina did not secede until after President Lincoln ordered their governors to raise regiments to invade the Southern Confederacy.

✖ To provide fair market value compensation to slaveholders would have cost the United States fifty times the entire 1860 federal budget.

and that those two warring parties would never have come to blows if one had not insisted on enslaving his fellow man while the other gently suggested that slaves be set free.

It was much more complicated than that.

A Dixie Fact

States' rights were so important in the South that it became a name. States Rights Gist was a brigadier general in the Confederate Army.

★ ★ ★ ★

There was no civil war

On strict definition, a civil war is between at least two political factions trying to take over the same government by violent means. The South had no intention of taking over the government of the United States when eleven states left the Union between December 1860 and May 1861. The Southern states' intention was to establish a confederacy of slaveholding governments that would peacefully co-exist with the United States on its northern border. The new Confederate leaders wanted peace, not war, and they believed the United States Constitution was written as a compact among states from which secession was an obvious option if the central government seemed overbearing. In other words, they did not think the Union was irrevocable.

The Ordinance of Secession adopted by South Carolina in December 1860 outlines in stark terms why it was the first state to secede. The document quotes both the Declaration of Independence and the Treaty of Paris (signed with Great Britain to end the American Revolution), both of which called the colonies "free and independent states." The Ordinance then quotes the first ruling document of the new United States, the Articles of Confederation: "that each State retains its sovereignty, freedom and independence, and every power, jurisdiction and right which is not, by this Confederation, expressly delegated to the United States in Congress assembled."

The Ordinance then points out that only nine of the original thirteen states immediately signed the Constitution, and only then with the promise that a Bill of Rights would be added. North Carolina and Rhode Island refused to ratify the Constitution until the Bill of Rights was added.

In the last paragraph of the Ordinance of Secession, South Carolina says it "has resumed its position among the nations of the world." South Carolina had no intention of taking over the government of the United States. It wanted to be its own nation.

The South wanted its independence

Six other states followed South Carolina out of the Union within a few weeks. On March 11, 1861, those seven states formed a new compact and adopted a constitution closely worded after the United States Constitution, with one big exception. The United States Constitution opens with: "We the people of the United States, in order to form a more perfect Union. . . . "

The Confederate Constitution opens with: "We the people of the Confederate States, each State acting in its sovereign and independent character. . . . "

The Southern states were careful to show in the wording of their preamble that they felt the United States government no longer recognized individual states' independence, but that the Confederate Constitution would.

A Book Y'all Aren't Supposed to Read

The Civil War: A Narrative by Shelby Foote; New York: Random House, 1974.

It took Foote, a Mississippi native, twenty years to write this three-volume history, which has a deliciously and decidedly Southern slant to it.

While the Confederate Constitution shared these similarities with the U.S. Constitution, it was marked with two significant differences. The major difference was that the Confederate Constitution specifically abolished the international slave trade. The second difference was that tariffs were permitted but were forbidden to benefit particular industries. This

★ ★ ★ ★ ★ ★ ★ ★ ★ ★ ★ ★ ★

Secession: The Redemption of Democracy

Sir John Dalberg Acton to Robert E. Lee, November 4, 1866:

"I saw in States Rights the only availing check upon the absolutism of the sovereign will, and secession filled me with hope, not as the destruction but as the redemption of Democracy. The institutions of your Republic have not exercised on the old world the salutary and liberating influence which ought to have belonged to them, by reason of those defects and abuses of principle which the Confederate Constitution was expressly and wisely calculated to remedy. I believed that the example of that great Reform would have blessed all the races of mankind by establishing true freedom purged of the native dangers and disorders of Republics."

★ ★ ★ ★

A Dixie Fact

Harriet Beecher Stowe, the author of *Uncle Tom's Cabin*, had never been to the South and had never even seen a plantation and how they were run.

★ ★ ★ ★

clause was a direct result of the South's belief that the import and export tariffs then imposed by the United States government heavily favored Northern industries over Southern agriculture.

By May 10, 1861, four more states had seceded, to make up a final eleven in the Confederacy. Significantly, the last four states (Virginia, Arkansas, Tennessee, and North Carolina) did not secede until after President Lincoln ordered their governors to raise regiments to invade the Southern Confederacy. Until Lincoln ordered an invasion, these four states hoped that a compromise could be worked out.

The Confederate capital was first established in Montgomery, Alabama, and was later moved to Richmond, Virginia, fewer than one hundred miles from Washington. Confederate leaders mistakenly believed that putting their capital so close to the U.S. capital would show that the two governments could live in peace and harmony. In reality, putting the Confederate capital one hundred miles from Washington just gave the North a tempting target. The North equated capture of Richmond with winning the war. If the war had been a true civil war, defending Washington, the national capital, would have been more important to the Union than capturing Richmond. But because the South merely wanted independence—it did not want to conquer the North—this was not a civil war.

In the South, the War Between the States has always been the popular description of the war, but a truer description is the War for Southern Independence. The states were not fighting each other. The North was fighting the South because the South wanted out of the Union.

Secession was an economic issue

Slavery did not suddenly crop up in 1860. Americans had always debated the Christian propriety of owning slaves—and how eventually they might be freed. On the latter point, Southerners asked: Would freed slaves roam the countryside begging for food? Would they lower the wages of white people by competing for paying jobs? If they couldn't find jobs, would they become violent thieves?

The answers to these questions were sobering and scary thoughts for Southerners and Northerners alike. Both regions had experienced slave uprisings and both wondered if lingering resentment among freed blacks would turn to violence. In 1820, six years before his death, Thomas Jefferson described the dilemma over slavery: "We have the wolf by the ear, and we can neither hold him, nor safely let him go. Justice is in one scale, and self-preservation in the other."

Because the U.S. Constitution specifically allowed slavery, many Southerners considered the morality of the institution irrelevant,

Even the Yankees Admired Lee

Robert E. Lee was "without any exception the very greatest of all the great captains that the English-speaking peoples have brought forth."

Teddy Roosevelt

and doubly irrelevant because the outfitting of slave ships was New York City's largest industry in 1860.

That was a mistake history would not forgive.

If nineteenth-century Confederate leaders could be asked today to name their biggest public relations mistake in seceding, they would probably say "talking so much about slavery and not enough about other grievances we had with the United States." Slavery is mentioned repeatedly in four states' "declaration of causes" for secession, though it is not mentioned at all or only in passing in the actual secession documents taking the eleven states out of the Union.

A Book Y'all Aren't Supposed to Read

The Glittering Illusion: English Sympathy for the Southern Confederacy by Sheldon Vanauken; Washington, D.C.: Regnery, 1989.

The South's chief grievances were always economic, of which the issue of slavery was a part, and which tied into concerns about security. Georgia's document of secession complains about tariffs and how Northern domination of the federal government was inflicting economic harm on the South. But it adds that if Northern abolitionists succeeded in freeing Georgia's slaves, the newly freed men would:

> subject us not only to the loss of our property but the destruction of ourselves, our wives, and our children, and the desolation of our homes, our altars, and our firesides. To avoid these evils we resume the powers which our fathers delegated to the Government of the United States, and henceforth will seek new safeguards for our liberty, equality, security, and tranquility.

Texas saw a conspiracy not only to abolish slavery, but also to grab land that Southerners had fought the Mexican War to obtain:

> By the disloyalty of the Northern States and their citizens and the imbecility of the Federal Government, infamous combina-

tions of incendiaries and outlaws have been permitted in those States and the common territory of Kansas to trample upon the federal laws, to war upon the lives and property of Southern citizens in that territory, and finally, by violence and mob law, to usurp the possession of the same as exclusively the property of the Northern States.

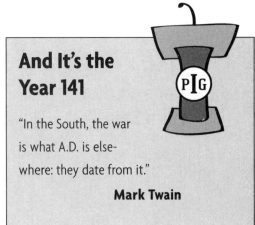

And It's the Year 141

"In the South, the war is what A.D. is elsewhere: they date from it."

Mark Twain

Virginia, one of the last four states to secede, did not issue a declaration of causes, but did point out that its people had ratified the Constitution only after giving the state an out should the United States became overbearing:

> The people of Virginia in their ratification of the Constitution of the United States of America, adopted by them in convention on the twenty-fifth day of June, in the year of our Lord one thousand seven hundred and eighty-eight, having declared that the powers granted under said Constitution were derived from the people of the United States and might be resumed whensoever the same should be perverted to their injury and oppression, and the Federal Government having perverted said powers not only to the injury of the people of Virginia, but to the oppression of the Southern slave-holding States. . . .

What concerned most Southern political leaders was the changing tone of abolitionist talk coming from the North. The demands were no longer slow, gradual, compensated emancipation of the Southern work force (discussed openly in Northern speeches at least as early as 1857), but sudden, total, and uncompensated emancipation.

The Southern planters listened to ideas on compensated emancipation, but the prewar numbers discussed were not realistic. The value of four million Southern slaves in 1860 was $3 billion—$60 billion today. The

What a Confederate Hero Said

"Secession belongs to a different class of remedies. It is to be justified upon the basis that the States are Sovereign. There was a time when none denied it. I hope the time may come again, when a better comprehension of the theory of our Government, and the inalienable rights of the people of the States, will prevent any one from denying that each State is a Sovereign, and thus may reclaim the grants which it has made to any agent whomsoever."

Jefferson Davis

average slave was purchased for $1,000—$20,000 today. Three billion dollars is not an insignificant sum, considering that the entire federal budget in 1860 was just $63 million ($12.6 billion today).

To provide fair market value compensation to slaveholders would have cost the United States fifty times the entire 1860 federal budget. The most any compensation plan ever formally offered was $300 per person in 1862—the price the federal government paid to slaveholders in the District of Columbia, more than a year after Lincoln had declared war on the South.

From this it is easy to see that in the South's view, the immediate abolition of slavery meant economic disaster.

Many Southerners demanded to know why Yankees were so interested in "our people," the term paternalistic planters routinely used to describe the slaves living on their farms. Most slaveholders made sure their slaves were properly fed and cared for because it was in their economic interest to do so (aside from any nobler motives). Plantation owners actually pointed out with pride that their slaves lived in family cabins without having to pay rent, ate fresh food for free, and led better lives than the poorly paid sweatshop workers who toiled away in Northern factories and slept in tenement slums at night.

Particularly vexing to Southerners was how abolitionists talked of slavemaster cruelty—which they had not seen firsthand. Harriet Beecher Stowe, author of *Uncle Tom's Cabin*, a hugely popular novel depicting cruelty inflicted on slaves working on a fictional plantation, had never actually seen a plantation. She had never been to the South and had no idea how plantations were run. But her novel firmly established in the minds of abolitionists, and many Northerners, that slavery had to be ended.

Most abolitionists made little effort to prove what they believed about slavery, which is why there was little understanding between Southerners and Northerners on the issue. Jefferson Davis was baffled by Northern views of slavery because they bore no relationship to his personal knowledge of life on his and his brother Joseph's Mississippi plantations. Slaves were not whipped on their plantations, and plantation management was actually left to the slaves, as were matters of justice (such as judging accused thieves and punishing them if convicted). For years after the war Davis's former slaves turned up at his speaking engagements as part of a friendly audience.

What a Confederate Hero Said

"There is a true glory and a true honor: the glory of duty done, the honor of the integrity of principle."

Robert E. Lee

When did abolition become a war aim?

The Corwin Amendment (introduced by Congressman Thomas Corwin of Ohio and endorsed by Senator William Seward of New York in the Senate) passed the House 133 to 65 in February 1861 and the Senate 24 to 12 on March 2, 1861. It stated: "No amendment shall be made to the Constitution which will authorize or give to Congress the Power to abolish or interfere, within any State, with the domestic institution thereof, including that of persons held to labor or service by the laws of said State."

In other words, Northern legislators (most Southerners had already left Washington) affirmed that they had no intention of abolishing slavery.

President-elect Abraham Lincoln told Congress in his inaugural address that he would support efforts to ratify the Corwin Amendment as the thirteenth amendment to the Constitution. He said, "I understand a proposed amendment to the Constitution . . . has passed Congress, to the effect that the Federal Government shall never interfere with the domestic institutions of the States, including that of persons held to service. To avoid misconstruction of what I have said, I depart from my purpose not to speak of particular amendments so far as to say that, holding such a provision to now be implied constitutional law, I have no objection to its being made express and irrevocable."

So Lincoln agreed that it was already "implied constitutional law" that slavery could not be abolished by federal law and had "no objection" to this "being made express and irrevocable."

But the South didn't trust Northern politicians.

In 1859 the violent abolitionist John Brown had invaded Harpers Ferry, Virginia, in a self-proclaimed attempt to start a race war in the South. Brown and his gang had been financed by at least six influential Northerners, who bought him a cache of Sharps rifles, a technologically advanced weapon that only a handful of U.S. Army soldiers carried because it was so expensive.

Brown's raid occurred just twenty-eight years after Nat Turner led a revolt southwest of Norfolk, Virginia, resulting in the murder of at least fifty-five white people, starting with a baby whose head Turner smashed against a stone fireplace. Such violent imagery stuck in the minds of

> ## What They Fought For
>
> "With all of my devotion to the Union and the feeling of loyalty and duty as an American citizen, I have not been able to make up my mind to raise my hand against my relatives, my children, my home."
>
> **Robert E. Lee**

slaveholders whenever they read newspaper accounts of Northerners calling for immediate abolition. And most Southerners thought that Northern talk about preserving slavery was just talk, while violence such as that instigated by Brown and Turner might be repeated.

The War wasn't about slavery; it was about states' rights

Slavery was an obvious issue. But how fervent were Southerners about defending something more nebulous like "states' rights"?

What a Confederate Hero Said

"Still a Union that can only be maintained by swords and bayonets, and in which strife and civil war are to take the place of brotherly love and kindness, has no charm for me."

Robert E. Lee

They were fervent enough that some families named their sons after the phrase, particularly in South Carolina. Brigadier General States Rights Gist was born in 1831. Gist, the nephew of the secession governor of South Carolina, was killed at the Battle of Franklin, Tennessee, in November 1864. His body was driven all the way home to Columbia by his faithful black servant.

The South used states' rights as a catchall to describe its sincere, fervent belief that the United States Constitution had been ratified by a compact of independent states. Almost every Southerner believed that his state was more important than the federal government, and almost every Southerner believed that states had the right to govern themselves. Slavery was just one such issue on which they believed state sovereignty was supreme. The other burning issue was the power to impose tariffs; the South wanted federal tariffs eliminated in favor of its own smaller, state-based tariffs and wanted to create free ports where no tariffs would be collected.

Nothing frightened Northern politicians with an interest in federal spending more than the thought of a nation without tariffs. A newspaper editorial in the *Chicago Daily Times* on December 10, 1860, nearly three weeks before South Carolina seceded, read:

> In one single blow our foreign commerce must be reduced to less than one-half what it is now. Our coastwide trade would pass into other hands. One-half of our shipping would lie idle at our wharves. We would lose our trade with the south, with all its immense profits. Our manufactures would be in utter ruins.

In his March 4, 1861, inaugural address, President Lincoln made it clear that he was not about to provoke a war over slavery: "I have no purpose, directly or indirectly, to interfere with the institution of slavery in the States where it exists. I believe I have no lawful right to do so, and I have no inclination to do so." But in the same speech, Lincoln made it very clear what would provoke war: "The power confided to me will be used to hold, occupy, and possess the property and places belonging to the Government and to collect the duties and imposts; but beyond what may be necessary for these objects, there will be no invasion, no using of force against or among the people anywhere."

The "property" to which Lincoln referred were federal forts like Fort Sumter, which were the primary means of enforcing the collection of tariffs. South Carolina was then demanding that the United States vacate Fort Sumter. But if Fort Sumter and others like it were abandoned to the Confederates, the United States would have no way of collecting the "duties and imports" on imported manufactured goods to the South and on Southern agricultural exports that Lincoln knew was the lifeblood of the ever-growing federal government.

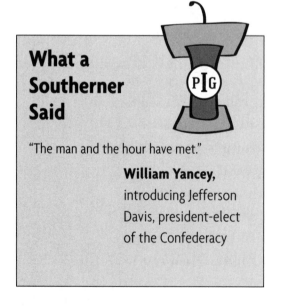

What a Southerner Said

"The man and the hour have met."

William Yancey,
introducing Jefferson Davis, president-elect of the Confederacy

One of the first laws signed by President Lincoln was the Morrill Tariff. It was designed to protect the industries in the North from European imports and to provide additional income to the federal government.

The Morrill Tariff, heartily endorsed by Northern congressmen and strongly opposed by Southern congressmen, passed the Senate with virtually no opposition, as all the Southern states had left the U.S. Senate by February 1861. It increased tariffs on virtually every imported and exported good from 15 percent to more than 37 percent on average, with an increase expected to be more than 47 percent within three years of passage. The tariffs were higher than the 1828 Tariff, which Southerners called the Tariff of Abominations and which had led directly to the South's first threat of secession.

The importance of the Morrill Tariff and expectations for the revenue it would generate were stated by Congressman John Sherman, the brother of future Union general William T. Sherman: "The Morrill tariff bill came nearer than any other to meeting the double requirement of providing ample revenue for the support of the government and of rendering the proper protection to home industries."

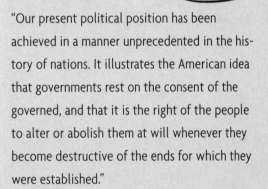

What a Confederate Hero Said

"Our present political position has been achieved in a manner unprecedented in the history of nations. It illustrates the American idea that governments rest on the consent of the governed, and that it is the right of the people to alter or abolish them at will whenever they become destructive of the ends for which they were established."

Jefferson Davis, inaugural address, February 18, 1861

Ironically, since the South seceded and the imports and exports that it accounted for were crippled by the war, the Morrill Tariff never created the cash flow that Lincoln had expected. In order to make up for the missing Southern money, Lincoln and Congress instituted the nation's first income tax.

Southerners have never liked taxes. Not then, and not now.

Chapter 11

TOTAL WAR VERSUS NOBLE WAR

Only a handful of people in Northern states like Indiana, Ohio, and Pennsylvania ever experienced even a small taste of what virtually every Southerner experienced between 1861 to 1865. Union general William T. Sherman foretold what he would do to the South when he said, "We are not fighting armies but a hostile people, and must make young and old, rich and poor, feel the hard hand of war."

Lincoln lied to everyone about Fort Sumter

Even before taking office, Lincoln talked about his intentions concerning Fort Sumter, just as he did afterward. But his opinions changed all the time. In one speech Lincoln said there was no reason for bloodshed in defending the fort. In another speech in New York City he stamped his foot and shouted, "It may be necessary to put the foot down firmly." When warned by a politician from Virginia that his state would leave the Union if the federal government moved against any Southern state, Lincoln offered, "If Virginia will stay in, I will withdraw the troops from Fort Sumter."

Tensions were high in Charleston, but manners were also high. After a Confederate cannonball was accidentally fired at the fort on March 8, 1861, hitting the wharf, the Confederate gun commander rowed out to the

Guess what?

- From April through December 1861, the Confederacy did not instigate a single aggressive action toward the United States.

- Union soldiers killed slaves who would not reveal Confederate positions.

- Robert E. Lee chose to surrender rather than conduct a guerrilla war that could have lasted for decades.

fort and profusely apologized to the U.S. Army officers. His explanation was he did not know the cannon was loaded.

On March 15, 1861, eleven days after his inauguration, Lincoln asked his cabinet if it would be wise to reinforce Fort Sumter, despite General Winfield Scott's advice that it be surrendered. Only one cabinet member suggested reinforcement. Lincoln sent one of his law partners to Charleston, who assured both the commander of Fort Sumter and Confederate officials that the fort would soon be vacated. Lincoln also sent a letter to South Carolina's governor assuring him that "no effort to throw in men, arms or ammunition will be made without further notice."

On March 28, Lincoln changed his mind. Against the advice of his top general and most of his cabinet, the president ordered a relief expedition of several ships to Fort Sumter, including two hundred troops that intended to land in direct violation of what he had been telling South Carolina authorities. Lincoln sent word that the captains of those vessels could use their cannons if they encountered any resistance. It was less than a week after Lincoln's lawyer had assured South Carolina officials that Fort Sumter would be evacuated.

★ ★ ★ ★ ★ ★ ★ ★ ★ ★ ★ ★ ★ ★ ★

What's That, Mr. Lincoln?

"I never have been, am not now, and probably never shall be, in a mood of harassing the people, either North or South."

Abraham Lincoln, December 15, 1860

"All we ask is to be let alone."

Jefferson Davis, First Message to the Confederate Congress, March 1861

On April 11, 1861, South Carolina officials rowed back and forth between Charleston and Fort Sumter, urging its commander to surrender the fort. If he did not, the Confederates would feel compelled to open fire on a potentially hostile fort within their harbor. Major Robert Anderson officially refused, but told the Confederates that the fort was out of food and he would soon be forced to surrender. Anderson held out hope that Lincoln would give him that order.

At about 4:30 AM on April 12, 1861, just as the Confederates had promised, the first shells were fired at Fort Sumter. The thirty-six-hour "battle" was uneventful. No battle casualties occurred though a crowd of Southern civilians watching the battle from Sullivan's Island was targeted by one vindictive Union gun crew tired of being ineffective in their shots on the Confederates' Fort Moultrie. Ships sent by Lincoln to resupply Fort Sumter arrived several hours after the battle started. Their crews watched the battle from the safety of the ocean.

Rather than batter Fort Sumter to the ground, a Confederate delegation asked for the surrender of the fort. Major Anderson accepted their terms.

The ninety-man garrison of Fort Sumter was not taken prisoner, because the South had not declared war on the North. Instead, the garrison was allowed to leave for New York City aboard one of the supply ships sent by Lincoln (the two hundred soldiers they carried never disembarked in South Carolina).

On April 15, 1861, President Lincoln called for 75,000 volunteers to "cause the laws to be duly executed." In the same message, Lincoln asked Congress to convene in July, a full three months after he had formed an army to invade the South.

Lincoln attacks early and often

Lincoln apparently believed that all he had to do was stamp his foot (as he had done in the New York City speech) and the South would return to the Union. That did not happen. The South simply went about its business of building a nation separate from the United States. The North, on the other hand, was the aggressor in all of the early battles. The South did not start a single battle in the first half-dozen engagements.

On June 1, 1861, the first true combat death of the war occurred when Union cavalrymen rode through Fairfax Court House, Virginia, shooting indiscriminately at everyone they saw. Captain John Quincy Marr, a militiaman who had not signed the oath of loyalty to the Confederacy, was shot down.

On June 3, Union forces attacked a Confederate recruiting camp at Philippi, Virginia (now West Virginia). No one was killed but several were wounded, including an enterprising young Southerner named J. E. Hanger, whose leg had to be amputated. Hanger designed his own artificial limb and founded a prosthetic company that remains in business today.

On June 10, Union forces attacked a Confederate encampment at Big Bethel Church, just northwest of Hampton, Virginia. Seeing a Union officer waving his sword while standing on a fence, a Confederate officer handed his rifle to his black servant and asked him to see if he could hit the man several hundred yards distant.

Calling attention to oneself on a battlefield is not a smart idea, as Union major Theodore Winthrop, a Yale graduate and the darling of the Northeastern literary set, learned. Winthrop, a descendant of the first governor of Massachusetts colony, was killed by a single bullet fired by a black servant. Sixteen other Federals died that day, but only one Confederate. Private Henry Wyatt of North Carolina was the first of more than 260,000 young Southerners to die in a war they had not started.

On July 11, Union general George McClellan attacked the Confederate camp at Rich Mountain, killing thirty-three Southerners while losing only twelve of his own. It was the first significant, if small, Union victory of the war, one which impressed Lincoln enough to endorse McClellan as the man he wanted to lead his army. Lincoln should have checked the battle rosters: McClellan had six times the numbers of the Confederates. A Union victory was a foregone conclusion. McClellan was not the military genius Lincoln first thought he was.

On July 16, Lincoln demanded that General Irvin McDowell use his 15,000-man army to attack the Confederate railroad junction at Manassas, Virginia, about twenty-five miles west of Washington. When McDowell pleaded that his army was "too green," Lincoln coldly replied that "so too are the Confederates green. You are all green together." McDowell left Washington with an army that was more interested and experienced in picking blackberries than it was in fighting. By the end of the day on July 21, the Union army was shattered. Most of its troops ran back to the capital, just as McDowell had worried they would.

A Book Y'all Aren't Supposed to Read

Robert E. Lee on Leadership: Executive Lessons in Character, Courage, and Vision by H. W. Crocker, III; New York: Three Rivers Press, 2000.

On August 27, a Union army landed on the Outer Banks of North Carolina, capturing two small dirt forts that were erected to protect the channels leading to inland rivers.

On November 6, a Union naval force shelled two Confederate forts protecting Port Royal Sound in South Carolina. Among the properties captured by the Federals was Hilton Head Island, which in November 1864 was promised to freed slaves by General William T. Sherman.

From April through December 1861, the Confederacy did not instigate a single aggressive action toward the United States.

The Union turns nasty

After successfully capturing Roanoke Island, North Carolina, on February 9, 1862, the Union moved inland toward the tiny river town of Winton. On February 19, Colonel Rush C. Hawkins of the Ninth New York

Regiment of Zouaves sacked and burned the town in retaliation for being attacked the previous day. It would be the first but certainly not the last Southern town burned to the ground by an invading Union army. One New Yorker wrote home: "court houses, churches, beautifully furnished dwellings with velvet carpets, pianos, etc., all sharing the same fate, and you may be sure that we gave it a pretty good ransacking while the flames were doing their work."

At almost the same time that Hawkins was burning Winton, Union General Ambrose Burnside assured North Carolinians that warnings from Confederate officials that Yankees intended them harm were false: "They impose upon your credulity by telling you of wicked and even diabolical intentions on our part; of our desire to destroy your freedom, demolish your property, liberate your slaves, injure your women, and such like enormities, all of which, we assure you, is not only ridiculous, but utterly and willfully false."

Regardless of General Burnside's words, it is doubtful that Colonel Hawkins lost sleep over his burning of Winton, or over what he did just before the April 19 Battle of South Mills, North Carolina. Hawkins had forced a local slave to show him a road leading to the area. When Hawkins suspected that the slave had intentionally taken him on a longer road, he shot and killed him. That nameless slave was not the last executed by invading Union armies. Written accounts on both sides tell similar tales of blacks being sometimes tortured and usually killed if they did not please the Union soldiers who forced them to reveal Confederate positions or show where a plantation family had hidden the family silver.

The Official Records of the War of the Rebellion, a multi-volume set of books cataloging reports and orders from both sides, is filled with accounts of Union atrocities in the South starting in 1862.

Movies Y'all Should Watch:

Gettysburg, 1993 (based on Michael Shaara's Pulitzer Prize–winning *The Killer Angels*)

Gods & Generals, 2003 (prequel based on Jeff Shaara's book of the same name)

On March 25, 1862, General Henry W. Halleck reported to Secretary of War Edwin Stanton about Union activities in relatively sedate Missouri: "It can not be denied that some of our own volunteer regiments have behaved very badly, plundering to an enormous extent. Many of the regiment officers are very bad men and participate in this plunder."

On May 27, 1862, General Thomas Williams, a Union general who was so hated that his own men killed him, wrote to General Ben Butler about pillaging in Louisiana: "These regiments, officers and men, with rare exceptions, appear to be wholly destitute of the moral sense, and I believe that they regard pillaging not only right in itself, but a soldierly accomplishment."

The next year, the Union Army put aside any sense of propriety about not making war on civilians. The Union made war on the civilian population of every Southern state. On October 7, 1864, General Philip Sheridan reported to General U. S. Grant: "I have destroyed over 2,000 barns ... over 70 mills, over 4,000 heads of stock and have killed and issued to the troops not less than 3,000 sheep. The destruction embraces the Luray Valley and Little Fort Valley."

A Book Y'all Aren't Supposed to Read

Stonewall Jackson: The Black Man's Friend, by Richard G. Williams, Jr.; Nashville: Cumberland House, 2006.

A fascinating book about the future Confederate general and his Sunday school where he taught slaves and free blacks to read.

President Lincoln sent Sheridan a letter after reading that report: "With great pleasure I tender to you and your brave army the thanks of the nation and my own personal admiration and gratitude for the month's operations in the Shenandoah Valley."

At about the same time that Sheridan was burning out the civilians of Virginia, General William T. Sherman was burning out the civilians of Georgia. In January 1865 he started on the civilians of South Carolina. From the summer of 1864 through February 1865, Sherman burned two large cities—Atlanta, Georgia, and Columbia, South Carolina—and scores of smaller towns. His own generals, such as Alpheus Williams, protested to deaf ears: "The houses in this vicinity, of free negroes even, have been stripped of the necessary bedclothes and of family apparel. These infamous practices are disgraceful to our arms and shocking to humanity."

Sherman's worst atrocity occurred at Ebenezer Creek, about thirty miles west of Savannah, Georgia, on December 7, 1864. Several thousand slaves had been following Sherman's army as it burned its way south toward Savannah. At rain-swollen Ebenezer Creek, Sherman and his immediate subordinate, General Jefferson C. Davis (no relation to Confederate president Jefferson Davis), saw their chance to get rid of these hangers-on. Davis told the slaves to wait patiently while his army crossed the pontoon bridge over the raging creek. They did. When the last white Union soldier crossed, the pontoon bridges were taken up.

Panicked slaves, fearful of pursuing Confederate cavalry, plunged into the river. Davis did not stick around to tally the bodies floating in the river, but it may have been hundreds. Those who did not jump into the river were rounded up by the Confederate cavalry.

One private wrote in his diary, "Where can you find in all the annals of plantation cruelty anything more completely inhuman and fiendish than this?"

A shocked Union officer reported Davis and Sherman to his congressman, who told Secretary of War Edwin Stanton. Stanton traveled to

What a Southerner Said

Zebulon Vance, a congressman from North Carolina in 1861, tried his best to keep his state in the Union. But after he thought Lincoln lied to him about resupplying Fort Sumter, he became an ardent secessionist. His job as executive of North Carolina, he said, was to **"fight the Yankees and fuss with the Confederacy."**

Savannah to put on a show of an investigation. Stanton met with a group of black ministers in Savannah, but apparently did not even mention the incident at Ebenezer Creek. Instead, Stanton asked the ministers if they liked General Sherman. They shrugged and said they did. The whitewash complete, Stanton returned to Washington with barely a cross word said to either general.

Northern atrocities were scattered around the South, but most have been neither explained nor even rated an apology. In 1864 in Marianna, Florida, raiding Union troops set fire to a church in which militiamen had taken refuge. As the men ran out of the flames, they were shot down and their bodies thrown back into the fire. In Alabama that same year, General John Turchin told his men, "I see nothing for two hours" when they captured the town of Athens—essentially giving them a free pass to behave as they wished. Had he cared to look, he would have seen white and black women raped and the town destroyed. In April 1865, with the war's end in sight, the University of Alabama was burned to the ground, including the thousands of books in its library.

The South was kinder to its enemies

In the fall of 1861, Robert E. Lee, commanding the Virginia state troops, discovered that General Thomas J. (before he was "Stonewall") Jackson had crossed the Potomac River at Harpers Ferry and put troops on Maryland Heights.

Lee ordered Jackson to remove his troops from the Heights because "it is considered advisable not to intrude on the soil of Maryland unless compelled by the necessities of war." At that time the Confederacy still hoped Maryland would secede, and Lee did not want to be impolite by invading another Southern state. What Lee had not counted on was that Lincoln had already imprisoned many of Maryland's legislators, which prevented them from voting the state out of the Union.

In June 1862, as McClellan's army was marching up the peninsula of Virginia toward Richmond, the Federals heard about a newfangled weapon called a torpedo. The torpedo, the invention of Confederate general Gabriel Rains, is now known as the land mine.

Rains wanted to place the land mines in the roads along the route the Federals would take. His commander, General James Longstreet, objected to the mines' use as unfair to the enemy, who would not suspect he was being targeted. The Confederate secretary of war, George Randolph (the grandson of Thomas Jefferson), finally stepped in to the debate and declared, "It is admissible to plant shells in a parapet to repel assault, or in a road to check pursuit. It is not admissible to plant shells merely to destroy life and without other design than that of depriving the enemy of a few men."

Randolph had declared that mines could only be buried where Federals might expect them to be, and that the mines had to serve some greater military purpose than merely killing the enemy. Randolph issued his order when McClellan was within a day's march of capturing Richmond with an army of more than 120,000 men, compared to Robert E. Lee's army of 75,000. Rains obeyed orders and the land mines did not play a significant role in either the Peninsula Campaign or the following Seven Days battles.

In June 1863, Lee crossed the Potomac River and made his way into Pennsylvania. He issued General Orders No. 73, which read in part:

> It must be remembered that we make war only upon armed men, and that we cannot take vengeance for the wrongs our people have suffered without lowering ourselves in the eyes of all whose abhorrence has been excited by the atrocities of our enemies, and offending against Him to whom vengeance belongeth, without whose favor and support our efforts must all prove in vain.

> The commanding general therefore earnestly exhorts the troops to abstain with most scrupulous care from unnecessary or wanton injury to private property, and he enjoins upon all officers to arrest and bring to summary punishment all who shall in any way offend against the orders on this subject.

Lee was so scrupulous about the enforcement of this order that he personally dealt with an irate hat shop owner in Chambersburg, Pennsylvania, who complained that some men in Lee's ranks had stolen hats from his shop. Lee found the culprits and returned the purloined hats to the shopkeeper. Although many in Lee's army were shoeless and hatless, he forced his men to return the items.

Not long after issuing the order, a Pennsylvania lady found her way into Lee's tent and asked for his autograph. A surprised and amused Lee reminded her that he was a rebel. The woman exclaimed that she was a good Union woman, but she still wanted that autograph.

"It is to your interest to be for the Union, and I hope you may be as firm in your principles as I am in mine," Lee said as he signed her autograph.

What a Confederate Hero Said

"It must be remembered that we make war only upon armed men and that we cannot take vengeance for the wrongs our people have suffered without lowering ourselves in the eyes of all whose abhorrence has been excited by the atrocities of our enemies, and offending against Him to whom benevolence belongeth, without whose favor and support our efforts must all prove in vain."

Robert E. Lee's Special Orders 73, issued as his army crossed into Pennsylvania in July 1863. Lee refused to war against civilians. No Union generals followed his example.

That sort of chivalry and respect for private citizens can be found repeatedly in Southern generals' encounters with Northerners. The only large-scale destruction of Northern property by Confederates during the war was the burning of Chambersburg, Pennsylvania, in 1864. That fire was set in retaliation for the thousands of homes and farms that had been burned in the Shenandoah Valley that summer. But unlike the raids of the Federals, it was an exception, not the execution of an official policy of waging war on civilians.

Defeat but not dishonor

On the morning of April 9, 1865, General Robert E. Lee was standing just west of Appomattox Court House, scanning the road to the southwest, when he turned to twenty-nine-year-old General Edward Porter Alexander to ask a question that could have changed history.

Alexander was one of the brightest young officers in the Army of Northern Virginia. He had played a key role in winning the first major battle of the war at Manassas and had contributed greatly to winning virtually every battle in which the Army of Northern Virginia had fought. Lee, twenty-nine years older than Alexander, valued the young general's opinion.

"Here we are at Appomattox, and there seems to be a considerable force in front of us. Now, what shall we have to do here today?" Lee asked.

Alexander replied, "We have only two alternatives to choose from. We must either surrender, or the army may be ordered to scatter into the woods and bushes and either to rally upon General Johnston in North Carolina, or make its way, each man to his own state, with his arms, and to report to his governor. This last course is the one which seems to me to offer us much the best chances. If there is any hope for the Confederacy, it is for delay."

Lee then asked how many would get away.

"Two-thirds of us. We would scatter like rabbits and partridges into the woods and they could not scatter to catch us," Alexander replied.

A Book Y'all Aren't Supposed to Read

Duty Faithfully Performed: Robert E. Lee and His Critics by John M. Taylor; Dulles, VA: Brassey's, 1999.

Lee lowered his head and thought for a moment. He then said, "The men would have no rations and would be under no discipline. They are already demoralized by four years of war. The country would be full of lawless bands. And as for myself, while you young men might afford to go bush-whacking, the only proper and dignified course for me would be to surrender myself and take the consequences of my actions."

Alexander later wrote, "I had never half known before what a big heart and brain our general had. I was so ashamed of having proposed to him such a foolish and wild cat scheme as my suggestion had been that I felt like begging him to forget that he had ever heard of it."

In one moment that lasted no more than twenty seconds, Robert E. Lee had chosen to spare the nation a guerrilla war that could have lasted for decades. Later that day Lee met with General Grant and signed a surrender agreement that allowed his men to return home without any further harassment from Union forces. No other political details were discussed.

Several weeks later and 140 miles to the south, the largest Confederate army still in the field was surrendered by Joseph E. Johnston. But the Union would not be satisfied.

The North threatens continued violence

The battered remnants of the Army of Tennessee, commanded by General Johnston, were camped around Greensboro, North Carolina, when Johnston heard that Lee had surrendered at Appomattox. Johnston had last

Civil War Reenacting

Lee may have surrendered at Appomattox Court House in April 1865, but that does not mean that the shooting has stopped.

There are at least 20,000 Union and Confederate reenactors scattered around the nation, and several hundred more in countries like Australia, England, Germany, and France. Just about any weekend of the year in any given state, men and women gather to spend the weekend recreating the lives of Johnny Reb and Billy Yank. They cook pork side meat over a wood fire, bake cornpone on rifle ramrods, massage their aching feet, and shoot at each other—just as the real soldiers did during the war.

There are some differences between the real soldiers of 1861–1865 and the facsimiles wearing blue and gray today. Most reenactors look nothing like the eighteen- to twenty-five-year-old, lean, mean, 5'5", 140-pound, fighting machines that made up the bulk of both armies. While there are a few who are young enough and thin enough to look the part, most reenactors today are middle-aged men. These men willingly call themselves TBGs (Tubby Bearded Guys). The weapons are different too. In 1861 Enfields were made in England and Springfields were made in the North. These days both are made in Italy. Most of the uniforms are very authentic, down to the period weave of the cloth and hand-stitched buttonholes. Shoes have leather soles fastened with wooden pegs.

The National Park Service allows many of the best, most authentic reenacting groups to camp on the original battlefields in exchange for drilling and firing demonstrations that bring in tourists who wonder how the original men survived the stress of combat in 100-degree weather while wearing wool-blend uniforms. Camping on the original battlefields is the ultimate thrill of reenactors because it was on that ground that their ancestors fought, bled, and sometimes died.

Most Union and Confederate reenactors share a common love of history and reading about the war. Modern-day politics, occupations, and economic status are all forgotten when the men and women end each day sitting around the campfire talking about the war, singing or joking with each other—in much the same way their ancestors ended each day.

One thing remains constant in reenacting. No one likes to play the bad guys: the Union, that is. Gettysburg holds an annual Remembrance Day in late November to commemorate Lincoln's Gettysburg Address. Regiments of Union and Confederate reenactors used to march separately, but now the units are interspersed. This came about after organizers realized that the Confederate regiments, with their battle flags waving high, were getting all the cheers while the Union troops were met with silence. Even in reenacting, everyone loves the underdog.

fought General William T. Sherman at Bentonville, one hundred miles to the east, a month earlier. Like Lee's men, Johnston's were exhausted, outnumbered, starving, and facing an enemy three times their numbers.

Johnston sent word to Sherman that he wanted to surrender. The two met at the Bennett family farmhouse just southwest of Durham Station. The two old adversaries who had fought each other in northern Georgia and at Bentonville, North Carolina, drew up plans over a bottle of whiskey. At Johnston's suggestion and with Jefferson Davis's approval, the two men discussed not only military surrender, but also how the peace would work. Among the terms agreed were that Johnston's men would turn in their weapons to state armories, state governments would be recognized, federal courts would be reestablished, political and civil rights would be restored, and there would be a general amnesty for all combatants. Johnston was negotiating for nearly 90,000 men stretching from North Carolina through Florida, and Sherman happily agreed to these terms.

On April 17, 1865, Sherman sent the terms to Washington, unaware that Lincoln had been assassinated three days earlier.

Secretary of War Edwin Stanton and the other Radical Republicans who had seized power from Vice President Andrew Johnson flew into a rage. Sherman had just agreed to let the South return to the Union without any punishment—a price that the Union fully intended to exact. Stanton sent Grant down on a train with clear instructions to Sherman— revoke the surrender terms he had signed. If Johnston balked at the renegotiations, Sherman's instructions were to start killing Confederates again.

A shocked but tired Johnston agreed to another meeting with Sherman—anything to end the war. He readily agreed to the same unconditional surrender terms that Lee had accepted. Now President Davis was livid that Johnston had signed such an agreement without checking with him, but Johnston ignored Davis. As far as Johnston was concerned, the war was over. He authorized men as far south as Florida and as far west as Texas to surrender. Like Lee, Johnston was loath to ask his men to become guerrilla fighters.

Sherman, a man of violent, unforgivable deeds against Southern civilians, but nonetheless a man of his word, told Grant that as regards Stanton: "I respect his office, but I cannot him personally."

Several weeks later, when forced to appear before the congressional Joint Committee on the Conduct of the War to explain why he had given the South such lenient surrender terms, Sherman replied that the terms seemed to him to be in compliance with Lincoln's request that the nation return to a quick peace. At some point Sherman told committee members that Stanton was "a two-faced scoundrel."

All over the South, Confederate commanders surrendered their men without sending them into the hills as insurgents. General Nathan Bedford Forrest told his men, "You have been good soldiers. You can be good citizens. Obey the laws, preserve your honor, and the government to which you have surrendered can afford to be and will be magnanimous."

Forrest was wrong on that account. It was May 1865 and Reconstruction had not yet begun.

Forrest was always a hard man to figure out. He had threatened his own Confederate commanding generals with death on more than one occasion. A prewar slave trader, he freed his own slaves on the agreement that they would fight with him. They did. After the war, he at first confessed sympathy for the early Ku Klux Klan, while denying being a member, and then later repudiated the Klan entirely and said that it should disband. In Memphis in 1868 Forrest was honored by an organization of blacks who presented him with a bouquet of flowers, which he accepted as a gift from his "brothers and sisters."

Colonel John Singleton Mosby, the famed "Gray Ghost," was a partisan ranger who operated behind Union lines in northern Virginia. He took a less conciliatory stand than Forrest and disbanded his battalion

The Great General Lee

"He was a foe without hate, a friend without treachery, a soldier without cruelty, a victor without oppression, and a victim without murmuring. He was a public officer without vices, a private citizen without wrong, a neighbor without reproach, a Christian without hypocrisy, and a man without guile. He was a Caesar, without his ambition; Frederick, without his tyranny; Napoleon, without his selfishness; and Washington, without his reward."

Benjamin H. Hill, Jr., spoken about Robert E. Lee

rather than surrender it. Mosby told his last assembly of his command, "The vision we have cherished of a free and independent country has vanished, and that country is now the spoil of a conqueror." Ironically, Mosby would become a trusted member of the Grant administration just a few years after Grant had tried to have him killed on the battlefield.

A Book Y'all Aren't Supposed to Read

Robert E. Lee by Allen Tate; New York: Minton, Balch, & Co., 1932.

All over the South, tens of thousands of Confederates simply put down their arms and went about the difficult task of trying to make a living in a despoiled land. Of the million men who had worn the gray, only a handful would take up the outlaw life. The best known of these Southerners who decided to continue fighting were brothers Frank and Jesse James and their cousins, the Youngers.

Meanwhile, in May 1865, the North planned a gaudy two-day parade, called the Grand Review, down Pennsylvania Avenue in Washington, D.C. The Army of the Potomac under General George Meade would march one day, and Sherman's Army of Georgia and Army of the Tennessee would be the star attractions on the next day. Grant, commander in chief of all the armies of the United States, oversaw the planning.

Only one "army" was pointedly not invited to the big party. They were the 180,000 men of the United States Colored Troops. Though scattered between the two theaters of operations in the east and west and never organized as a single command, the USCT regiments were larger in total numbers than the armies taking part in the Grand Review.

The reason that the hundreds of regiments of black troops who had fought and died on battlefields like Port Hudson, Battery Wagner, Olustee, Natural Bridge (Florida), New Market Heights, and Fort Fisher were not allowed to march was because Grant specifically ordered them to stay away. Sherman had told Grant that if black troops marched in any proximity to his army, he would pull his soldiers out of the ranks in protest.

Grant agreed.

The only black men who marched in the Grand Review were freed slaves employed by Sherman to dig ditches and fell trees. They were civilians dressed in the same clothes they had been wearing when they had fled the plantations. Sherman did not believe that black men deserved to wear blue uniforms.

Sherman was blunt in his opinion of black troops. When a subordinate said, "They can stop a bullet as well as a white man," Sherman replied, "A sandbag is better."

In a letter to a friend, Sherman wrote, "A nigger as such is a most excellent fellow, but he is not fit to marry, to associate, or vote with me or mine."

Grant reorganized many of the black regiments into the Twenty-fifth Corps, and just days before the Grand Review ordered the entire corps shipped to Texas to serve as occupation troops. The Twenty-fifth Corps boarded ships on the Potomac River and started their long voyage to Texas just as preparations for the Grand Review were being wrapped up.

The Twenty-fifth Corps' commander was General Godfrey Weitzel, one of the few generals in the Union Army who seemed to genuinely appreciate the abilities of black soldiers. He had personally led some black regiments into Richmond the previous month. He was also a gentleman. One of his first acts was to send an armed guard to the residence of Mrs. Robert E. Lee so she would not be disturbed. He also offered to loan the Lee family money until their finances could be straightened out now that Confederate money was worthless.

While Weitzel was a gentleman, the secretary of war he served, Edwin Stanton, was not. And at the Grand Review, Sherman treated Stanton as such. When Sherman strode onto the podium, Stanton stuck out his hand. Sherman not only didn't shake it, but did not even look at the man who was Grant's boss and his ultimate superior.

Sherman didn't know it, but Stanton was actually spreading a rumor that Sherman was crazy and was planning a military coup. It might have been better for the South if he had.

Chapter 12

THE SECRET HISTORY
OF THE WAR

The politically correct fable is that President Lincoln waged war on the South to emancipate the slaves. Not only is this incorrect, but it also ignores a much more complex reality that turns some preconceived ideas of racial and religious prejudice upside down.

How many people know that Lincoln twice refused—or actually revoked—orders for emancipating slaves, or that slavery continued to exist in states aligned with or occupied by the Union?

The first instance was in August 1861, when General John C. Fremont—who had been the 1856 Republican Party candidate for president—officially ordered that slaves in his military district in Missouri be freed. Lincoln demanded Fremont rescind his emancipation proclamation, fearing that border states (like Missouri) would join the Confederacy. Fremont refused. Lincoln summarily sacked him and revoked Fremont's proclamation, so Missouri, officially a Union state, kept its slaves.

The second instance was on April 25, 1862, when Union general David Hunter, commander of the district based at Port Royal, South Carolina, covering South Carolina, Georgia, and Florida, declared slaves in those three states "forever free." An alarmed Lincoln revoked Hunter's order. Curiously, Lincoln questioned—in print—if Hunter's order was even "authentic." The president wrote that he would only free the slaves if it became "a necessity indispensable to the maintenance of the government."

Guess what?

- The South missed its greatest public relations opportunity when it turned down the enlistment of hundreds of blacks willing to fight early in the War.

- Lincoln planned to send the freed slaves back to Africa.

- Lincoln issued the Emancipation Proclamation primarily to stop European countries from recognizing the Confederacy.

Not only did he refuse to free slaves in a Union state, but he also refused to free them in territory captured from the Confederates.

Nor was President Lincoln in favor of enlisting black soldiers. It would not be until July 1863, more than two years after the war started, that the first black troops entered the war for the Union. The United States Colored Troops were paid less than white soldiers, were charged for their uniforms, and were assigned white officers. And they fought bravely. (At national cemeteries scattered around the nation, the dead of the USCT are segregated into their own sections.)

Around 2.8 million men served in the Union Army. Of that number, 180,000 (about 6 percent) were black, half of them free blacks recruited from the North and the other half former slaves recruited from occupied areas of the South. All of the USCT were formed into regiments, and those regiments were brigaded together and put into mostly black corps, such as the Tenth and Eighteenth Corps, which served in the eastern theater, and the Corps d'Afrique that served in the western theater.

While they saw heavy action in several battles, black troops were never welcomed into the ranks of the two main armies commanded by Ulysses S. Grant and William T. Sherman. Grant reluctantly agreed that black men could one day become soldiers, but he never allowed them to be part of his Army of the Potomac. The blacks who served in the east were in the Army of the James.

Sherman was unapologetic in his racism and dislike of black soldiers, and he never allowed them to be part of his army. "All the Congresses on earth can't make the Negro anything else than what he already is," Sherman said in late 1860 in commenting on abolitionists. Four years later he dressed down General Rufus Saxton, an abolitionist then in command at Beaufort, South Carolina, with the biting comment that "Massachusetts and South Carolina had brought on the war and I would like to see them cut off from the rest of the continent and hauled out to sea together."

In 1863, while commenting about why he refused to allow black soldiers in his army, Sherman said, "I would prefer to have this a white man's war and provide for the negroes after the time has passed.... With my opinion of negroes and my experience, ye prejudice, I cannot trust them yet. Time may change this, but I cannot bring myself to trust negroes with arms in positions of danger and trust."

Grant and Sherman, the two men who actually freed the most slaves during the war, refused to enlist them to fight for their own freedom.

Contrast this with the Confederate army, which paid black Confederates the same wages, gave them free uniforms and rations, and allowed them to march side by side with the rest of the Confederate army, even if this was not authorized by the Confederate government, which did not approve the raising of black regiments until the very end of the war.

Frederick Douglass, a former slave himself, was one of those who bullied the Lincoln administration to recruit soldiers from the black male

A Quotation the History Books Leave Out

"I will say then that I am not, nor ever have been, in favor of bringing about in any way the social and political equality of the white and black races—that I am not, nor ever have been, in favor of making voters or jurors of Negroes, nor of qualifying them to hold office, nor to intermarry with white people; and I will say in addition to this that there is a physical difference between the white and black races which I believe will forever forbid the two races living together on terms of social and political equality. And inasmuch as they cannot so live, while they do remain together there must be the position of superior and inferior, and I as much as any other man am in favor of having the superior position assigned to the white race."

Abraham Lincoln, 1858

population to counter the Confederates' recruitment of blacks. In 1862 Douglass wrote to the president, "There are at the present moment, many colored men in the Confederate Army doing duty not only as cooks, servants and laborers, but as real soldiers, having muskets on their shoulders and bullets in their pockets, ready to shoot down ... and do all that soldiers may do to destroy the Federal government."

As Douglass was demanding action from a reluctant Lincoln, a *Harper's Weekly* engraving made from a Union officer's observations through a telescope depicted two armed black Confederate pickets. There are no white Confederates in the engraving keeping watch to make sure that the black pickets didn't run to the Union lines.

Horace Greeley, the famous abolitionist editor of the *New York Tribune* (who had once argued that for the sake of peace the South should be allowed to secede), was also lobbying Lincoln to arm blacks after hearing of black Confederates. Greeley wrote, "For more than two years, Negroes have been extensively employed in belligerent operations by the Confederacy. They have been embodied and drilled as rebel soldiers and paraded with white troops at a time when this would not have been tolerated in the armies of the Union."

No one knows how many black Confederates served alongside white soldiers, but reports of them from official records are too numerous to ignore. Certainly there were scores, maybe hundreds of black Confederates in uniform and maybe thousands in civilian clothes, if slaves who helped prepare earthworks are counted. Critics are often desperate in their insistence that black Confederates did not exist because that would spoil a carefully cultivated image that black Southerners were sitting around pining for the day when "Father Abraham" would rescue them.

Most official accounts of black Confederates describe small numbers or individuals serving in ranks rather than large units, but one famous account filed by a Union doctor observing Stonewall Jackson's Second Corps on the march to the Battle of Sharpsburg in September 1862 put the number of "Negroes" he saw in Jackson's corps alone at more than three thousand. The doctor called the armed black Confederates "an integral part of the army," implying both that they were numerous and were scattered through the ranks.

One of the more interesting accounts of black Confederates is that of the forty-five slaves who rode with Confederate general Nathan Bedford Forrest, a prewar slave trader. Forrest promised his people freedom if they fought with him. He later described the black men as among the best Confederates he had ever known.

A Book Y'all Aren't Supposed to Read

Stonewall Jackson: The Good Soldier by Allen Tate; New York: Minton, Balch, & Co., 1928.

It is known that black Confederates fought all the way to the end of the war. One account from a Union witness described how a small number of black soldiers fought off a Union cavalry attack on Lee's wagon train just days before he surrendered at Appomattox. At least thirty black Confederates were granted paroles at Appomattox.

The South missed its greatest public relations opportunity when it turned down the enlistment of hundreds of blacks willing to fight early in the war.

The Louisiana Native Guard was a militia unit made up of elite free blacks in New Orleans, who formed themselves into a military unit to prove their loyalty to the Confederacy. In November 1861, more than seven hundred soldiers and thirty-three black officers paraded down the streets of New Orleans, marching in front of and behind white Confederate regiments. The men had even paid for their own arms, equipment, and uniforms, as New Orleans in those days boasted a larger black professional class than did New York City.

The Native Guards never got their chance to prove their loyalty. The Confederate government in Richmond was wary of showcasing armed regiments made up entirely of blacks, and the Native Guard was never given the status of officially joining the Confederate Army. When New Orleans was captured in April 1862, many of the same men who had been willing to fight for the Confederacy signed up to fight for the Union. They first saw action in the bloody battle of Port Hudson, Louisiana, in July 1863.

The Native Guards proved their value on the battlefield, but General Nathaniel Banks, a former governor of Massachusetts, believed their officers were incompetent. His aide filed a report detailing his opinion of black officers: "The experiment of officering colored troops with colored men has proved a distressing failure." Banks discharged the black officers and replaced them with white officers, one of whom sent the Native Guards into a disastrous, stupid attack at Port Hudson. If the original black officers of the Louisiana Native Guards had been good enough to serve in the state militia, they should probably have been good enough to serve in the Union Army.

A Book Y'all Aren't Supposed to Read

Nashville 1864 by Madison Jones; Chicago: J.S. Sanders & Co, 2005.

A novel with a boy's-eye view of the War; it's a modern classic.

Though there were far more blacks in the Union Army, the devotion of black Confederates to their own cause is rarely ever mentioned. Here are a few individuals you probably haven't read about in politically correct history books.

Henry "Dad" Brown of Darlington, South Carolina, was a free black when the war started. He joined a South Carolina regiment as a drummer and was at both the firing on Fort Sumter and at First Manassas, where he was credited with calling his regiment to arms without orders when he saw a Union force approaching. When he died in 1907 his funeral was preached by two pastors, one white and one black. His pallbearers were white former Confederates and black former slaves. Accounts of Brown's life after the war say he never missed a United Confederate Veterans reunion, and he often loaned money to his white Confederate comrades.

Adam Miller Moore of Lincolnton, North Carolina, brought his dead master home after Chancellorsville, then rejoined the army. When asked in a newspaper interview at age 108 why he had not run away rather than bring his master's body home, he replied, "If the South had won, my master promised me freedom and if the North won, the Yankees promised freedom." The most recognized black Confederate is seventeen-year-old free black Silas Chandler, who was photographed with his fifteen-year-old white friend and former owner, Andrew Chandler. Silas holds a large knife and a musket and has a pistol stuck in his coat pocket. The two friends fought together, and Silas is credited with saving Andrew's life by bringing his wounded friend home from a battlefield hospital.

Only one Native American was appointed general on either side during the war. He was a Cherokee Indian named Degataga, better known by the English translation of his name, Stand Watie. Confederate general Watie and his Indians fought in nearly twenty engagements, including the crucial Battle of Pea Ridge, Arkansas, in 1862. Watie surrendered the last Confederate army in the field in June 1865.

The several thousand Confederate Indians, mostly Cherokee and Creek, who fought against the Union would find that the war did not end for them in 1865. Many of the same Union generals who had burned the South later fought to drive the Indians from the Great Plains.

An army of immigrants

While both sides enrolled immigrant soldiers, the Union Army was disproportionately an immigrant army, while the Confederate Army was almost entirely native born. Barely half of the Union Army was native born. More than 216,000 Germans, 200,000 Irish, 90,000 Dutch, and 20,000 Scandinavians were pressed into service by the Lincoln administration, with the promise that they would be welcomed as citizens after they had proven their loyalty to the nation by fighting the Confederates.

To help control the diverse populations of immigrant soldiers flooding into the ranks, Lincoln scouted around for officers of the same ethnic group. It made little difference to Lincoln if they were good generals; if they spoke the language that was qualification enough. That explains how Prussian August von Willich, a Communist and personal friend of Karl Marx, Prussian Alexander Schimmelfennig, and Germans Louis Blenker and Franz Sigel got their stars. All turned out to be terrible leaders in the field.

Most of the Eleventh Corps (15,000 men) spoke only German. Orders from higher-ranking officers had to be translated for them. The Eleventh was thrown into battle without competent training and paid for it at Chancellorsville in May 1863, and then at Gettysburg two months later.

On at least one occasion, at Fredericksburg, Virginia, in December 1862, Union Irish (of the famed Irish Brigade) fought Georgia Irish. But the Georgia Irish were native Southerners; the Union Irish were immigrants. Many surviving Irish folk songs, including "Paddy's Lamentation," describe the immigrants' anger at being thrust into a war not of their making: "When we got to Yankee land, they shoved a gun into our hands / Saying 'Paddy, you must go and fight for Lincoln.'"

A Book Y'all Aren't Supposed to Read

The Unvanquished by William Faulkner; New York: Vintage (reissue edition), 1991.

A classic novel about the War.

Texas contributed a number of Mexicans to the Confederate ranks. Louisiana sent men from France, Belgium, and Italy. There were even at least two Confederate soldiers of Asian descent. Those were two of the sons of Eng and Chang Bunker, the original Siamese Twins who had married sisters and settled in North Carolina.

Jewish communities had long been present in the South. Roughly 3,000 Jews are believed to have served in the Confederate Army, which is about 12 percent of the 25,000 Jews who lived in the South before the war. Compare that to the 8,000 Jews who served in the Union Army, out of a population of 200,000 Northern Jews, and you'll see that Confederate Jews served at three times the rate of their Northern brethren.

No Jew was considered for general in the Union Army, but one almost made it in the Confederate Army. That was Colonel Abraham C. Myers, who served as the Confederate Army's quartermaster general. He was recommended for a brigadier general's slot, but his wife insulted the wife of Confederate president Jefferson Davis. Mrs. Davis told the story to her husband and the president refused to approve Myers's promotion. Still, Myers's name lives on—Fort Myers, Florida, is named after him.

Another prominent Jew in Confederate gray was Marcus Baum, an aide to South Carolina general Joseph Kershaw. Baum was accidentally killed by a Confederate volley at the Battle of the Wilderness. His tombstone reads: "The qualities of his nature, well constructed like his brief career in defense of his adopted country, formed a fitting tribute to his life."

A high-ranking Jew who survived the war was Major Raphael Jacob Moses. He was entrusted with guarding and distributing the last of the Confederate gold by President Jefferson Davis. Moses is considered the founder of Georgia's iconic peach industry because he was the first to ship Georgia peaches from the South to the North.

Rabbi Max Michelbacher of the Congregation Beth Ahabah in Richmond composed a prayer distributed to Jewish Confederates. One paragraph read: "O Lord, God, Father, Give unto the officers of the Army and of the Navy of the Confederate States, enterprise, fortitude and undaunted courage; teach them the ways of war and the winning of victory."

Robert E. Lee, always considerate of his soldiers' religion, wrote to a rabbi in Richmond, saying, "I will gladly do all in my power to facilitate the observance of the duties of the religion by the Israelites in the army and will allow them every indulgence consistent with safety and discipline," including allowing them to return home for religious observances when possible.

★ ★ ★ ★

The Civil War: Also Known As

The War of Northern Aggression

The War Between the States

The Late Unpleasantness

The War for Southern Independence

★ ★ ★ ★

Jewish civilians were even more prominent in the Confederacy. The first two Jewish United States senators were Judah P. Benjamin of Louisiana and David Levy Yulee of Florida. Both men resigned their senatorial seats to join the Confederacy. Benjamin became the most trusted and competent member of the Confederate cabinet (serving at various times as attorney general, secretary of war, and secretary of state). Yulee served in the Confederate Congress.

While Jews were scattered through the Confederate Congress, Davis's cabinet, and the Confederate Army officer ranks, there were no Jews in positions of power in the Lincoln administration. And there was at least one notorious Union action that reeked of anti-Semitism.

On December 17, 1862, General U. S. Grant issued General Orders No. 11: "The Jews, as a class violating every regulation of trade established by the Treasury Department, are hereby expelled from the department within twenty-four hours of the receipt of this order." Grant had just given all Jews twenty-four hours to leave the states of Tennessee, Kentucky, and Mississippi (130,000 square miles of territory), and he refused permission for Jews to visit his headquarters to ask for permits to stay.

Grant's officers enforced the law by confiscating Jewish property. Some Jews were accosted on the road, arrested, and their horses and buggies confiscated. Thirty Jewish families were forcibly removed from their homes in Paducah, Kentucky. One of the few Jewish officers in the Union Army resigned when he saw the order, writing to his commanding officer: "I can no longer, bear the Taunts and malice, of those to whom my religious opinions are known, brought on by the effect that, that order has instilled into their minds."

When Lincoln was visited by an irate delegation of Jews, his first response was to make a crude joke: "And so the children of Israel were driven from the happy land of Canaan?!"

When no one laughed but him, Lincoln was forced to send a note to General Henry Halleck, Grant's commander, to have Grant rescind the order.

★ ★ ★ ★

A Dixie Fact

Mary Todd Lincoln's brother was a Confederate surgeon, and her three sisters were married to Confederate soldiers.

★ ★ ★ ★

Halleck reluctantly complied by dashing a letter off to Grant. In a separate note, Halleck wrote, "The President has no objection to your expelling traitors and Jew peddlers, which, I supposed, was the object of your order; but, as it is terms proscribed by an entire religious class, some of whom are fighting in our ranks, the President deemed it necessary to revoke it."

No such order was ever issued by the Confederacy. But do politically correct history books ever tell you that?

War for cotton?

In 1861 President Lincoln said he was invading the South to preserve the Union. In 1863 he said the Union was fighting to end slavery. But some New England mill owners thought the real reason to fight the war was to hold onto the "cotton kingdom."

Before the war started, the South's politicians believed the Yankees would be cutting their own throats if they attacked the South. They thought the North couldn't survive without the South's cotton—and Confederate blockade runners could take the cotton bales to Europe, sell them, and use the money to return to the South loaded with arms and supplies.

"Cotton is king!" cried South Carolina senator James Hammond on the Senate floor in 1857. Hammond pointed out that of $279 million worth of exports in the previous year, $185 million was produced by the South and most of that value was cotton. He gleefully pointed out that in the latest Northern recession, the South had rushed cotton to the North and put $35 million "into the charity box of your magnificent financiers, your cotton lords, your merchant princes." Hammond declared that no one would make war on cotton. It was too important to the world's economy.

Nearly four years later, on December 6, 1860, Senator Louis Wigfall of Texas opened a short speech on the Senate floor with Hammond's same words: "Cotton is king!" Wigfall told the Senate that he soon expected to meet in a different type of body (the Confederate Congress), and predicted that the South would do just fine on its own—with the export of five million bales of cotton at an average of $50 per bale. Wigfall defended secession and ridiculed the Northern belief that under the Constitution "there is a consolidated government; that there are no states, that there is a national government . . . that the boundaries of Massachusetts, have, by some hocus pocus, been extending themselves until they embrace the remainder of the Union . . . and we are under the control of the Massachusetts school of politics."

A Book Y'all Aren't Supposed to Read

Jefferson Davis: His Rise and Fall by Allen Tate; New York: Minton, Balch, & Co., 1929.

Hammond and Wigfall were right that cotton was vital to the North—and that the North believed that "the Massachusetts school of politics" needed to rule everywhere. In fact, in 1861 a wealthy New England mill owner published a pamphlet calling for "the confiscation of the lands of all rebels, individuals and states, and the bestowal of them as a bounty to our soldiers [as a] necessary step in the reconstruction of southern society which must be accomplished, to render the reconstruction of the Union solid and enduring." Another Massachusetts politician praised the suggestion and said it would be necessary to "ruin them completely and settle their lands with Yankees."

Cotton-producing states were targeted first

As early as August 1861 Union war planners were focusing on attacking Texas—not to bring the state back into the Union or free any slaves, but to appropriate its cotton-growing land. The reason was obvious. By the spring of 1862 more than two-thirds of the Yankee cotton mill spindles were idle because there was no cotton flowing up from the South. The news media noticed. The *New York Times* urged the rapid capture of Texas, Florida, and Arkansas to grab their cotton crops.

The Red River Campaign of March–May 1864, named after the river separating Texas and Louisiana, had only one purpose—to capture cotton-growing land. The operation was led by Union general Nathaniel Banks, a former governor of Massachusetts who was deeply beholden to cotton mill owners. Banks was a terrible general who led both his army and an accompanying river squadron of ironclads to disaster before finally turning around and going back downriver.

In November 1864 a Union naval blockade intercepted a cotton-laden ship off Texas. That was not unusual. Most blockade-running ships left Texas with cotton. What made this ship unusual was that it had just finished running guns into Texas in exchange for cotton. Papers were found onboard indicating that one of the partners owning the ship was William Sprague, a former Union army colonel, former governor of Rhode Island, sitting United States senator from Rhode Island, and son-in-law of Salmon Chase, the current chief justice and former treasury secretary.

Chase went to Secretary of War Edwin Stanton urging him to suppress any news of the incident. Stanton, always willing to bend the rules of honesty and legality when it suited him, sanitized the War Department files. As far as the War Department was concerned, the cotton-carrying Yankee ship had never existed. The incident remained secret until 1870, when a political rival of Sprague described it in a speech. Newspapers like the *New York Times* swept the scandal under the rug, telling its readers that their focus should be punishing the South, not impugning Union heroes. Sprague's "Texas Adventure" remains a well-documented but little-known fact to this day.

Lincoln planned to colonize freed slaves

Confederate President Jefferson Davis had a black foster son, and enjoyed taking care of and being around "his people." Lincoln intended to ship them back to Africa.

As early as 1854 in a speech eulogizing Kentuckian Henry Clay, Lincoln called for returning blacks to Africa because "we cannot make them our equals." In the 1858 Lincoln-Douglas debates, candidate Lincoln made the same suggestion that blacks be shipped to Liberia, the country founded in 1822 as a home for freed slaves from America.

In August 1862 Lincoln summoned a group of black ministers to his office—but pointedly did not invite famed black abolitionist Frederick Douglass. The president shocked the ministers when he casually told them, "It is better for us both to be separated." He asked the leaders if they could gather some volunteers to move to Central America to prove to other blacks that the idea would work. It would be "for the good of mankind," Lincoln said, if blacks left the United States. In his 1863 State of the Union address to Congress, Lincoln proposed appropriations for "colonizing free colored persons, with their own consent, at any place or places without the United States."

Lincoln funded experimental colonies in Haiti and what is now Panama and Belize, all of which failed miserably, with a death rate of more than 50 percent among the several hundred slaves who had been persuaded to leave their homes to try to blaze the trail for others. The establishment of the colonies had been suggested to Lincoln by swindlers who were more interested in collecting federal subsidies than they were in supplying food and equipment to resettling former slaves. Curiously, *Harper's Weekly* newspaper recognized the swindle even if Lincoln did not. Lincoln had been telling black leaders that they could support themselves by mining coal in Panama. *Harper's Weekly* claimed the quality of the coal found in the region was too poor to be used in Navy ships. The newspaper also called the local natives of Panama "greasers" who would not appreciate newcomers to their land.

Lincoln never repudiated his stand on colonization, and because of his assassination (on April 14, 1865), we can never know what his postwar policy on freed slaves would have been.

★ ★ ★ ★

Southern Writers You Can't Afford to Miss

William Faulkner

Shelby Foote

Joel Chandler Harris

Harper Lee

Carson McCullers

Margaret Mitchell

Flannery O'Connor

Walker Percy

Edgar Allan Poe (born in Boston, but grew up in Richmond, Virginia, and lived in Baltimore, Maryland)

John Kennedy Toole

Mark Twain

Robert Penn Warren

Eudora Welty

Thomas Wolfe

Tom Wolfe

★ ★ ★ ★

But we do know that Jefferson Davis remained a popular figure in the black community, and that everywhere he went after the war, Davis was swamped by men claiming to be his former slaves who wanted to shake his hand. Bet your children aren't learning that in their history schoolbooks.

Lincoln was no defender of civil rights

If you think Abraham Lincoln was a defender of civil rights, you haven't read your history.

In his inaugural address in March 1861, President Lincoln sounded a conciliatory tone:

> In your hands, my dissatisfied countrymen, and not in mine, is the momentous issue of civil war. The government will not assail you. You can have no conflict without yourselves being the aggressors. You have no oath registered in Heaven to destroy the government, while I shall have the most solemn one to preserve, protect and defend it. . . . We are not enemies, but friends.

Within a month President Lincoln was arresting thousands of his "friends" without warrants, and without even telling them what they had done. Most of his early illegal arrests were in reaction to the pro-Confederacy sentiment in Baltimore, Maryland, where on April 18, 1861, crowds of civilians tried to prevent newly raised regiments of Union Army volunteers from passing through the city. The soldiers fired on the civilians, and the civilians attacked back with clubs. At least ten were killed on each side.

Lincoln reacted to the Baltimore Massacre by issuing an order that anyone who looked like a troublemaker could be arrested on a line between Baltimore and Philadelphia, the primary route Union volunteers from the North would be taking to reach Washington. Lincoln feared an undefended Washington would be attacked by swarms of secessionists. That threat never materialized, because taking over Washington was not a Confederate war aim.

U.S. Supreme Court chief justice Roger B. Taney demanded to know by what authority Lincoln could suspend habeas corpus (not telling someone the reason for his arrest). Lincoln's response could have been to cite Article 1, Section 9 of the Constitution as his defense ("The Privilege of the Writ of *Habeas Corpus* shall not be suspended, unless when in Cases of Rebellion or Invasion the public Safety may require it.") Instead of citing the Constitution, Lincoln issued an arrest warrant for the eighty-four-year-old chief justice. The warrant was never carried out, as Lincoln could not find a U.S. marshal willing to arrest the highest-ranking judge in the nation.

Over the course of the war, Lincoln arrested more than 14,000 civilians without charging them with specific crimes. Among those arrested were at least thirty members of the Maryland legislature known to favor secession. Those men were detained so they could not debate the idea of taking slaveholding Maryland out of the Union. The president also threw one Ohio congressman out of the country entirely for making a speech on the floor of the House of Representatives criticizing the suspension of habeas corpus. In addition, Lincoln violated the First Amendment by arresting newspaper editors who irritated him with their editorials or news coverage.

In the November 1862 statewide Maryland election, Lincoln sent troops to monitor the polls to keep Democrats and other nefarious characters

Books Y'all Aren't Supposed to Read

Black Southerners in Gray: Essays on Afro-Americans in Confederate Armies, John McGlone, ed., Journal of Confederate History Series, Vol. XI; Murfreesboro, TN: Southern Heritage Press, 1994.

Forgotten Confederates: An Anthology about Black Southerners, Charles Kelly Barron, J. H. Segars, and R. B. Rosenburg, eds., Journal of Confederate History Series, Vol. XIV; Murfreesboro, TN: Southern Heritage Press, 1995.

Black Southerners in Confederate Armies: A Collection of Historical Accounts, J. H. Segars and Charles Kelly Barrow; Atlanta: Southern Lion Books, 2001.

from voting for anyone but Republicans. Lincoln gave Maryland troops serving in the Union Army furloughs to cast their ballots in the election— and provided instructions on which candidates deserved their votes.

Davis ignored his critics

While Lincoln chose to imprison his newspaper-owning critics, Confederate president Jefferson Davis chose to abide by the Confederate Constitution, which stated: "Congress shall make no law respecting an establishment of religion, or prohibiting the free exercise thereof; or abridging the freedom of speech, or of the press; or the right of the people peaceably to assemble and petition the Government for a redress of grievances."

Davis had plenty of people telling him how to do his job, including men like Robert Barnwell Rhett, owner of the *Charleston Mercury*, and Edward Pollard and John Moncure Daniel, both editors of the *Richmond Examiner*.

But however much he was criticized, Davis never ordered any newspaper editor, or any member of the Confederate Congress, arrested for disagreeing with him. Jefferson Davis better defended civil rights than Abraham Lincoln did.

Why Lincoln's Emancipation Proclamation was a sham

For nearly 150 years the public has been told that the war was "to free the slaves" and that President Lincoln freed those slaves when he issued his Emancipation Proclamation.

Actually, he didn't.

The only slaves Lincoln freed were the slaves he did not control, the ones living in the Confederacy. The slaves the president did control— more than 800,000 men, women, and children living within captured

Confederate territory and in Delaware, Maryland, Kentucky, Missouri, and unoccupied parts of Tennessee—were specifically left out of the document. Lincoln's proclamation even gets down to specific counties. He writes that he is not freeing the slaves in twelve Louisiana parishes, including the city of New Orleans, and not freeing them in seven Virginia counties and the thirty-eight counties making up West Virginia. All of those places were in Union hands.

Lincoln privately explained to his friends that the document really did not mean much, because it had "no constitutional or legal justification, except as a military measure. The exemptions were made [meaning the specified areas where the slaves were not freed] because the military necessity did not apply to the exempted localities."

Near the end of the proclamation, Lincoln writes that freed slaves will be accepted into the armed forces. The document details how the freed slaves will be used to "garrison forts, positions, stations, and other places, and to man vessels of all sorts in said service." Curiously, Lincoln says nothing about actually putting black soldiers into battle.

The reaction in Northern states was interesting. The Illinois legislature, in which Lincoln had served, passed a resolution calling the proclamation a "gigantic usurpation" of the war's purpose and that freeing the slaves:

> invites servile insurrection as an element in this emancipation crusade—a means of warfare, the inhumanity and diabolism of which are without example in civilized warfare, and which we denounce, and which the civilized world will denounce, as an uneffaceable disgrace to the American people.

Others accused Lincoln of being timid. Horace Greeley of the *New York Tribune* said, "While the Proclamation leaves slavery untouched where his decree can be enforced, he emancipates slaves where his decree cannot be enforced. Friends of human rights will be at a loss to understand this discrimination."

Months earlier Lincoln had chastised Greeley for getting involved in the slavery issue. Lincoln wrote the newsman a letter saying that if he could end the war without freeing any slaves, he would do it, because preservation of the Union was all-important.

The Union Army's reaction was dangerous.

General Joseph Hooker wrote, "A majority of the officers, especially those high in rank, were hostile to the policy of the government in the conduct of the war.... A large element of the army had taken sides antagonistic to it, declaring that they would never have embarked in the war had they anticipated this action of the government." One entire regiment from Illinois, Lincoln's home state, had to be disbanded because the men were so against it.

Lincoln's primary motivation in issuing the Emancipation Proclamation was to make it difficult for any European countries to recognize the Confederacy. Granting legitimacy to the slaveholding Confederacy would give the United States a black eye. Lincoln counted on Europeans staying clear of the American conflict once he issued his proclamation. It worked—but it did not free a single slave.

Blacks get the "presidential" treatment

One will not encounter the name Jim Limber when reading PC-approved biographies of the life and career of Confederate president Jefferson Davis. That is because the existence of Jim Limber destroys the theory that Davis was a racist Confederate president.

Jim Limber was a black child the Davis family raised as their own.

Jefferson Davis's wife, Varina, was riding in her carriage in downtown Richmond in 1864 when she chanced upon a black man whipping a

What a Confederate Hero Said

"Nothing fills me with deeper sadness than to see a Southern man apologizing for the defense we made of our inheritance. Our cause was so just, so sacred, that had I known all that has come to pass, had I known what was to be inflicted upon me, all that my country was to suffer, all that our posterity was to endure, I would do it all over again."

Jefferson Davis

child. The appalled First Lady grabbed the four-year-old and put him into the carriage with her.

For the next year Jim Limber lived in the Confederate White House as a ward of the Davis family. The child was too young at the time to explain much about himself other than that he was an orphan. He took the name his foster brothers and sisters gave him, Jim Limber Davis, though it is not known if the family legally adopted him.

Jim Limber lived and played with the Davis children and celebrated Christmas 1864 with them. When the Davis family fled Richmond in April 1865, Jim Limber was with them. He stayed with the Davises until May 10, 1865, when Union cavalry caught up to the Davis party in southeastern Georgia. Jim Limber was snatched from Varina Davis's grasp. He was dragged away screaming and crying from his loving adopted mother.

Despite repeated pleas and letters to Union officials, the Davis family never found out what had happened to Jim Limber. It was not in the Union's best interests to let the public know that the Confederate president was raising a black foster son in the Confederate White House. And so Jim Limber, whom the Davis family had educated and raised as a free black child and one of their own, was lost to history.

Contrast this with the story of Elizabeth Keckley, Mary Todd Lincoln's dressmaker and only friend in Washington. Mrs. Keckley was so close to the First Lady that when the Lincolns' son Willie died, she took the responsibility of dressing his body for display and burial. After Lincoln was assassinated, only Mrs. Keckley walked out of the White House with

Mrs. Lincoln. Washington's politicians disliked the First Lady so much that they could not even bring themselves to help her in her time of grief.

After the war, Mrs. Keckley wrote a book called *Behind the Scenes: Thirty Years as a Slave and Four Years in the White House.* It was the forerunner of the "tell-all" autobiography, in which Mrs. Keckley described some conversations between the president and Mrs. Lincoln, including the famous comment from Lincoln that he would put his wife in an insane asylum if she did not get over Willie's death.

When the book was published, Robert Lincoln, the family's oldest son, questioned in public why anyone would want to read a book written by a "mulatto." He approached the publisher and tried to have the book pulled out of circulation. Mrs. Keckley, once the most famous dressmaker in the nation, never recovered from the attacks on her by the Lincoln family. She died poor in Washington; even her gravesite is unknown.

Andersonville and the horror of the prison camps

More than 140,000 Union soldiers and more than 200,000 Confederate soldiers were captured during the war. Of those numbers about 30,000 of each side died in prison camps.

At the beginning of the war, captured prisoners were treated as gentlemen. The Union prisoners captured at Fort Sumter were allowed to board a ship and sail to New York City. During the first year of the war, the two sides negotiated the numbers of men to be exchanged according to rank. For instance, a general was worth forty-six privates—even though the general was often a drunken lout who did not know how to shoot a rifle and the privates were probably country boys who knew how to hunt.

The Union ended the exchange system on May 25, 1863, on the grounds that the Confederacy would not exchange black prisoners for white prisoners. But the real reason was to cripple the Confederacy's manpower. According to General U. S. Grant, "Every man we hold when released on parole or otherwise, becomes an active soldier against us at once either directly or indirectly. If we commence a system of exchange which liberates all prisoners taken, we will have to fight on until the whole South is exterminated. If we hold those caught they amount to no more than dead men."

Suddenly, prison camps that had been designed as temporary holding facilities became permanent prisons. The numbers of prisoners swelled immediately after any battle. Formerly manageable prisons became hell-holes where fresh water was scarce, food was precious, and crime was sometimes rampant. Throughout most of 1864 prisoners and guards in Southern camps were on the same diet and suffered the same percentages of death and disease. Union raids on Confederate farms made food shortages even worse.

But conditions were just as bad up North—though with less excuse, because those camps had access to all the food, water, and medicines that they needed. In Elmira, New York, the commander delayed issuing winter blankets to prisoners. When asked for funds to build more barracks at Camp Douglas outside Chicago (described as "Forty Acres of Hell"), Secretary of War Edwin Stanton's secretary replied that Stanton "is not disposed at this time, in view of the treatment our prisoners of war are receiving at the hands of the enemy, to erect fine establishments for their prisoners in our hands." At Point Lookout, Maryland, and Fort Delaware, on an island in the Delaware River, the camps were surrounded by water, and men froze to death during the winters.

Remarkably, Union officials, including President Lincoln and Secretary of War Stanton, refused personal appeals from five paroled Union prisoners from Andersonville in July 1864 to restart the exchange. The men had presented a petition signed by most of the prisoners asking for help. When the men returned they said that in no meeting with any Union official was the subject of black prisoners brought up. It was obvious to these men that their government had abandoned them in hopes of wearing down the Confederacy.

Immediately after the war the commander of Andersonville, Confederate major Henry Wirz, a wounded native of Switzerland, was given a show trial and executed for crimes against the Union prisoners in his care. Despite little real evidence that he had ever intentionally harmed any prisoner, the outcome of the trial was never in doubt. Wirz was executed to show an angry Union civilian population that their government did care about the men who had perished in Confederate prison camps.

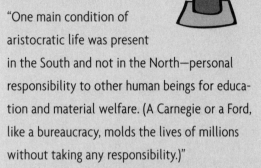

The Southern Mentality

"One main condition of aristocratic life was present in the South and not in the North—personal responsibility to other human beings for education and material welfare. (A Carnegie or a Ford, like a bureaucracy, molds the lives of millions without taking any responsibility.)"

Marshall McLuhan,
"The Southern Quality"

While Andersonville was horrible and remains notorious, and is maintained by the National Park Service as an historic site, how often do you hear about the *intentional* suffering inflicted in Union prisons, like Elmira, which today is only a cemetery?

God recognized the Confederacy

One of the long-term goals the South desperately desired but never achieved during the War for Southern Independence was recognition by the major European powers. Jefferson Davis and his cabinet believed that if Europe recognized the Confederacy, the United States would either be forced to lift its blockade or would run the risk of setting off a war with Europe. The South believed that Europe would be so anxious to secure a stable supply of cotton that it would readily recognize the Confederacy.

Books Y'all Aren't Supposed to Read

Forced into Glory: Abraham Lincoln's White Dream by Lerone Bennett, Jr.; Chicago: Johnson Publishing Company, 2000.

This book, little noticed or reviewed by the mainstream media, examined Lincoln's deep-rooted racism and his plans to colonize blacks to Central America and back to Africa.

The Devil's Own Work: The Civil War Draft Riots and the Fight to Reconstruct America by Barnet Schecter; New York: Walker & Company, 2005.

This book looks at the bloody riot in New York City in which hundreds, perhaps thousands, of blacks were attacked, beaten, and killed as the objects of hatred by New Yorkers who blamed them for being drafted into the War Between the States.

After the North passed its conscription laws, draft agents descended upon captured Confederate territory so they could sign up former slaves as substitutes for the draft-age sons of wealthy Northern families. The law allowed a man to pay the government $300 to shift his draft burden to someone else.

The South was wrong.

Expecting North and South would eventually come to blows, the Europeans had imported and stockpiled record amounts of cotton in the years leading up to the war. Rather than recognize the Confederacy, Europe decided to await the outcome, confident in its hoarded supplies of cotton.

Another aspect of international relations the South had not counted on was Europe's reluctance to recognize a country that still practiced slavery. England had outlawed slavery in its home islands and in all of its colonies in 1833. France had outlawed slavery in 1848. The governments of both countries did not want to appear to be backpedaling on what had become an emotional issue in the Western world.

Only one European country endorsed the new Confederacy. It was a small country with an armed force that consisted of a handful of Swiss mercenaries, but its leader reported to an even higher authority than the king of England or the president of France: he reported to God.

Pope Pius IX, the longest-serving pope in the Vatican's history (1846–1878), must have felt some affinity with Confederate president Jefferson Davis. The two never met, but they established a long-distance friendship through letters, starting early in 1862 when Davis wrote to the pope asking him to discourage European Catholics who were enlisting in the Union army in exchange for American citizenship. The pope agreed and instructed his bishops to remind their parishioners that they had no stake in a foreign war. The Vatican newspaper even editorialized on the Confederacy's behalf. And at the top of all correspondence with Davis, the pope addressed him as: "His Excellency, Jefferson Davis, President of the Confederate States of America." It was an official recognition of the Southern nation by the world leader of the Catholic faith.

There were other similarities in the lives of the two men. Just as Davis's South was invaded by the North, the Papal States were under constant threat from other European powers, most especially from violent Italian nationalism that eventually reduced the area of the Papal States to Vatican City. Like Davis, Pope Pius allowed his political enemies to speak freely against him. And Davis, as a young man, had attended a Catholic school and had even considered converting to Catholicism.

For Christmas 1866, Pope Pius sent Davis, then imprisoned at Fort Monroe, an autographed photograph of himself with a Latin verse: "Come unto me all ye that labor and are cast down, and I will refresh you." Attached to the wooden frame was a crown of thorns woven by the pope himself.

Davis was moved by the gift from his faraway friend. He remarked that the gifts came at a time "when the invention of malignants was taxed to the utmost to fabricate defamations to degrade me in the estimation of mankind."

Both the framed photograph and the crown of thorns can be found at the collection of the Confederate Memorial Museum in New Orleans.

Pope Pius was one of many religious people who sided with the Confederacy. Leonidas Polk, the Episcopal bishop for the state of Louisiana, had been a friend of Davis at West Point, but had resigned his commission almost immediately after graduation to become an Episcopal priest. When the war started, he removed his clerical robes and put on the gray uniform of the Confederacy.

Polk was a great bishop and a great inspiration for young men. He was the principal founder of the University of the South at Sewanee, Tennessee. Unfortunately for the South, he was a terrible general. Though the man had served only a month as a second lieutenant in the 1820s, his old friend Jefferson Davis appointed him a major general. Later he would be promoted to lieutenant general, the rank held by the commander of an army. Polk had to be the least experienced army leader in American history. His career, and his life, ended in the summer of 1864 when a well-placed Union artillery shell tore him apart on a battlefield north of Atlanta.

Father Abram Ryan was a Catholic priest who joined the Confederate army as a chaplain. After the war he won even greater fame as a poet, concentrating on poems that extolled the virtues of the Confederate fighting men. His most famous poem was "The Conquered Banner," which urged those who fought under the flag to put it away carefully. The poem ends with the lines:

> Furl that Banner, softly, slowly,
> Treat it gently it is holy
> For it droops above the dead.
> Touch it not, unfold it never,
> Let it droop there, furled forever,
> For its people's hopes are dead!

Why did religious men like Father Ryan, the pope, and Bishop Polk support the Confederacy? Many reasons, but one that is as true today as it was then is that they recognized in the South a traditional conservative religious society being attacked in an aggressive war by a modern centralized state that put state-enforced, coercive law ahead of the dispersed authority of families, churches, and localities. A lot of folks up North still think the federal government should tell us how to live our lives; folks down South think that's the job of families, preachers, and local officials we know and can hold accountable.

Southern women were the backbone of the Confederacy

Northern intellectuals always claim that they were the first to launch the women's movement with the 1848 Seneca Falls, New York, convention. In reality all that convention of disgruntled women produced was a proclamation that consisted of a laundry list of why women were supposed to hate men, such as "He has made her, if married, in the eye of the law, civilly dead." While Northern women were drawing up their protest placards, Southern women were already operating farms, running plantations, tending to the sick, raising families, and being hospitable to boot. Southern history is full of women who filled the roles of men, or were as brave as men. None were braver or more devoted than Sally Tompkins of Virginia, the first woman in history to hold a military commission.

Sally Tompkins was an attractive, single young woman of means visiting relatives in Richmond in July 1861 when the first train cars loaded with the wounded of the Battle of Manassas began rolling into town. Though she had no medical training, she saw the chaos created by the sudden influx of soldiers. She boldly walked to the home of Judge John Robertson and demanded the keys to an empty home she knew he had. She opened the house as a hospital. For the next four years Miss Tompkins headed the Robertson Hospital, treating 1,333 wounded men and losing only seventy-three of them to death. The untrained hospital matron had the lowest death rate of any hospital in the South—or the North.

Miss Tompkins had no medical secrets. She believed in throwing open the windows and letting sunlight and fresh air into the house. She made sure the food was fresh, hot, and plentiful. She was a stickler about the cleanliness of soldiers' wounds and of their bed linens. She allowed no malingering in her hospital—she believed that soldiers should be up and moving around to help them recuperate.

But what Sally Tompkins was doing was radical in the eyes of doctors assigned to regular Confederate hospitals. She was also embarrassing—a nurse matron with no previous experience who had a lower death rate than doctors with years of medical training. Those doctors forced a law through the Confederate legislature that required all military hospitals to have a Confederate officer in charge. As a civilian and a woman, Miss Tompkins would be forced to close her hospital.

Undaunted, Miss Tompkins went directly to President Jefferson Davis and described to him both her high rate of patient recovery and the fact that the doctors of Richmond were trying to shut down her hospital out

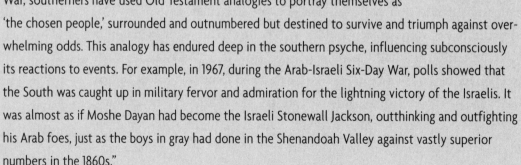

What a Southerner Said

"I have for years been intrigued with the ways in which Jews and southerners are alike—stepchildren of an anguished history. From the period before the Civil War, southerners have used Old Testament analogies to portray themselves as 'the chosen people,' surrounded and outnumbered but destined to survive and triumph against overwhelming odds. This analogy has endured deep in the southern psyche, influencing subconsciously its reactions to events. For example, in 1967, during the Arab-Israeli Six-Day War, polls showed that the South was caught up in military fervor and admiration for the lightning victory of the Israelis. It was almost as if Moshe Dayan had become the Israeli Stonewall Jackson, outthinking and outfighting his Arab foes, just as the boys in gray had done in the Shenandoah Valley against vastly superior numbers in the 1860s."

Eli N. Evans, *The Lonely Days Were Sundays: Reflections of a Jewish Southerner* of jealousy. Davis had the solution. Before she left the Confederate White House, Miss Sally Tompkins was commissioned an officer in the Confederate cavalry. From that moment on she was officially Captain Sally Tompkins of the Confederate Army. It was the first time in history that a woman had been formally inducted into an army on American soil.

Captain Sally never took a dime for her service to the Confederacy. In fact, she depleted the family fortune caring for her "boys" in Richmond. She never married, and lived to be an old woman. Her tombstone bears the lines of Matthew 25:35–36: "I was hungry and you gave me meat. I was thirsty and you gave me a drink. I was sick and you visited me."

Another Confederate nurse was Phoebe Yates Pember, a thirty-eight-year-old Jewish widow from Charleston. In 1861 she moved from Charleston to Richmond to take over matron duties in Chimborazo Hospital, a huge complex of hospital buildings in the city. When someone told her that a military hospital was no place for a woman she replied: "In the midst of suffering death, hoping with those almost beyond hope in this world; praying by the bedside of the lonely and heartsicken; closing the eyes of boys hardly old enough to realize man's sorrow, much less suffer man's fierce hate, a woman must soar beyond the conventional modesty considered correct under different circumstances." After the war she wrote her memoirs, *A Southern Woman's Story*, which is still considered one of the best accounts of the war written by a woman because of its rich details and unflinching assessment of war in the South.

Both Tompkins and Yates were acting as nurses and ignoring medical bureaucracies long before more famous Union nurses like Clara Barton and Dorthea Dix had even taken the field. Unlike Northern feminists who often seemed to hate men, no one ever accused a Southern lady of being anything other than a lady. Southern women can treat the wounded and mind their manners while they're doing it. Courage and grace go together in the South.

Chapter 13

RECONSTRUCTION...
OR DECONSTRUCTION?

The assassination of Abraham Lincoln was the worst thing that could have happened to the South, if one assumes that Honest Abe was uncharacteristically as good as his word. Lincoln was, if nothing else, a masterful politician, and so one has to wonder what he would have done with the South after the war.

It might surprise some, but according to Confederate vice president Alexander Stephens, the Emancipation Proclamation was up for negotiation.

Stephens met with Lincoln aboard a ship at Hampton Roads, Virginia, on February 3, 1865, hoping to negotiate an end to the war. According to Stephens, Lincoln said that the proclamation was a war measure and as soon as the war ceased, its effect would also cease. Lincoln had said the same thing to at least one congressman and a close friend before his meeting with Stephens. Even though the United States Congress had just passed the Thirteenth Amendment, ending slavery, President Lincoln wanted to keep his options open. Lincoln even offered to pay slaveholders up to $400 per slave (the going rate in 1860 for a prime field hand had been $1,000), saying that "it was wrong in the North to carry on the slave trade and sell them to the South." Stephens and the astonished Confederates at the meeting left unsure of Lincoln's sincerity.

Guess what?

- No Confederate leaders were ever charged with treason, because a trial could show secession was constitutional.

- There had been no segregation in the antebellum South.

- A Southern congressman proposed the desegregating of the armed forces seventy years before it happened.

Was the War Worth It?

On a per capita basis, the costs to the Northern population were about $150, roughly equal to a year's income. The Southern burden was two and a half times that: $376 per man, woman, and child.

The total cost of the war was around $7 billion, roughly twice what it would have cost to buy and free every Southern slave at market value.

Roger Ransom, *The Economics of the Civil War*, University of California–Riverside, 2005

But Lincoln made good on that promise at his next cabinet meeting by suggesting a bill that would pay the South $400 million in compensation if hostilities immediately ceased. The cabinet unanimously rejected Lincoln's idea. Lincoln grumbled to his cabinet, "You are all against me."

Lincoln and Grant still had dreams of a negotiated peace. The president met with Grant and Sherman on March 28, 1865, and told them, "I want no one [referring to Confederate leaders] punished; treat them liberally all around. We want those people to return to their allegiance to the Union and submit to the laws." He hinted to Sherman that he would prefer that any Confederate leaders trying to avoid capture be allowed to leave the country.

At about the same time Lincoln told a visiting French government official that he intended to "stand for clemency [for Confederates] against all opposition." When Richmond fell and Lincoln made a surprise visit to the city, General Godfrey Weitzel asked the president what he should do with the civilians of the city. Lincoln replied, "Let them up easy." On April 8, the day before Lee met Grant at Appomattox, Lincoln asked a band to play "Dixie," saying, "With us in power, they [Southerners] will be free to hear it again."

On April 10, after learning that Lee had surrendered, Lincoln made a speech and told another band to play "Dixie," saying, "It is one of the best tunes I have ever heard." In the same speech he hinted that he might back the idea that black men in Louisiana, particularly those who were soldiers, would be allowed to vote. At that time, only three states in New England (with very small black populations) allowed blacks to vote.

The South will never know what Lincoln had in store for it. He was shot on April 14 and died on April 15. On April 19, Jefferson Davis read a telegram describing the president's assassination. Davis said, "I certainly have no special regard for Mr. Lincoln, but there are a great many men of whose end I would much rather hear than this. I fear it will be disastrous to our people."

Confederates were accused of treason, but never tried

Davis was captured on May 10, 1865, near Irwinville, Georgia. He would spend the next two years imprisoned at Fortress Monroe in Hampton, Virginia. For several months of that time he was chained and kept in a damp windowless cell. A light was kept on twenty-four hours a day. He was granted better conditions only when a doctor told General Nelson Miles, his captor, that Davis would likely go insane from such inhumane treatment. Miles reluctantly let Davis move into better quarters and get fresh air and exercise. Miles later earned a reputation as one of the more ruthless generals fighting the Plains Indians.

Many Confederates, including Davis, virtually demanded that they be tried for treason, believing that secession was constitutional. Their demands were never granted. In 1869 Chief Justice Salmon Chase wrote the majority decision in the obscure case of *Texas* v. *White* (involving the issuing of government bonds), ruling that secession was unconstitutional. But no Confederate leaders were ever charged with treason, leading some historians to speculate that Chase conspired with Congress to specifically avoid bringing such high-profile men to trial, out of fear that intense scrutiny of the case would find language in the Constitution supporting the Confederacy.

One thing that *Texas* v. *White* did do was put Congress, rather than President Andrew Johnson, in charge of Reconstruction. Congress had tried to do that in 1864 with the passage of the Wade-Davis Bill, but Lincoln rejected Congress's harsh plans to punish the South after the war and pocket-vetoed the bill. After Lincoln's assassination, Congress first made Lincoln a martyr and then enforced the policies of the Wade-Davis Bill that Lincoln had rejected.

Little "reconstruction" was done during Reconstruction

"Reconstruction" is the most misnamed period in American history. Nothing of the sort went on from 1865 to 1876, the officially recognized period when the South was occupied by federal soldiers on the grounds that Southern states had to be "reconstructed" before they could be readmitted into the Union.

There was little left to reconstruct. The urban infrastructure was gone. Charleston had been shelled mercilessly for more than two years and Vicksburg for two months by heavy Union cannons. Atlanta and Columbia had been intentionally burned to the ground by invading Union armies, as had dozens of smaller towns. All of the Southern railroads had been destroyed, with the rails twisted around telegraph poles into "Sherman's neckties." The small manufacturing plants were gone, targeted to prevent them from producing military equipment. Southern public and private property had been gleefully destroyed by the Union invaders during the war in order to punish the South. One Union general sent a note to Sherman that Barnwell, South Carolina, would have to be renamed "Burnswell" thanks to the skill of his men and their matches.

A Book Y'all Aren't Supposed to Read

I'll Take My Stand: The South and the Agrarian Tradition by 12 Southerners; New York: Harper & Brothers, 1930.

The rural infrastructure was also gone. The farmlands of the Shenandoah Valley had been so successfully destroyed that the generals joked with each other that a crow flying over the valley would have to bring his own rations. In every Southern state livestock had been slaughtered for food and target practice and to demoralize the civilians. Just days before Lee surrendered, one little girl's pony was shot in front of her, so she would always remember the day the Yankees came to Boone, North Carolina—a mountain town that had seen no fighting.

Rebuilding the South was not an issue for Congress. The real issue was how to punish the South. Congressman Thaddeus Stevens of Pennsylvania had one idea that sounded great to him: he filed a bill to confiscate all of the Southern states' land and redistribute it to the freed slaves. That idea was so radical that even Stevens's friends in Congress rejected it.

One thing was clear. President Johnson—a Democrat Lincoln had brought on to his 1864 ticket for bipartisan appeal—and the Radical Republicans in Congress hated each other. The president and Congress were locked in a battle over who would administer Reconstruction.

"I have been fighting the South, and they have been whipped and crushed, and now, as I go around the circle, having fought the traitors at the South, I am prepared to fight the traitors at the North. He who is opposed to the restoration of this government and the reunion of the states is as great a traitor as Jeff Davis," said Johnson in an 1866 speech in Cleveland, Ohio.

What a President Said

"We have heard all of our lives how, after the Civil War was over, the South went back to straighten itself out and make a living again. It was for many years a voiceless part of the government. The balance of power moved away from it—to the north and the east. The problems of the north and the east became the big problem of the country and nobody paid much attention to the economic unbalance the South had left as its only choice."

Lyndon Baines Johnson

Under Johnson's early leadership, many Southern states quickly abolished slavery as a condition of being readmitted to the Union. All of them ratified the Thirteenth Amendment, ending slavery. But they also began to enact "black codes" that tried to control blacks' ability to work and travel. Freedmen were paid a contracted wage, but Southern states were still wary of giving blacks total freedom.

When the Radical Republicans saw the black codes being made into state law under President Johnson's watch, they moved against him to take over Reconstruction. Among their first efforts was to refuse admission to any former Confederate in the U.S. House and Senate. Congress passed bills governing Reconstruction and Johnson vetoed them. In 1868 Congress finally impeached Johnson on a minor, trumped-up charge and he barely avoided conviction by the Senate. He was finished in his efforts to bring about the Reconstruction Abraham Lincoln had envisioned.

Instead, the Radical Republicans invaded the South again, using the military to take over the states' governments. On March 2, 1866, the South was divided into five military districts. The treatment of former Confederates ranged from the expected (excluding them from holding office) to the ridiculous (forbidding men from wearing their old brass military buttons on their civilian clothes).

What They Fought For

"During all these years the conduct of the southern people has been admirable.... Accepting the harshest conditions and faithfully observing them, they have struggled in all honorable ways, and for what? For their slaves? Regret for their loss has neither been felt nor expressed. But they have striven for that which brought our forefathers to Runnymede, the privilege of exercising some influence in their own government."

General Richard Taylor, son of President Zachary Taylor

In June 1866, the Radical Republicans brought the Fourteenth Amendment up for ratification. This amendment sounded much like the Thirteenth: "nor shall any State deprive any person of life, liberty, or property, without due process of law; nor deny to any person within its jurisdiction the equal protection of the laws."

But buried down in Section 4 of the amendment was language banning any man from serving in Congress who "shall have engaged in insurrection or rebellion against the same, or given aid or comfort to the enemies thereof. But Congress may by a vote of two-thirds of each House, remove such disability."

The Fourteenth Amendment was a public relations trap set by the Radicals for the South. Any Southern state that wanted to do the right thing by agreeing that black men should be equal to whites would also have to agree that no former Confederate would be able to serve in Congress. Several Southern states initially rejected the Fourteenth Amendment, but after their legislatures were reconstituted by the Radicals, it passed.

The Fifteenth Amendment, passed in 1870, said the right to vote could not be denied because of race. Oddly, it did not guarantee the right to vote. So states could otherwise determine a voter's qualifications. Even the majority of Northern states did not yet allow blacks to vote, but the Fifteenth Amendment passed in all the Southern state legislatures, which were mere puppet governments of the Radical Republicans. (Curiously, Oregon and California refused to ratify the Fifteenth Amendment until 1959 and 1962, and Oregon four times refused to remove a clause in its

And We're All Better Off

"One of the most singular facts about the unwritten history of this country is the consummate ability with which Southern influence, Southern ideas, and Southern ideals have from the very beginning even up to the present day, dictated to and domineered over the brain and sinew of this nation."

Anna Julia Cooper, a North Carolinian born into slavery, became a leading black educator.

own constitution specifically denying blacks' right to vote, even though federal law made that clause inactive.)

Reconstruction: the good

One good thing that came from Reconstruction was that blacks got an exhilarating taste of electoral freedom—which, unfortunately, wouldn't last. But it did put some positive arguments in play. One of the first black congressmen elected, Robert Smalls of South Carolina, a former slave, proposed legislation desegregating the armed forces. But his amendment was not considered by the Radical Republican Congress. Smalls was seventy years ahead of his time. Eventually another Southerner, President Harry Truman, ordered the armed forces desegregated.

Many all-black schools, such as Tuskegee University in Alabama, Morehouse College in Georgia, Fisk University in Nashville, Howard University in Washington, D.C., and Jackson State University in Jackson, Mississippi, were all started during Reconstruction to satisfy a pent-up demand for education among blacks. Men like Booker T. Washington and George Washington Carver used their positions at Tuskegee to further the education of blacks, and Carver used the school to break new ground in the field of agricultural research. Later, Tuskegee would serve as the home training base of the Tuskegee Airmen, a wing of fighter pilots who escorted bombers during World War II.

Reconstruction: the bad

There had been no segregation in the antebellum South. Plantation slaves lived in cabins within feet of their owner's house. City slaves lived in brick houses behind their owner's house. While whites in the North often lived far away from black people, Southern whites and blacks lived and worked (and their children played) side by side and thought nothing of it.

That changed after the war, when the Radical Republicans sent armed regiments of black soldiers into the South as occupation troops and installed black politicians into local and state government slots, while barring all former Confederates from holding office. Former Confederates resented what

A Book Y'all Aren't Supposed to Read

From Eden to Babylon by Andrew Nelson Lytle; Washington, DC: Regnery, 1990.

they saw as interference from the North that overthrew responsible government and created a sense of entitlement among blacks. It also bred racial animosity and led to the creation of the vigilante group the Ku Klux Klan, which expressed the bitterness of former Confederates who had lost their right to vote.

Racial violence was an extreme reaction to Reconstruction, but almost equally damaging was the development of segregation in the previously unsegregated South: whites-only bathrooms, drinking fountains, restaurants, and seats on public transportation.

Within twenty-five years of the war's end, all of the gains that blacks had made in the South were lost, as white power brokers emerged to take their places in state government. Because white Southerners could not fight the North again or fight Reconstruction through their own elected legislatures, black Southerners became the unfortunate victims of white Southerners' anger at Reconstruction's wrongs. That was the sad legacy of Reconstruction.

Chapter 14

THE SOUTH RISES AGAIN

It took another war for the North to welcome the South back into the fold. In the winter of 1897–1898 the New York City newspapers published by William Randolph Hearst and Joseph Pulitzer were filled with stories of atrocities committed in Cuba by occupying Spaniards against native Cubans. The papers competed against each other to produce the day's most lurid headlines. Soon congressmen were demanding that President William McKinley do something to save the tiny country just ninety miles from Florida. President Grover Cleveland had successfully deflected similar calls. Neither Cleveland nor McKinley saw how American interests were threatened by Spain's actions.

Then on February 15, 1898, the USS *Maine*, a battleship that had been sent to Havana to impress the Spaniards, was sunk by an explosion. More than 225 sailors were lost. New Yorkers Hearst and Pulitzer speculated that Spaniards had put an underwater mine beneath the ship's keel. (Some historians think the explosion was an accident.)

By late April Congress had passed a resolution forcing a reluctant McKinley to declare war. More than 182,000 men from both North and South volunteered to join the United States Army. The army, only 28,000 strong, was at that time mostly scattered around the West, fighting Indians. Most of the training camps for the new army volunteers were established

Guess what?

✖ A Jewish Southerner, Moses Jacob Ezekiel, sculpted the Confederate Memorial at Arlington National Cemetery.

✖ A former Confederate general, Joseph Wheeler, held the black troops under his command in higher regard than Teddy Roosevelt's famous "Rough Riders."

in the South, including one large camp on the old Chickamauga, Georgia, battlefield; another almost within sight of the battlefield of Manassas, Virginia; and another at Mobile, Alabama, which had seen a large naval battle in 1864. The influx of federal money was welcomed in those regions, still mired in a thirty-year depression.

Among the generals leading 15,000 U.S. troops into Cuba was Joseph Wheeler, a congressman from Alabama who had resigned his seat to take command. Wheeler had previously resigned from the U.S. Army in 1861 to gain fame as a Confederate cavalry leader. When asked how it felt to wear the blue uniform of the United States Army again at age sixty-two, Wheeler replied, "I feel as though I have been away on a three weeks' furlough and I have just returned to my own colors." Joining Wheeler were two other former Confederates, Matthew Butler, who had lost a foot in 1863, and Fitzhugh Lee, Robert E. Lee's nephew, who had been serving as the counsel in Cuba.

On July 1, thirty-five years to the day after the start of the Battle of Gettysburg, the Americans took San Juan Hill, the most famous battle of the Spanish-American War. Lieutenant John J. Pershing, a native of Missouri (a state that had supplied 40,000 troops to the Confederacy), later wrote: "White regiments, black regiments, regulars and Rough Riders, representing the young manhood of the North and South, fought shoulder to shoulder, unmindful of race and color, unmindful of whether commanded by an ex-Confederate or not, and mindful only of their common duty as Americans." Pershing, then a line officer with the Tenth United States Cavalry, a unit of black troops, would later command the American Expeditionary Force in World War I.

The Southern Mentality

"Most Southerners of my parents' era were raised to feel that it wasn't respectable to be rich. We felt that all patriotic Southerners had lost everything in defense of the South, and sufficient time hadn't elapsed for respectable rebuilding of financial security in a war-impoverished region."

Sarah Patton Boyle, Virginian and civil rights advocate

By the fall, "the splendid little war" was over. More than 3,000 Americans had died, but only 365 of those were combat deaths. The rest had succumbed to diseases, mostly yellow fever. Not long after the war, Dr. Walter Reed, a native of Virginia, determined while assigned in Cuba that mosquitoes spread yellow fever. With that knowledge, the mosquito population was targeted and deaths from the disease were greatly reduced.

Wheeler praises his black soldiers

General Wheeler, the old Confederate, knew good soldiers when he saw them, and he knew what he had in the "Buffalo Soldiers." When asked to compare their performance to Colonel Theodore Roosevelt's hand-picked Rough Riders (a volunteer regiment of cowboys and Ivy Leaguers), Wheeler said the Rough Riders "were brave, determined, and chivalrous men, but the truth impels me to say that in effectiveness in battle they could not be expected to be equal to trained regular soldiers" (like the regular Army units of the Ninth and Tenth Cavalry, both black regiments).

When Wheeler disbanded his division in September 1898, he told them, "Whatever may be my fate, wherever my steps may lead, my heart will always burn with increasing admiration for your courage in action, your fortitude under privation, and your constant devotion to duty in its highest sense, whether in battle, in bivouac, or upon the march."

Bygones are finally bygones

The Spanish-American War seemed to break the ice between North and South. Until 1898, the chill had been real.

In 1887 President Grover Cleveland tried to return more than 440 Confederate battle flags that were stored at the War Department. Cleveland, who had not fought in the war, thought nothing of signing an executive order to clean out the closets of the War Department. The Grand Army of the Republic, an organization of Union Army veterans, turned the executive order into a national outrage. The GAR commander publicly prayed for God to "palsy the brain" of the president. A chagrined Cleveland quickly rescinded his executive order.

But after the Spanish-American War, President William McKinley wanted to do something to recognize the South's newfound patriotism. McKinley had fought in the war as a soldier from Ohio. He had won a curious kind of fame at the Battle of Sharpsburg for bravely delivering coffee and pastries while under fire (while acting as commissary sergeant for his regiment).

In December 1898 McKinley traveled to Atlanta for a speech. After a rousing round of "Dixie," during which McKinley jumped up and waved his hat, the president announced that "every soldier's grave during our unfortunate civil war is a tribute to American valor." He then announced that the United States would take responsibility for caring for more than four thousand Confederate graves scattered around several national cemeteries in the North.

In 1900, by presidential order, Arlington National Cemetery set aside a section of land for the collection and reburial of nearly five hundred Confederate bodies. Arlington National Cemetery itself had been founded in 1864, after Robert E. Lee's home and property had been confiscated by the Union Army. The section chosen was next to the 1,500 graves of United States Colored Troops. The government adopted a new tombstone, with an angular top, to distinguish Confederate graves from Union graves, which had a rounded top. Southern humorists quickly declared that the pointed Confederate gravestones prevented living Yankees from sitting on them.

After McKinley's assassination, President Theodore Roosevelt continued making overtures to the South. In 1905 Roosevelt asked Congress to pass another law to return the Confederate battle flags, an idea that had not been discussed since Cleveland's aborted executive order in 1887. A joint resolution bill to that effect was passed unanimously in both houses of Congress. The law included the lines: "The loyalty of the Southern states is nowhere questioned" and "We think it will be a graceful act of the Congress to return these flags."

This time there were no objections either from the Grand Army of the Republic or the press. The Confederate battle flags were returned to their

---

Defend the Flag!

The Rebel flag never flew over a slave ship. It is a military flag. Designed by General P. G. T. Beauregard, it was the Confederate battle flag. And its symbolism is Christian. It is modeled on St. Andrew's Cross (seen in the national flag of Scotland and in the Union Jack of Great Britain).

Half this nation fought for the Confederate battle flag. And to Confederate soldiers the flag represented their country, their families, and their homes, as well as a desire for the same sort of independence, the freedom to go their own way, that motivated the patriots of 1776.

That flag was defended with honor, courage, and self-sacrifice on battlefields across this country, many of which are now national or state parks.

For Southerners today, the flag is a symbol of Southern pride, a symbol of independence of mind, and a memory of Southern military valor.

Yet this noble flag—part of the family heritage of many Southerners, who are descended from Confederate veterans—is under assault nearly everywhere by the forces of political correctness who want to erase history, erase regional pride, and erase a heritage of Southern military service that used to be valued by all Americans. Robert E. Lee and Stonewall Jackson were once not just Southern heroes, but American heroes, and the flag they fought for should bear no shame.

Wave it proudly and defend it from those who would dishonor it, and from the politically correct who want to stuff down the memory hole of forbidden thoughts, forbidden history, and forbidden truth.

respective states, where they were received with solemn ceremonies by the aging veterans.

After the return of the flags Roosevelt followed McKinley's strategy and scheduled a Southern tour to bask in the region's appreciation. At every stop, the president, who had two uncles who had served in the Confederate navy, extolled the virtues of Confederate soldiers. At one stop Roosevelt said, "Only a heroic people could have battled successfully against the conditions with which the people of the South found themselves face to face at the end of the Civil War." In another speech Roosevelt declared, "All Americans must ever show high honor to the men of the War Between the States, whether they wore the blue or the gray, as long as they did their duty as the light was given them to see their duty with all of the strength that was in them." Like McKinley, Roosevelt often shouted "Charge!" when he heard "Dixie" played. He always stood up and took his hat off.

A Book Y'all Aren't Supposed to Read

The Complete Tales of Uncle Remus.

These African American folk tales were compiled by Joel Chandler Harris.

1906 was a heady time to be a Southerner. One Northern-born U.S. president had tried to return captured Confederate battle flags, another had promised the South that the United States would start caring for Confederate graves, and a third had made good on the old promise of returning the battle flags—and had praised Southern courage to boot.

Realizing that the time was ripe, the United Daughters of the Confederacy—a 60,000- member organization dedicated to memorializing the valor of Confederate soldiers—approached President Roosevelt's secretary of war, William Howard Taft, to ask permission to erect a memorial to the Confederates interred at Arlington. Taft readily agreed, with the stipulation that the ladies raise the money for the monument themselves.

After spending several years raising money, the design committee knew who they wanted to sculpt their monument. They approached a thickset, short-legged, big-eyed, sixty-seven-year-old sculptor with an impressive handlebar mustache, who was making one of his rare visits to the United States from his studio in Rome.

Moses Jacob Ezekiel met with the UDC and readily agreed to their request if they could raise the money, saying, "I have been waiting for forty years to have my love for the South recognized." He even offered to sculpt the monument for the cost of materials rather than tacking on the commission he usually received from European kings and queens.

Born to a middle-class Jewish family in Richmond in 1844, Ezekiel was just sixteen when the war began. He begged his parents to send him to the Virginia Military Institute in Lexington, wanting to become a soldier so he could defend his home state. He never officially joined the Confederate Army, but he did fight as a young cadet at the Battle of New Market, Virginia, where his roommate was killed. Ezekiel held his hand until he died.

Ezekiel had met Robert E. Lee shortly after the war, and had asked the general what he should do with his life. The old general, who had relaxed in his early Army days by sketching the unusual animals he encountered, such as alligators and armadillos, replied, "I hope you will be an artist, as it seems to me you are cut out for one. But, whatever you do, try to prove to the world that if we did not succeed in our struggle, we are worthy of success, and do earn a reputation in whatever profession you undertake."

In 1900, Ezekiel offered to cast a statue to commemorate the deaths of his fellow VMI cadets at New Market. The resulting bronze was "Virginia Mourning Her Dead," a life-size casting of the classical female figure from the Virginia state seal. The figure sits with her head in her hands, lamenting the deaths of the young men. Ezekiel made several other Confederate statues, including one of Stonewall Jackson. Though honored by the kings and queens of Europe for his bronzes (he was knighted by the king of Italy), Ezekiel still revered his Southern roots.

The central figure of the memorial he built for Arlington Cemetery shows a woman representing (and facing) the South, leaning back on a plow, holding in her hand a laurel wreath representing peace. Below the woman is a quote from Isaiah 2:4: "They will beat their swords into plowshares and their spears into pruning hooks."

Circling the round base of the memorial are thirty-two figures, starting with Minerva, the Roman goddess of war. Minerva holds up a mortally wounded woman, representing the South at the beginning of the war, clutching a shield embossed with "United States Constitution."

Behind the wounded woman are two lines of soldiers marching into battle. In the far rear rank of the second column, a focal point of the work, is an unarmed but Confederate cap–wearing black man marching shoulder to shoulder with the Confederate soldiers. Next to the marching soldiers is a black nanny lifting a baby for a Confederate officer to kiss goodbye. A small child clings to the nanny's legs. Other images on the sculpture memorialize the wealthy, the poor, and the religious who served the Confederacy.

Ezekiel and the ladies of the UDC had accomplished much more than erecting a memorial to the Confederate dead in Arlington National Cemetery. They had erected a defense of the Lost Cause.

Chapter 15

THE SOUTH SAVES THE WORLD

Could World Wars I and II have been won without Southerners? Maybe . . . but not likely. The most important American soldier in World War I was General John J. Pershing, the overall commander of the American Expeditionary Force (AEF), which would eventually number more than one million men by the summer of 1918. Pershing's father was a non-serving Unionist from central Missouri, a border state where young John had plenty of contact growing up with former Confederate soldiers.

After graduating from West Point, Pershing served with the Tenth United States Cavalry, one of two units made up of black soldiers, leading them during the Spanish-American War. Pershing was so closely associated with his black regiments that he earned the nickname "Black Jack" Pershing.

One lesson Pershing took from Cuba was the disadvantage his army faced by using outdated equipment. Many Army cartridges were filled with black powder that when ignited created clouds of smoke, revealing American positions. The Spaniards used modern smokeless powder, allowing them to remain hidden. American uniforms were wrong for fighting in a tropical climate. And he noted the need for a better quartermaster department.

Guess what?

- Had Southern generals not followed in the footsteps of their Confederate ancestors and the Confederate they admired, the United States might not have won the two major wars of the twentieth century.

- Several famous generals—including Eisenhower and Patton—while not Southern by birth can be considered "honorary" Southerners.

By the time the United States entered World War I, Pershing had been promoted general ahead of scores of other officers and given command of the American Expeditionary Force.

Pershing's task was formidable. His AEF had been rushed to France so quickly that most of the men were not properly trained. That did not matter to the French or the British, who were desperate for more troops.

Pershing's first task was to maintain his independent command. The French and British wanted the Americans integrated into European corps. Pershing refused.

Pershing's insistence on keeping control of his men paid off, first at Château-Thierry, where an American machine gun battalion kept the Germans from advancing on Paris. Then, at Belleau Wood, the U.S. Marines suffered heavy casualties in a battle that had been planned by the French. Pershing repeatedly refused French demands that he turn over his army to their officers.

When Pershing's army stopped the German offensive at Verdun in the Argonne Forest, the Germans realized that the might of the Americans—one million fresh soldiers—was too much. They began surrender negotiations. Pershing wanted to defeat the Germans on German soil rather than negotiate surrender terms on French soil, but he was overruled. He would later say that had Berlin been taken in 1918, there would have been no need to take it in 1945.

Pershing wrote a 1932 Pulitzer Prize–winning history of his European experience. The book criticized the old generals back in Washington for not giving the men the modern equipment they needed in Europe. It was the same complaint he had made in the Spanish-American War twenty years earlier.

When Pershing died in 1948, "Taps," at his request, was blown by a black soldier in memory of Pershing's service with the Tenth United States Cavalry. Pershing was buried in Arlington National Cemetery under the same simple white tombstone that rank-and-file soldiers received. He had retired as General of the Armies, a title previously held only by George Washington, and one that entitled him to wear six stars. No other general since has had a higher rank.

After Pershing, the two best-known American heroes from World War I were Ohioan air ace Eddie Rickenbacker and Tennessee-born Sergeant Alvin York.

York was nearly thirty years old and a devout Christian who believed war was evil when he was drafted in 1917. But he was also a crack shot who had used a muzzle-loading rifle to hunt back in the hills of Tennessee. During the battle of the Argonne Forest, York and six other survivors of an ambushed American unit destroyed several machine gun emplacements and captured 132 Germans. York's natural shyness, his initial pacifism, and his backwoods background made him a newspaper reporter's dream. Promoted to sergeant after the Argonne Forest, York became the spokesman hero for America's soldiers, traveling the country. In 1942 Gary Cooper won an Academy Award for portraying Sergeant York in the eponymous film.

Southerners won World War II in the Pacific theater

In the Pacific theater, the highest-ranking generals in the Army and Marine Corps and the highest-ranking Navy admiral were all Southerners. But even before the United States entered World War II, Southerners were fighting the Japanese.

In 1940, Claire Chennault of Louisiana, a relative of Robert E. Lee and former Army officer who had resigned after butting heads with superiors (a typical Southern trait), was organizing an air assault group in China. The unit of P-40 fighters, dubbed the "Flying Tigers" by a newspaper, was staffed by American mercenaries who later rejoined the Army Air Corps after the attack on Pearl Harbor. Chennault's tactic of attacking Japanese bombers in the air with fighters firing machine guns was deemed impossible by his superiors—but Chennault's success proved him right. When the war became fully engaged, the Flying Tigers were absorbed into the Army Air Corps. Chennault was again forced to retire from the Air Corps early in 1945 when he complained that generals back in Washington were impeding the war effort. One ace pilot who flew with the Flying Tigers was Georgian Robert Lee Scott, who wrote the bestselling book *God Is My Co-Pilot*. Another Flying Tiger was Texan David Lee "Tex" Hill, one of the unit's top aces with ten air victories.

In China at the same time was General Joseph W. Stilwell, of Palatka, Florida, who was one of the first officers to be officially assigned to help the Chinese fight the Japanese. When the war broke out, Stilwell fought in Burma, far from supply lines. Stilwell, who detested the trappings of rank and was known as "Vinegar Joe" for his Southern outspokenness, eventually rose to four-star general and often trekked through the jungle on foot alongside his much younger men.

Little Rock–born Douglas MacArthur came from a mixed marriage. His father was a Union officer who won the Congressional Medal of Honor. His mother was a fiercely proud, fiercely protective, and still more fiercely independent sister of four Confederate soldiers. The two met in New Orleans in 1874 when Arthur MacArthur was on duty occupying the city and Mary "Pinky" Hardy was visiting relatives. Her brothers were so shocked when she accepted a marriage proposal from the Massachusetts Yankee that they refused to attend the 1875 wedding. The birth of Douglas helped soften their hard feelings.

By 1930 Douglas MacArthur was the Army chief of staff. Then the Depression hit, and his pleas to modernize and expand the U.S. Army to address Japanese expansion in the Far East went unheeded. But MacArthur's strategy to win the ground war in the Pacific—"island hopping"—led to victory in New Guinea and the Philippines and eventually over Japan itself.

While MacArthur was leading the Army, the United States Marines and Navy were also being led by Southerners.

Marine Lieutenant General Lewis "Chesty" Puller of West Point, Virginia, was a descendant of a Confederate major in J. E. B. Stuart's Fifth Virginia Cavalry. Puller dropped out of the Virginia Military Institute in 1917, hoping to fight in World War I, and after the war, reenlisted as a private. By 1942 he had made general and commanded part of the First Marine Division battling the Japanese on Guadalcanal, one of the first U.S. ground victories in the war. When informed that the Japanese had surrounded his division, Puller said, "All right, they're on our left, they're on our right, they're in front of us, they're behind us…they can't get away this time!" Puller fought again in the Korean War and volunteered for Vietnam when he was well into his sixties. He was turned down. Puller accumulated more than fifty medals, including five Navy Crosses for bravery during World War II and Korea.

★ ★ ★ ★ ★ ★ ★ ★ ★ ★ ★ ★ ★ ★ ★

Southern Patriotism

The only two surviving surviving military colleges in the nation are the Virginia Military Institute in Lexington, Virginia, and The Citadel in Charleston, South Carolina. Both have sent students and graduates into every war since the War Between the States. Stonewall Jackson was an instructor at VMI in the ten years prior to the war. Cadets at The Citadel fired on *The Star of the West*, a supply ship trying to reach Fort Sumter, several days before the official attack. Both schools have lost hundreds of graduates in wars right up through the ones being fought in Iraq and Afghanistan.

General Alexander Vandegrift of Virginia was also on Guadalcanal. Vandegrift, the grandson of a Confederate soldier wounded at Sharpsburg and Gettysburg, remembered being surrounded by Confederate veterans as he grew up in Charlottesville. The tales the men told whetted his appetite for a military career. Vandegrift would earn four stars as a combat general in World War II before returning to the U.S. to head the entire Marine Corps.

The Navy's top admiral in the Pacific was Chester Nimitz of Fredericksburg, Texas. Appointed commander of the Pacific Fleet within days of Pearl Harbor, Nimitz proved himself a great strategist by anticipating where the Japanese would strike. Husbanding his resources until more ships could be built and more men trained, Nimitz kept the Japanese at bay for two years and then overwhelmed them. One of his top commanders was Raymond Spruance of Maryland, who led the task force that sank four Japanese carriers at Midway, the turning of the tide in the Pacific War. Spruance would later plan the naval assaults on the Gilbert Islands, Iwo Jima, and Okinawa.

Southerners won the European theater

Truthfully, Generals George Marshall, Dwight Eisenhower, and George Patton were Southerners in name only, but all of them were heavily influenced by the military tradition of the South.

Few generals win both a world war and the Nobel Peace Prize, but that is what happened to General George Marshall.

By accident of birth, George Marshall was a Pennsylvanian, though his ancestry included John Marshall, the Virginian who was the longest-serving and most influential chief justice of the U.S. Supreme Court. Marshall became an honorary Southerner by attending the Virginia Military Institute. While on campus he soaked up the history of the school, including tales of how the ghost of Stonewall Jackson, an instructor at the school through the 1850s, could sometimes be seen drawing on a chalkboard in his old classroom.

Marshall excelled at strategic planning, as shown in his successful transfer of more than 400,000 soldiers from one front to another in World War I, which won the praise of General Pershing. When World War II began, Marshall brought the nation's neglected armed forces up to strength. And it was on his prewar watch that many of the fighter and bomber aircraft that eventually dominated the skies in the Atlantic and Pacific theaters were designed. During the war, Marshall suggested Douglas MacArthur and Dwight Eisenhower as commanders in the Pacific and Atlantic theaters, respectively. MacArthur was a natural choice, but Marshall spotted Eisenhower's abilities virtually by himself.

Immediately after the war, Marshall helped develop a plan to rebuild Europe. In 1947 he drew up the plans for the Berlin Airlift to fly supplies into the city, after the Russians blockaded it. Later he proposed the European Recovery Plan—also know as the Marshall Plan—which became a multi-billion-dollar effort to rebuild the European economies. For this he was awarded the Nobel Peace Prize in 1953.

Marshall's pick for commander in Europe, General Dwight David Eisenhower was a Southerner thanks to his birth in Denison, Texas, though his family had lived in Kansas and soon returned to Kansas with the infant future general and president.

Like Marshall, Eisenhower had served under "Black Jack" Pershing in World War I, and then under Douglas MacArthur in the Philippines. When he returned to the United States, he was still a staff officer who had never commanded his own unit. That never bothered Marshall, who recognized that Eisenhower was like Robert E. Lee—a humble man with a gift for handling egotistical generals. Marshall saw to it that Brigadier General Eisenhower, who had been promoted to that position in September 1941, was made commander of all Allied operations in Europe.

Eisenhower met with Douglas Southall Freeman, Robert E. Lee's biographer, in 1946 to tell him how much he had enjoyed the four-volume biography of Lee for which Freeman had won the Pulitzer Prize. Freeman urged Eisenhower to run for public office, insisting that he owed it to the nation. Eisenhower scoffed at the idea, saying it would never happen because congressmen would be suspicious of a military man in high office. Freeman, a Virginian, might have been the first person to put the idea of running for public office into Eisenhower's head.

In 1950 Eisenhower purchased a Gettysburg farm on the reverse slope of Confederate Ridge, from where Lee had launched the Pettigrew-Pickett-Trimble Assault on July 3, 1863. He reveled in showing the battlefield to such visitors as Winston Churchill. He even filmed a show for a television network describing the battlefield. When showing British field marshal Bernard Montgomery around Gettysburg, the two looked at the Pettigrew-Pickett-Trimble ground and Eisenhower commented that Lee must have been so angry with Meade that "he must have wanted to hit him with a brick."

In 1960, after President Eisenhower addressed the Republican convention, he received a letter from a dentist in New Rochelle, New York, complaining that Eisenhower had mentioned during a television appearance that he admired Robert E. Lee. Eisenhower, though obviously busy as president of the United States, felt the need to answer the complainant personally. The text of the two letters, now on file at the Eisenhower Library in Abilene, Kansas, reads:

> Dear Mr. President: At the Republican Convention I heard you mention that you have the pictures of four (4) great Americans in your office, and that included in these is a picture of Robert E. Lee. I do not understand how any American can include Robert E. Lee as a person to be emulated, and why the President of the United States of America should do so is certainly

beyond me. The most outstanding thing that Robert E. Lee did, was to devote his best efforts to the destruction of the United States Government, and I am sure that you do not say that a person who tries to destroy our Government is worthy of being hailed as one of our heroes. Will you please tell me just why you hold him in such high esteem? Sincerely yours, Leon W. Scott

Eisenhower's response, written from the White House on August 9, 1960:

Dear Dr. Scott: Respecting your August 1 inquiry calling attention to my often expressed admiration for General Robert E. Lee, I would say, first, that we need to understand that at the time of the War Between the States the issue of Secession had remained unresolved for more than 70 years. Men of probity, character, public standing and unquestioned loyalty, both North and South, had disagreed over this issue as a matter of principle from the day our Constitution was adopted. General Robert E. Lee was, in my estimation, one of the supremely gifted men produced by our Nation. He believed unswervingly in the Constitutional validity of his cause which until 1865 was still an arguable question in America; he was thoughtful yet demanding of his officers and men, forbearing with captured enemies but ingenious, unrelenting and personally courageous in battle, and never disheartened by a reverse or obstacle. Through all his many trials, he remained selfless almost to a fault and unfailing in his belief in God. Taken altogether, he was noble as a leader and as a man, and unsullied as I read the pages of our history. From deep conviction I simply say this: a nation of men of Lee's caliber would be unconquerable in spirit and soul. Indeed, to the degree that present-day American youth will strive to emulate his rare qualities, including his devotion to this land as revealed in his painstaking efforts to help heal the nation's wounds once the bitter struggle was over, we, in our own time of danger in a divided world, will be strengthened and our love of freedom sustained. Such are the reasons that I proudly display the picture of this great American on my office wall. Sincerely, Dwight D. Eisenhower

Eisenhower, an accidental Southerner, not only eloquently defended his admiration of Lee, but, as president of the United States, former supreme Allied commander in World War II, and a five-star general in the United States Army, used the term "War Between the States" rather than "Civil War," and he urged America's youth to follow in Lee's footsteps. If any man deserves to be called an honorary Southerner, it's President Eisenhower.

Among the most popular generals in World War II was Missouri-born Omar Bradley, grandson of a Confederate Missouri sharpshooter. Bradley earned the sobriquet "the soldier's general" during the war because he cared so much about his troops. One war correspondent marveled that Bradley always said "please" when he issued an order to a soldier of any rank. Even mild-mannered Tennessean Alvin York once told Bradley that he would not go far in the Army because he was "too nice." Bradley became a five-star general, and his men attacked North Africa, took Sicily, landed at Utah and Omaha beaches at Normandy, and faced down the Germans during the Battle of the Bulge.

Certainly the most colorful general of World War II was honorary Southerner George S. Patton, Jr. Patton was born in California, but his grandfather was a Confederate killed at the Third Battle of Winchester in 1864. His great-uncle, Tazewell Patton, was killed at Gettysburg in 1863. While George Jr. was growing up, he listened to war stories told by a family friend, John Singleton Mosby, the famed Confederate "Gray Ghost." Patton's family hung paintings of Robert E. Lee and Stonewall Jackson in their home, and his daughter once said that her father was fifteen years old before he realized the two Confederates on the wall were not God the Father and God the Son.

Patton spent one year at his grandfather's alma mater, the Virginia Military Institute, before transferring to West Point. In World War I, Patton was a tank officer. He served under MacArthur and Eisenhower during peacetime, but he would hit his stride in World War II when his forces invaded North Africa.

Patton's tactics were those of his heroes John Singleton Mosby and Stonewall Jackson, who believed in moving fast and hitting hard before the enemy had a chance to learn your weaknesses. Time after time, Patton was ordered to slow down his advances in Sicily, France, and Germany in order to allow the British to catch up and win some of the glory he was taking from them. Patton's tanks moved so fast that at times they ran out of fuel, because the rest of the army, including his supplies of gas, couldn't keep up.

In 1943 the politically correct mavens of the day finally stopped Patton in his tracks when he slapped two soldiers in a field hospital for displaying what he believed to be cowardice. Newspaper editorialists, appar-

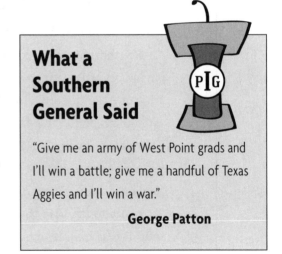

What a Southern General Said

"Give me an army of West Point grads and I'll win a battle; give me a handful of Texas Aggies and I'll win a war."

George Patton

ently forgetting that the Germans and Italians were the real enemy, demanded that Patton apologize to the two men or be relieved of command. Eisenhower forced him to do just that.

The Germans were so afraid of this Confederate son that whenever Patton lingered in any location too long, the Germans assumed he was planning the invasion of Europe. Knowing this, Eisenhower used Patton's reputation against the Germans. For weeks, Patton agreed to pose as general of a fictitious army training to invade France at Calais. The real invasion force was training to land at Normandy. German spies paid so much attention to Patton's activities that the invasion at Normandy on June 6, 1944, was a complete surprise.

Southerners fought in the air as well. General Ira Eaker, first commander of the Eighth Air Force bomber command and the Texas-born grandson of a Confederate cavalryman, was the architect of the dangerous but necessary strategy of bombing German targets by daylight. He led the first B-17 bombing mission himself. General Bill Lee of North Carolina developed the idea of airborne assault and was the first commander of the 101st Airborne Division. He was replaced by General Maxwell Taylor of Missouri, who led the 101st behind the lines on D-Day. General Matthew Ridgeway, commander of the 82nd Airborne during the D-Day invasion, hailed from Virginia.

Southerners also commanded the seas. Vice Admiral Royal Eason Ingersoll of Washington, D.C., made up for his Unionist roots by marrying an Atlanta native who came from a long line of Confederates. Ingersoll commanded the Atlantic fleet during most of World War II. It was on his watch, starting in 1943 and 1944, that the U.S. Navy began to hunt down and destroy the German U-boats that had inflicted so much damage on American shipping in 1942.

Every top spot in the U.S. military chain of command in World Wars I and II was held by a native Southerner, or by a descendant of Confederate soldiers or by someone who had some other strong link to the South. Even if the officer was a Northerner by birth, he still had some ties to the Confederacy, usually by marriage. Even men who were all-but-Yankees, such as Eisenhower and Marshall, expressed deep admiration for the leaders of the Confederacy. They visited and studied the battlefields on which Confederate generals had fought.

It is safe to say that had these sons of the South not followed in the footsteps of their Confederate ancestors and the Confederates they admired, the United States might not have won the two major wars of the twentieth century.

THE NATION SHOULD
THANK GOD FOR THE SOUTH

The South embodies the very spirit of the United States. Texans have a phrase: "Don't mess with Texas!" That could be applied to all Southern states. The South has always been the founding light of the nation. A Southern Founding Father, Thomas Jefferson, wrote the Declaration of Independence. A Southern Founding Father, James Madison, wrote the United States Constitution. A Southern Founding Father, George Mason, insisted on the Bill of Rights.

The South resisted an isolationist Northeast that wanted to retain power for itself, while Southerners wanted to expand from the Atlantic to the Pacific.

The South has always been the first region to jump to the nation's defense. The first victory in the American Revolution occurred in the South, at Moore's Creek Bridge in North Carolina. When Texas declared independence from Mexico, Tennesseans and Carolinians rushed to the Alamo. Conservative Southern politicians and military officers won the Mexican War, which brought Texas, California, and much of the West into the union. When Northern politicians allowed the United States Army to wither so much that the nation's defense was in danger, a Southern secretary of war, Jefferson Davis, pushed through laws that made the United States Army the best equipped in the world.

The one major blemish on the South's record, the one mistake for which it is still blamed and on which its image is still cast, was that the region depended on slaves to fill out its work force. No Southerner alive today disputes that slavery was wrong. Every Southerner now agrees that the South should have followed the North's lead and freed its slaves. The South should have adopted wages for work, the same economic concept on which business is run today. Had the slaves been freed peacefully and a plan set up to spread their labor nationwide rather than dumping more than four million human beings on a defeated and devastated South in 1865, the nation would have been much better off and there would have been none of the ravages and bitterness engendered by Reconstruction, and likely none of the segregation and racism that followed. Instead, it took the South a century to recover, but recover the South has.

Since 1865 it's often been said that "the South will rise again!" Well, guess what? It's happened. The South has risen and it now flies above all other regions, including its old enemy, the North. Census records indicate that Florida, Georgia, Texas, and North Carolina, all Confederate states, will be gaining congressional seats. Losing seats to the South (and to other western states like Utah and Arizona) will be New York, Massachusetts, Pennsylvania, Ohio, Iowa, and Michigan—all states that invaded the South in 1861. All those Yankees are leaving their home states and moving to the South because we have things the North doesn't: lower taxes, a family-friendly atmosphere, and a culture of faith and hard work rather than strident social liberalism and a sense that the state should take care of everything. More people are moving to the South because the South remains more American—fuller of traditional American virtues—than the increasingly liberal, secular, high-tax and big government Northern states.

And yet, we can't trust all those Northern transplants not to turn the conservative South into a version of the liberal states they left behind. And there are plenty of Southern scalawags who will assist them in banning the song and the very name "Dixie." When 1996 Atlanta Olympics officials heard a young gymnast practicing to the tune, they forced her to change her entire routine lest anyone be offended. In Fayetteville, North Carolina, Little League officials are renaming the Dixie League. And city officials in Winston-Salem, North Carolina, have considered renaming the Dixie Classic Fair to be more politically correct.

The Confederate battle flag, which never flew over a slave ship, which is based on the St. Andrew's Cross (the national flag of Scotland), and is a matter of familial pride of military service and of region and of heritage for many Southerners, has been virtually forced from public view.

Statues of Confederate soldiers are under threat of being hauled down from places of honor on county courthouse lawns and on college campuses. Southern heroes, flesh and blood men, are being demeaned. A Boy Scout council in Richmond renamed itself from the Robert E. Lee Council out of concern that minority Scouts could not relate to the Virginian. A Northern transplant to Lee County, Florida, has demanded that the county rename itself because he considers Lee to be a traitor for resigning from the Union Army. Protesters in Kentucky have demanded the removal of the statue of Jefferson Davis, a Kentucky native, from the state capitol.

Even the words "South" and "Confederate" are sometimes deemed offensive. The president of the University of the South in Sewanee, Tennessee, founded by Confederate lieutenant general Leonidas Polk, is rebranding the university under the Sewanee name. At Vanderbilt University in Nashville, the president of the college tried to sandblast the word "Confederate" from a dorm. A court ruled that Vanderbilt would have to repay the United Daughters of the Confederacy in modern dollars what it had cost them to build the dorm. Vanderbilt's president thought better of paying $1 million to remove the word. Still, he got cheap revenge. Campus maps used to label the dorm Confederate Memorial Hall. Now the maps just say Memorial Hall.

Politicians are the most cowardly of all when it comes to protecting our Southern heritage. While serving as Texas governor, George W. Bush removed a brass plaque honoring the contributions of Confederates who built the Texas Supreme Court building. His brother, Governor Jeb Bush, removed a display of all the flags that had flown over Florida because one of them was a Confederate flag. Though politicians now routinely issue proclamations for Kwanzaa and Cinco de Mayo, they equally routinely ignore Confederate History Month in April.

Even our movies are being banned. Who would have thought that the 1930s Disney classic *Song of the South* would disappear? *Song of the South* introduced the characters of Georgia writer Joel Chandler Harris: Brer Rabbit and Uncle Remus. Though the movie shows a black man's loving, grandfatherly relationship with a lonely white child who sees him as a father figure, Disney refuses to offer the movie for sale. The only explanation is that some scenes show black people picking cotton, and in some scenes Uncle Remus (who in the movie is never called a slave) shows respect for the woman who owns the plantation. I guess that's supposed to be offensive. The only available copies of the movie are bootlegs from China, complete with the occasional Chinese subtitle during the singing of songs like "Zip-a-Dee-Doo-Dah."

That's crazy. But that's the North for you.

It's time we demanded back our "Zip-a-Dee-Doo-Dah," because the South has much to offer the nation. Even visitors can take back a little spirit of the South to make the world a better place.

Just look at what the South gives the United States on a daily basis:

- A strong sense of patriotism that protects the rest of the nation. According to a 2005 study of military enlistments conducted by the Department of Defense, Southerners enlist in the armed forces at a much higher rate than anyone else, particularly than Northeasterners. In 2003, the South represented about 35 percent of the nation's population but accounted for more than 41 percent of military recruits. Expressed as a percentage of recruits divided by total population, the enlistment figures are even more dramatic. The 2003 recruit/population ratio for North Carolina, one of the last states to leave the Union for the Confederacy, was 1.05. South Carolina, the first state in the Confederacy, had a ratio of 1.13. Virginia, the capital state of the Confederacy, had a ratio of 1.23. Every single Confederate state ranked above 1.0. By contrast, the recruit/population ratio for New York state, where the World Trade Center Towers were brought down, was .79. Massachusetts, the home of John Kerry, the last Democratic presidential contender and where two of the terrorist planes originated, was a dismal .62.

The facts don't lie. Southerners are more willing than any other region to settle scores against enemies of the United States. Proportionally, Virginia sends more than twice as many willing souls to defend America as does Massachusetts.

- A sense of tradition. The South loves its old ways, its old speech patterns and accents, its old buildings, its old battlefields. While much of the rest of the world is rushing forward to shrug off the memories of the past, much of the South is doing what it can to preserve those memories. Mount Vernon has just opened a multi-million-dollar museum dedicated to George Washington. The foundation that owns Montpelier, the home of James Madison, is renovating the house of the man who literally created the concept of the United States of America. Monticello, the home of Thomas Jefferson, is looking for ways to remind Americans of the contributions of the man who wrote the Declaration of Independence. The National Civil War Trust is buying up endangered battlefields throughout the South to keep them from being bulldozed. The Friends of the *Hunley* are painstakingly cleaning and restoring the Confederate vessel that won the distinction of being the first submarine to sink a warship.

- A conscience about race relations. The South has never denied its role in perpetuating slavery. The South, and only the South, has apologized profusely for its role in slavery. In the intervening 140 years since slavery was abolished in the South, black income in the region has steadily increased, neighborhoods have been integrated, black politicians have been elected to major offices, and black businesspeople have emerged to head national corporations. In the South, regional patriotism trumps race any old day.

- A sense of morals and religion. Others can joke about the "Bible Belt" all they want, but the nation needs at least one region willing to speak up about what is right and what is wrong. The South always has and always will speak up on religious and moral topics. We don't care that Hollywood actors laugh at our dedication to doing the right thing. We like to think that God cares more about folks going to church on Sunday (or synagogue on Saturday), saying their prayers, being polite, looking out for their neighbors, and being kid- and family-friendly than He does about the Academy, the latest fashions, and the gossip sheets. We believe that He prefers folks who trust in His ways over those who want to use liberal judges to redefine marriage and morality. And that's not going to change. Even though liberals are moving to the South and turning some parts of it "bluer," overall it appears that the South is winning more converts to conservatism than liberals are winning over Southerners. That's because in the South conservatism is not just a collection of opinions that can easily change. It's rooted in who we are, in faith and family and tradition.

- A welcoming environment for business. New York City proclaims itself the center of U.S. commerce, but it really is Bentonville, Arkansas, home of Wal-Mart. Wal-Mart didn't need Wall Street, didn't need skyscrapers, didn't need investment bankers, didn't need any of the trappings of big-city finance in order to become the single largest company in the United States. It just needed Sam Walton, a native Southerner, and his vision for selling products to average Americans at affordable prices. Other Southern companies have also made a name for themselves, including Exxon, Federal Express, Coca-Cola, Lowe's, Delta, Krispy Kreme, and Home Depot.

  Thanks to a long-standing tradition of employees ignoring union drives, the South is leading the nation in revitalized manufacturing. Toyota, Honda, Saturn, Nissan, BMW, and Mercedes have all opened factories in the South in the last twenty years. Tens of thousands of jobs have been created in these large factories. While the Rust Belt rusts, the South's business clout is growing like kudzu on a clay hillside.

- A creative atmosphere. Few folks think about "Northern literature," but there is an abundance of Southern literature. There is no such thing as Northern music, but there is country music, Southern rock, Southern jazz, Southern blues, and bluegrass. There is something about Southern lovers, rivers, dogs, ex-wives, ex-husbands, magnolias, pine trees, eccentrics, and soldiers that keep writers and musicians inspired. New York City might have the Metropolitan Opera, but such highfalutin' music still can't hold a candle or a crowd like the Grand Old Opry in Nashville, Tennessee. Southern music gets your feet tappin' like nothing else can.

✖ Real men. Southern men are gentlemen, but they're also uncompromising, opinionated, and won't defer to what "the group" wants. That Southern hard-headedness is what motivated Memphis native Fred Smith to push ahead with his idea of creating an overnight delivery company, even though a Yale business professor told him the idea was unworkable. Smith went on to create Federal Express.

America needs men who stick by their guns, and Southerners do just that. We need more men of honor and depth and fewer business and political leaders who flip-flop on their "convictions" and "principles." Southern men don't do that. Southern men are taught strong principles by their families and they stick with them. Even though they might lose in the end, they stick with what they believe is right. That's why the Confederacy fought to the bitter end—and why if the South has its way, we won't ever lose a war again. Our boys grow up with tales of our military heroes, they grow up with fishing rods and hunting rifles, and, as Hank Williams Jr. says, "Country Boys Will Survive."

✖ Real women. Southern women are as ladylike and charming as can be, but, like their menfolk, they have backbones of steel. During the War most of the able-bodied men were away fighting the Yankees. Women were left behind to deal with the rigors of running the farm and caring for immediate family and slaves (if they owned any). Those women did a remarkable job. There were no slave revolts during the War, one indication that the slaves left behind on the plantation respected Southern women and understood that they were all Southerners, and all family.

Any Yankee who tries to push a Southern woman around is likely to learn the same lesson one did when he tried to challenge Scarlett O'Hara and her Colt revolver. But Southern boys know how to treat Southern girls. And you can see why the rest of the nation is jealous of us when those handsome football players and gracious belles get married and have batches of great-looking kids.

The South is truly rising again. In fact, it has already risen and will keep on rising. If you are born in the South, consider yourself one of the luckiest individuals on the face of the earth. If you moved here, you can also consider yourself one of the luckiest individuals on the face of the earth. Just be sure to raise your children to fit right in with their courageous, God-fearing Southern neighbors.

In Dixie land we'll take our stand!

★ ★ ★ ★ ★ ★ ★

ACKNOWLEDGMENTS

Thanks to Joe Valley, a Southern-born agent forced to live in New York City, who recognized the value of this book when it was in a different form, and who found a place for it.

Thanks to the folks at Regnery Publishing for seeing how my original idea could fit into their Politically Incorrect Guide™ Series.

Specific mention should go to my editor, Miriam Moore, a Louisiana native educated at the University of Georgia who inexplicably also found the need to study in France. She put the book into its present form.

Thanks also to senior editor Harry Crocker, a lover of the South, who saw the potential in the idea. Thanks, Harry, for mentioning the Floridians' defense of Fredericksburg in your book, *Don't Tread on Me—A 400-Year History of America at War from Indian Fighting to Terrorist Hunting*. One of my ancestors lost an arm down on the Rappahannock River in December 1862 when those selfish Mississippians hogged all the good houses for cover. Harry surprised me with the favor of giving some long overdue recognition to the 8th Florida regiment when most histories of that battle only mention the Mississippi Brigade.

Thanks too to Barb, my Wisconsin Yankee wife, for not objecting to my thirty years of traipsing around battlefields as a member of the 26th Regiment of North Carolina Troops Reactivated reenactors.

Finally, thanks to all my teachers in Arcadia, Florida, who instilled in me the love of reading, writing, and history. Miss Frances Pooser, the fourth-grade teacher who first taught me about "The War" still remembers the spark of interest she instilled in me. Miss Margaret Hays taught me to read in the first grade. Mrs. Joy Barnard taught me English in the eighth grade (though I still don't understand conjugating verbs and all that stuff). Mr. Sam McDowell in the eighth grade taught me to be a creative writer. Miss Sydney Anderson taught me to be a reporter in high school. All these teachers did what they were supposed to do—inspire a young student to learn to do more. We need more teachers like I had growing up.

★ ★ ★ ★ ★ ★ ★

BIBLIOGRAPHY

Adams, Charles. *When in the Course of Human Events: Arguing the Case for Southern Secession*. Lanham, MD: Rowman & Littlefield Publishers, 2000.

Allen, Felicity. *Jefferson Davis: Unconquered Heart*. Columbia, MO: University of Missouri Press, 1999.

Ambrose, Stephen E. *Eisenhower: Soldier, General of the Army, President-Elect 1890–1952*. New York: Simon & Schuster, 1983.

Anonymous (Editors of the *Army Times*). *The Yanks Are Coming: The Story of General John J. Pershing*. New York: G. P. Putnam's Sons, 1960.

Anonymous (Editors of Combined Books). *The Civil War Book of Lists*. Conshohocken, PA: Combined Books, 1993.

Barrow, Charles Kelly, J. H. Segars, and R. B. Rosenburg, eds. *Forgotten Confederates: An Anthology about Black Southerners*. Atlanta: Southern Heritage Press, 1995.

Batson, Ann Barrett. *Having It Y'All*. Nashville: Rutledge Hill Press, 1988.

Belden, Thomas Graham and Marva Robins Belden. *So Fell the Angels*. Boston: Little, Brown & Company, 1956.

Belin, Ira and Leslie M. Harris, eds. *Slavery in New York*. New York: New York Historical Society, 2005.

Bennett, Jr., Lerone. *Forced into Glory: Abraham Lincoln's White Dream*. Chicago: Johnson Publishing Company, 2000.

Blight, David W. *Race and Reunion: The Civil War in American Memory*. Cambridge, MA: Belknap Press of Harvard University Press, 2001.

Blue, Frederick J. *Salmon Chase: A Life in Politics*. Kent, OH: Kent State University Press, 1987.

Bradley, Omar and Clay Blair. *A General's Life*. New York: Simon & Schuster, 1983.

Breen, T. H. and Stephen Innes. *Myne Owne Ground: Race and Freedom on Virginia's Eastern Shore, 1640–1676*. New York: Oxford University Press, 1992.

Chidsey, Donald Burr. *The Spanish-American War: A Behind-the-Scenes Account of the War in Cuba*. New York: Crown Publishers, Inc., 1971.

Cornish, Dudley Taylor. *The Sable Arm: Black Troops in the Union Army, 1861–1865*. Lawrence, KS: University Press of Kansas, 1987.

Corse, Corita Doggett. *Dr. Andrew Turnbull and the New Smyrna Colony of Florida*. Jacksonville, FL: The Drew Press, 1919.

Coski, John. *The Confederate Battle Flag: America's Most Embattled Emblem*. Cambridge, MA: Belknap Press of Harvard University Press, 2005.

Cray, Ed. *General of the Army George Marshall: Soldier and Statesman*. New York: W. W. Norton, 1990.

Current, Richard N., ed. *Encyclopedia of the Confederacy* (four volumes). New York: Simon & Schuster, 1993.

DiLorenzo, Thomas J. *The Real Lincoln: A New Look at Abraham Lincoln, His Agenda, and an Unnecessary War*. Roseville, CA: Prima Publishing, 2002.

Donald, David Herbert. *Lincoln*. New York: Touchstone Books, 1995.

Dufour, Charles. *The Mexican War: A Compact History*. New York: Hawthorn Books, 1968.

Farrow, Anne, Joel Lang, and Jennifer Frank. *Complicity: How the North Promoted, Prolonged, and Profited from Slavery*. New York: Ballantine Books, 2005.

Fellman, Michael. *Citizen Sherman: A Life of William Tecumseh Sherman*. New York: Random House, 1995.

Flood, Charles Bracelen. *Grant and Sherman: The Friendship That Won the Civil War*. New York: Farrar, Straus & Giroux, 2005.

Fogel, Robert and Stanley Engerman. *Time on the Cross: The Economics of American Negro Slavery*. New York: W. W. Norton & Company, 1995.

Foster, Gaines M. *Ghosts of the Confederacy: Defeat, the Lost Cause, and the Emergence of the New South*. New York: Oxford University Press, 1987.

Freeman, Douglas Southhall. *R. E. Lee* (four volumes). New York: Charles Scribners & Sons, 1937.

Freidel, Frank. *The Splendid Little War: The Dramatic Story of the Spanish-American War*. Short Hills, NJ: Burford Books, Inc., 1958.

Gilbert, Martin. *The First World War: A Complete History*. New York: Henry Holt & Company, 1994.

Goldfield, David. *Still Fighting the Civil War: The American South and Southern History*. Baton Rouge: Louisiana State University Press, 2002.

Goldstone, Lawrence. *Dark Bargain: Slavery, Profits and the Struggle for the Constitution*. New York: Walker & Company, 2005.

Goodwin, Doris Kearns. *Team of Rivals: The Political Genius of Abraham Lincoln*. New York: Simon & Schuster, 2005.

Guelzo, Allen C. *Lincoln's Emancipation Proclamation: The End of Slavery in America*. New York: Simon &Schuster, 2004.

Heidler, David S. and Jeanne T. Heidler, eds. *Encyclopedia of the American Civil War* (five volumes). Santa Barbara, CA: ABC-CLIO, 2000.

Hinkle, Don. *Embattled Banner: A Reasonable Defense of the Confederate Battle Flag*. Paducah, KY: Turner Publishing Company, 1997.

Hirshson, Stanley P. *General Patton: A Soldier's Life*. New York: HarperCollins, 2002.

Hirshson, Stanley P. *White Tecumseh: A Biography of William T. Sherman*. New York: Wiley, 1998.

Hollandsworth, Jr., James G. *The Louisiana Native Guards: The Black Military Experience during the Civil War*. Baton Rouge: Louisiana State University Press, 1995.

Horton, James Oliver and Lois E. Horton. *Slavery and the Making of America*. Oxford, UK: Oxford University Press, 2005.

Hurst, Richard. *Pipe Clay & Drill: John J. Pershing—The Classic American Soldier*. New York: Readers' Digest Press, 1977.

Johnson, Charles and Patricia Smith. *Africans in America: America's Journey through Slavery*. San Diego: Harcourt, Brace & Company, 1998.

Johnson, Michael P. and James L. Roark. *Black Masters: A Free Family of Color in the Old South*. New York: W. W. Norton, 1984.

Keegan, John. *The First World War*. New York: Alfred Knopf, 1999.

Keys, Thomas Bland. *The Uncivil War: Union Army and Navy Excesses in the Official Records*. Biloxi, MS: Beauvoir Press, 1991.

Koger, Larry. *Black Slaveowners: Free Black Slave Masters in South Carolina, 1790–1860*. Columbia, SC: University of South Carolina Press, 1985.

Kolchin, Peter. *American Slavery 1619–1877*. New York: Hill & Wang, 1993.

Lamphier, Peg. *Kate Chase & William Sprague*. Lincoln, NE: University of Nebraska Press, 2003.

Lepore, Jill. *New York Burning: Liberty, Slavery, and Conspiracy in Eighteenth-Century Manhattan*. New York: Alfred Knopf, 2005.

Livermore, Thomas L. *Numbers & Losses in the Civil War in America 1861–1865*. Carlisle, PA: John Kallman Publishers, 1900.

Louvish, Simon. *Stan and Ollie: The Roots of Comedy—The Double Life of Laurel and Hardy*. New York: St. Martins Press, 2001.

Manber, Jeffrey and Neil Dahlstrom. *Lincoln's Wrath: Fierce Mobs, Brilliant Scoundrels, and a President's Mission to Destroy the Press*. Naperville, IL: Sourcebooks, Inc., 2006.

McCabe, John. *Laurel & Hardy*. New York: Barnes & Noble Books, 1996.

McCombs, Don and Fred Worth. *World War II: 4,139 Strange and Fascinating Facts*. New York: Wings Books, 1983.

Miller, Edward A. *Gullah Statesman: Robert Smalls from Slavery to Congress 1839–1915*. Columbia, SC: University of South Carolina Press, 1995.

Murphy, Audie. *To Hell and Back*. New York: Owl Books, 1949.

O'Connor, Richard. *Black Jack Pershing: A Candid Biography of the United States' Only Six-Star General since George Washington*. Garden City, NY: Doubleday & Company, 1961.

Panagopolus, Epaminondas. *An Eighteenth-Century Greek Odyssey*. Gainesville, FL: University of Florida Press, 1966.

Reeder, Red. *The Story of the Spanish-American War*. New York: Duell, Sloan & Pewarce, 1966.

Rollins, Richard, ed. *Black Southerners in Gray: Essays on Afro-Americans in Confederate Armies*. Murfreesboro, TN: Southern Heritage Press, 1994.

Sacks, Howard L. and Judith Roe Sacks. *Way Up North in Dixie*. Washington, DC: Smithsonian Institute Press, 1993.

Schecter, Barnet. *The Devil's Own Work: The Civil War Draft Riots and the Fight to Reconstruct America*. New York: Walker & Company, 2005.

Segards, J. H. and Charles Kelly Barrow. *Black Southerners in Confederate Armies: A Collection of Historical Accounts*. Atlanta: Southern Lion Books, 2001.

Soodalter, Ron. *Hanging Captain Gordon: The Life and Trial of an American Slave Trader*. New York: Atria Books, 2006.

Sterling, Dorothy. *Captain of the Planter*. Garden City, NY: Doubleday & Company, 1958.

Thomas, Hugh. *The Slave Trade: The Story of the Atlantic Slave Trade 1440–1870*. New York: Simon & Schuster, 1997.

Trudeau, Noah Andre. *Like Men of War: Black Troops in the Civil War*. Boston: Little Brown & Company, 1998.

Webb, James. *Born Fighting: How the Scots-Irish Shaped America.* New York: Broadway Books, 2004.

Werstein, Irving. *Turning Point for America: The Story of the Spanish-American War.* New York: Julian Messner, Inc., 1964.

Werstein, Irving. *War with Mexico.* New York: Norton, 1965.

Websites

http://www.army.mil/cmh-pg/books/revwar/contarmy/CA-05.htm.

http://www.usconstitution.net/consttop_ccon.html#slavery.

http://www.archives.gov/publications/prologue/2000/winter/garrisons-constitution-2.html.

http://www.cr.nps.gov/history/online_books/dube/inde3.htm.

INDEX

A

Absalom, Absalom! (Faulkner), 9
ACC. *See* Atlantic Coast Conference
Acton, Sir John Dalberg, 138
Adams, John, 93, 114, 119
Adams, Samuel, 87, 89
Adkins, Trace, 41
Afghanistan, 221
African Burial Ground, N.Y., 39, 125
agrarianism, 10
Alabama, barbecue tradition in, 36
Alabama, University of, 68–69, 157
Alabama Gang, 41
Alexander, Edward Porter, 19, 160–61
Alien and Sedition Acts, 114
Allen, Henry, 39
Allison brothers, 41
*The All-New Ultimate Southern Living
Cookbook*, 44
American Idol, 40–41
American Legend: The Real-Life Adventures of David Crockett (Levy), 118
American Revolution: debt from, 10, 101; English taxation and, 87–89; Morgan, Daniel and, 95–97; patriotism, Southern and, 97–99; South and, 1, 87, 93–95, 231; Southern readiness to fight in, 90–93; Washington, George and, 93–94

"The American Scholar" (Emerson), 41
Anderson, Robert, 151
Andersonville, Ga., 66–67, 190–91
Andrew, Rod, Jr., 29
Andy Griffith Show, 43
Annapolis Conference (1786), 103
Anti-Federalists, 107, 114
anti-Semitism, 178
Appomattox Court House, 160–61
Aristotle, 41
Arkansas, 11, 18, 135, 138
Arlington National Cemetery, 60, 212, 218; Confederate Memorial at, 59, 61–62, 209, 214–16
Articles of Confederation, 102–3, 107
Atlanta Falcons, 23
Atlanta Olympics (1996), 233
Atlantic Coast Conference (ACC), 53
Augusta National, 72

B

Baltimore Massacre, 183–84
Banks, Nathaniel, 174, 181
barbecue tradition, 31, 35–37
Barron, Charles Kelly, 184
Barton, Clara, 197
baseball, college, 24
Baum, Marcus, 177
Beauregard, P. G. T., 213

Behind the Scenes: Thirty Years as a Slave and Four Years in the White House (Keckley), 188

Being Dead Is No Excuse: The Official Southern Ladies' Guide to Hosting the Perfect Funeral (Metcalfe and Hays), 44

Benjamin, Judah P., 178

Bennett, Lerone, Jr., 192

Bennett Place, N.C., 28

Bergen, Candice, 26

Berry, Chuck, 56–57

Bible, 20, 130

Bierce, Ambrose, 10

Bill of Rights, 107, 231

Biltmore Estate, N.C., 73

Birmingham, Ala., 13

The Birth of a Nation, 58

Black Hawk War, 119–20

Black Southerners in Confederate Armies: A Collection of Historial Accounts (Segars), 184

Black Southerners in Gray: Essays on Afro-Americans in Confederate Armies (ed. McGlone), 184

Blenker, Louis, 176

BMW, 237

Boone, Daniel, 27

Borglum, Gutzon, 66

Boston, Mass., 13, 99

Boyle, Sarah Patton, 210

Boy Scouts, 233

Bradley, Omar, 226

Breen, T. H., 124

Brown, Henry "Dad", 174

Brown, John, 126, 144–45

Brown University, 125–26

Bryant, Paul "Bear," 53, 68–69

Buffalo Soldiers, 211

Bullock, Sandra, 26

Bunker, Eng and Chang, 176

Burr, Aaron, 115, 116

Bush, George W., 234

Bush, Jeb, 234

Butler, Ben, 155

Butler, Matthew, 210

Byrd, William, II, 13–14

C

Calhoun, John C., 70, 118

Carolina Hurricanes, 24

Carson, Kit, 121

Carver, George Washington, 206

Cary, N.C., 27

Cash, Johnny, 40, 56

Cash, June Carter, 40

Cash, W. J., 9–10

Castiglione, 41

Castor, John, 83

Catalogue for Philanthropy, 11

Census Bureau, 11

Chancellorsville National Military Park, Va., 66

Chandler, Andrew, 175

Chandler, Silas, 175

"The Character of Summer" (Allen), 39

Charleston, S.C., 13, 70

Charleston Mercury, 185

Charleston Receipts (Junior League of Charleston, S.C.), 44

Charlotte, N.C., 13

Checker, Chubby, 57

Chennault, Claire, 219–20

Chicago Daily Times, 146

Churchill, Winston, 224

Church Suppers, 44

Cicero, 41

Circular Letter of 1768 (Adams), 87, 89

The Citadel, 221

civil rights, Lincoln, Abraham and, 183–85

The Civil War: A Narrative (Foote), 137

The Clansman, 58

Clark, George Rogers, 111–12, 116

Clark, William, 116, 117

Clay, Henry, 118, 182

Cleveland, Grover, 209, 211–12

Clinton, George, 93

Coca-Cola, 237

Coercive Acts of 1774, 87, 91

Colonial Williamsburg Foundation, 63

Columbus, Christopher, 78

Columbus, Diego, 78

Committee of Five, 92, 93

The Complete Tales of Uncle Remus (Harris), 214

Complicity: How the North Promoted, Prolonged, and Profited from Slavery (Farrow, Lang, and Frank), 131

Confederacy: aggressive action by, 149, 153; capital of, 138–39; Constitution, U.S. and, 201; European recognition of, 169, 191–93; secession and, 138; symbols of, 3, 56, 233–34; women, Southern and, 195–97. *See also* secession; War for Southern Independence

Confederate Avenue, Gettysburg, Pa., 65–66

Confederate Constitution, 137–38, 185

Confederate flag, 3, 56, 59, 212–14

Confederate Heroes Day, 3

Confederate Memorial (Arlington National Cemetery), 59, 60, 61–62, 209, 214–16

Confederate Memorial Hall, La., 63–65, 71

Confederate White House, Va., 60

Connecticut, University of, 51

Connecticut Courant, 114

"The Conquered Banner" (Ryan), 194

Constitution, U.S., 68, 114–15, 231; Bill of Rights and, 107–8, 231; Confederacy and, 201; Confederate Constitution vs., 137; Constitutional Convention and, 103–4; election process and, 114–15; federalism and, 106–7; Fifteenth Amendment, 205; First Amendment, 114, 184; Fourteenth Amendment, 205; ratification of, 101, 107; secession and, 136–37, 199, 201–2; slavery and, 104–6, 119, 139–40, 144, 199; states' rights and,

145; Thirteenth Amendment, 144, 199, 204, 205; War for Southern Independence and, 225

Constitutional Convention, 103–4

Continental Monthly, 126

Cooper, Anna Julia, 205

Cornwallis, Lord Charles, 94, 97, 101

Corwin, Thomas, 143

Corwin Amendment, 143–44

Crocker, H. W., III, 83, 153

Crockett, David, 27

Corps d'Afrique, 170

culture, Southern: barbecue tradition and, 31, 35–37; defining, 10–12; eating and, 34–37; friendliness and, 12–13, 16; gentility and good manners and, 13–17, 32; guns, personal ownership of and, 26–28; hospitality in, 17; moonshine and, 39–40, 42; religion and, 20–23; sense of place and, 5, 17–20; sports and, 23–26; symbols of, 28–29; tradition, sense of and, 235–36. *See also* South

Custis, George Washington Parke, 60–61

Custis, Mary Anna, 60–61

Custis-Lee Mansion, 60–61

D

Dallas, Tex., 13

Dallas Morning News, 3

Daniel, John Moncure, 185

Daniels, Charlie, 41

Dare, Virginia, 80

Davenport House Museum, Ga., 73–74

Davis, Jefferson, 60, 63, 142, 146, 147; Black Hawk War and, 120; criticism of, 185; Lincoln, Abraham, assassination of and, 201; Pius IX and, 63, 192–93; as racist, 187–88; slavery and, 143; War for Southern Independence and, 32

Davis, Jefferson C., 156

Davis, Joe, 60

Davis, Joseph, 143

Davis, Varina, 131, 187

Day, Thomas, 131

Dayan, Moshe, 196

Declaration of Independence: Jefferson, Thomas and, 87, 92–93, 102, 231; secession and, 136; slavery and, 93; Virginia documents and, 87

Declaration on the Causes and Necessity of Taking Up Arms, 91

Deen, Paula, 44

Degataga, 175

Delta Airlines, 237

Democratic Party, Democrats, 10

Democratic-Republican Party, 114

Destruction & Reconstruction: Personal Experiences of the Late War (Taylor), 121

The Devil's Own Work: The Civil War Draft Riots and the Fight to Reconstruct America (Schecter), 192

Dickey, James, 72

Dickinson, John, 91, 93, 102, 107

Dix, Dorothea, 197

Dixie Chicks, 41

"Dixie" (Emmett), 49–50, 52, 200

Dixie League, 233

Don't Tread on Me: A 400-Year History of America at War from Indian Fighting to Terrorist Hunting (Crocker III), 83

Douglass, Frederick, 127, 171–72, 182

Drake, Sir Francis, 80

Drawl, Southern, 32–35

Drayton Hall, S.C., 73

Duke, Washington, 28

Duke University, 52

Duty Faithfully Performed: Robert E. Lee and His Critics (Taylor), 161

E

Eaker, Ira, 228

The Economics of the Civil War (Ransom), 200

Edison, Thomas, 5, 57

Edmonston-Alston House, S.C., 73

Edmund Pettus Bridge, Ala., 67–68

education, Southern: blacks and, 18, 52, 206; football and, 53–56; Reconstruction and, 206; slavery and, 131–32; universities and, 49, 50–56

Edwards, John, 10

Eisenhower, Dwight D., 217, 222, 223–26, 228

Elizabeth I, 78

Ellison, William, 133–34

Ellsworth, Oliver, 105

Elmira, N.Y., 66–67, 190

Emancipation Proclamation, 199; Lincoln, Abraham and, 169, 169–70, 185–87; as sham, 185–87

Emerson, Ralph Waldo, 41

Emmett, Dan, 49–50

Emory University, 52

Engelhard, Joseph, 51

Esquire magazine, 42

Etiquette: In Society, in Business, in Politics, and at Home (Post), 14

European Recovery Plan, 223

Evans, Eli N., 196

Exxon, 237

Ezekiel, Moses Jacob, 209, 215–16

F

Fanning, Edmund, 90

Farrow, Anne, 131

Faulkner, William, 9, 64, 74, 176, 182

Federal Express, 237

Federalists, 107, 114, 115–16, 118, 119

feminism, 72–73

Ferdinand, 78–79

Ferguson, Patrick, 95

Ferris, William, 43

Fifteenth Amendment, 205

First Amendment, 114, 184

Fisk University, Tenn., 206

Flock brothers, 41

Florida, 77, 84–86

Florida, University of, 52

Flying Tigers, 219–20
food: barbecue tradition and, 31, 35–37; Southern, 34–37, 44; Southern mentality and, 43
football, college, 23, 53–56
Foote, Shelby, 135, 182
Forced into Glory: Abraham Lincoln's White Dream (Bennet Jr.), 192
Forgotten Confederates: An Anthology about Black Southerners (ed. Barron, Sergars, and Rosenburg), 184
Forrest, Nathan Bedford, 165, 173
Fort Apache, 109
Fort Sumter, War for Southern Independence and, 18, 32, 146, 149–51, 156
Founding Fathers, 102
Fourteenth Amendment, 205
France, Bill, 26
Frank, Jessica, 131
Franklin, Benjamin, 102, 113
Fraser, Simon, 96
Freeman, Douglas Southall, 224
Fremont, John C., 121, 169
French and Indian War, 94, 96
Friends of the *Hunley*, 236
From Eden to Babylon (Lytle), 207

G

Gadsden, James, 121
Gadsden Purchase, 121
Gately, Ian, 113
Gates, Horatio, 94
Generosity Index (2005), 11
George III, 87, 88, 91, 93, 97
George Rogers Clark National Memorial, Ind., 113
Georgetown University, 52
Georgia, 36, 77, 140
Georgia, University of, 51
Georgia Institute of Technology, 52
Gerry, Elbridge, 104–5, 107
Gettysburg, 154
Gettysburg, Pa., 65–66
Girl Scouts, 73

Gist, States Rights, 136, 145
The Glittering Illusion: English Sympathy for the Southern Confederacy (Vanauken), 140
globalization, 17
God Is My Co-Pilot (Scott), 220
Gods & Generals (Shaara), 154
Gone with the Wind (Mitchell), 14–15, 21, 23, 27, 239
Gordon, Nathaniel, 127–29
government: Southern creation of, 101–9; South vs. North and, 10; state sovereignty and, 102
Graceland, Tenn., 69
Grand Ole Opry, Tenn., 69–70, 238
Grant, Ulysses S., 155, 161, 164, 166; anti-Semitism and, 178; black soldiers and, 170–71; Lee, Robert E. vs., 45; prisoners of war and, 189–90; Reconstruction and, 200
The Gray Ghost, 4
Great Compromise of 1790, 109
Great Depression, 35, 220
The Great Train Robbery, 57
Greeley, Horace, 172, 186–87
Greene, Nathanael, 97
Griffith, D. W., 58
Grizzard, Lewis, 29, 35
guns, personal ownership of, 26–28
Guthrie, John, 127

H

Haggard, Merle, 41
Haley, Bill, 57
Halifax Resolves, 92
Halleck, Henry W., 155, 178–79
Hamilton, Alexander, 103–4, 106, 107, 108–9
Hammond, James, 179–80
Hanger, J. E., 152
Hanging Captain Gordon: The Life and Trial of an American Slave Trader (Soodalter), 131
Hardy, Babe, 57

Hardy, Mary "Pinky," 220
Harper's Weekly, 128, 172, 182
Harris, Joel Chandler, 182, 214, 234
Harris, Richard, 109
Harrison, William Henry, 118
Harris Poll, 26
Hartford Convention, 118–19
Harvard University, 46, 52
Hawkins, Rush C., 153–54
Hays, Charlotte, 44
Hearst, William Randolph, 209
Hemings, Sally, 114
Henrico, University of, 51
Henry, Patrick, 87, 88–89, 91, 99, 107, 109, 117
heroes, Southern, 44–47
Heston, Charlton, 109
Heyward-Washington House, S.C., 73
Hill, Benjamin H., Jr., 165
Hill, David Lee "Tex," 220
hockey, 24
Holly, Buddy, 56
Hollywood, 49, 57–58, 117, 236
Home Depot, 237
homes, Southern, 73–74
Honda, 237
Hooker, Joseph, 187
Houmas House, La., 73
Howard University, Washington, D.C., 125, 206
Huckleberry Finn (Twain), 73
Hull, Isaac, 118
Hunter, David, 169–70
Husky, Ferlin, 41

I

I'll Take My Stand: The South and the Agrarian Tradition, 202
immigration, 35
industrialization, 10
Industrial Revolution, 41
Ingersoll, Eason, 228
Innes, Stephen, 124

Intercollegiate Studies Institute (ISI), 54, 55
Intolerable Acts of 1774, 87, 91
Intruder in the Dust (Faulkner), 64
Iraq, 221
Isaac, Bobby, 41–42
ISI. *See* Intercollegiate Studies Institute

J

Jackson, Alan, 41
Jackson, Andrew, 118, 135
Jackson, Thomas J. "Stonewall," 19, 60, 66, 71; black soldiers and, 172–73; slavery and, 132; as Southern hero, 44, 46, 47, 213; VMI and, 221; War for Southern Independence and, 157
Jackson State University, Miss., 206
James, Frank and Jesse, 166
Jamestown, Va., 81–84
Jefferson, Thomas, 108–9, 114, 116, 117, 158; American Revolution and, 92; Declaration of Independence and, 87, 92–93, 102, 231; religion and, 22–23; slavery and, 139
Johns Hopkins University, 52
Johnson, Andrew, 164; impeachment of, 204; Reconstruction and, 202, 203–4
Johnson, Anthony, 81–84
Johnson, Frank M., 67–68
Johnson, Junior, 41, 42
Johnson, Lyndon B., 68, 203
Johnston, Albert Sidney, 19
Johnston, Joseph E., 28, 160, 161, 163–64
Jones, Madison, 174
Junior League, 44

K

Kantor, Elizabeth, 40
Keckley, Elizabeth, 131, 188–89
Keith, Toby, 41
Kentucky, 36, 37, 111–12

Kentucky Derby, 72
Kerry, John, 10, 234–35
Kershaw, Joseph, 177
The Killer Angels (Shaara), 154
King, Florence, 21
King, Martin Luther, Jr., 68
King, Rufus, 105, 116
KKK. *See* Ku Klux Klan
Krispy Kreme, 237
Ku Klux Klan (KKK), 37–38, 58, 165, 207

L

The Lady & Sons Savannah Country Cookbook (Deen), 44
Lang, Joel, 131
language, 31, 32–34
Lanterns on the Levee: Recollections of a Planter's Son (Percy), 121
The Late Unpleasantness. *See* War for Southern Independence
Laurel, Stan, 57
Laurel and Hardy, 57
Lee, Bill, 228
Lee, Fitzhugh, 210
Lee, Harper, 182
Lee, Richard Henry, 92
Lee, Robert E., 3, 51, 60, 61, 66, 71, 92, 139, 143, 158; Eisenhower, Dwight D. and, 224–26; secession and, 18–19; slavery and, 132; soldiers' religion and, 177; as Southern hero, 44–47, 213; surrender by, 149, 160–61; War for Southern Independence and, 144, 145, 157–61
The Lee Bros. Southern Cookbook (Lee and Lee), 44
Lee, Matt and Ted, 44
Lepore, Jill, 131
Letcher, John, 132
Levy, Buddy, 118
Lewis, Jerry Lee, 56
Lewis, Meriwether, 116, 117

Lexington, Va., 71
Limber, Jim, 187–88
Lincoln, Abraham, 128; assassination of, 164, 182, 199, 201; Black Hawk War and, 119–20; black inequality and, 172; civil rights and, 183–85; colonization of freed slaves and, 169, 181–83; compensated emancipation and, 142; Corwin Amendment and, 144; "Dixie" and, 49, 52; Emancipation Proclamation and, 169, 169–70, 185–87; Fort Sumter and, 18, 149–51, 156; Lee, Robert E. and, 45; Mexican War and, 121; Morrill Tariff and, 147; prisoners of war and, 190; Reconstruction and, 199–201, 202; secession and, 135, 138; slavery and, 146, 169; War for Southern Independence and, 146, 151–53, 155, 157, 169–70, 179
Lincoln, Mary Todd, 131, 178, 188–89
Lincoln, Robert, 188
Lincoln, Willie, 188
literature, Southern, 42, 237
Livingston, Robert R., 93
The Lonely Days Were Sundays: Reflections of a Jewish Southerner (Evans), 196
Long Gray Lines (Andrew, Jr.), 29
Longstreet, James, 158
Lost Colony, 79–81
Louisiana Purchase, 111, 115–17
Louisiana State University (LSU), 55–56
Lowe, Juliette Gordon, 73
Lowe's, 237
LSU. *See* Louisiana State University
Lumbee Indian tribe, 80–81
Lytle, Andrew Nelson, 207

M

MacArthur, Douglas, 220–21, 223
Madison, James, 104, 106–9, 114, 118, 231

Major Dundee, 109

manifest destiny, 120

Marion, Francis "the Swamp Fox," 98

Marr, John Quincy, 152

Marshall, George, 222–23, 228

Marshall, John, 109

Marshall Plan, 223

Marx, Karl, 176

Maryland, 107, 157

Mason, George, 93, 101, 107–8, 109, 114, 231

Massachusetts, 11, 78, 105

Massachusetts, University of, 51

Massachusetts Circular Letter, 97

Masters Golf Tournament, Augusta, Ga., 72–73

Mather, Cotton, 124

Mayberry, N.C., 43

Mayflower Society, 77

McClellan, George, 152–53, 158

McCullers, Carson, 182

McDowell, Irwin, 153

McGlone, John, 184

McGuire, Hunter, 60

McKinley, William, 209, 212, 214

McLuhan, Marshall, 191

Meade, George, 166

Mecklenburg Declaration, 92

men, Southern: gentility and good manners and, 238; *Gone with the Wind* and, 14–15; as handier, 9, 29

Mercedes, 237

Metcalfe, Gayden, 44

Mexican War, 27, 120, 121, 140–41, 231

Michelbacher, Max, 177

Middleton Plantation, S.C., 73

Miles, Nelson, 201

Miller, Adam, 175

The Mind of the South (Cash), 9–10

Miss America pageants, 25

Miss Congeniality, 26

Mississippi, 11, 36

Mississippi, University of, 56

Mitchell, Margaret, 14–15, 182

Monroe, James, 109

Montgomery, Ala., 138

Montgomery, Bernard, 224

Monticello, 235–36

Montpelier, 235

moonshine, 39–40, 42

Morehouse College, Ga., 206

Morgan, Daniel, 95–97

Morrill Tariff, 147

Mosby, John Singleton, 165–66, 227

Moses, Raphael Jacob, 177

Mount Rushmore, 59, 66

Mount Vernon, 62, 235

movie-making, 49, 57–58

"Mr. Madison's War." *See* War of 1812

"Mr. Polk's War." *See* Mexican War

Murphy, Audie, 32

Museum of the Confederacy, Va., 60, 63

music: bluegrass, 238; blues, 56–57, 71, 237; country, 40–41, 69–70, 237; gospel, 41; jazz, 56–57, 65, 71, 237; rock and roll, 56–57, 237

Myers, Abraham C., 177

Myne Owne Ground: Race and Freedom on Virginia's Eastern Shore, 1640–1676 (Breen and Innes), 124

N

Namath, Joe Willie, 53

Napoleon Bonaparte, 115

Narrative of the Life of Frederick Douglass, an American Slave (Douglass), 127

NASCAR. *See* National Association for Stock Car Auto Racing

Nashville 1864 (Jones), 174

National Association for Stock Car Auto Racing (NASCAR), 26, 41–43, 71–72

national bank, 10, 108

National Civil War Trust, 236
National Park Service, 63, 162, 191
New Hampshire, 11
New Jersey, 11
New Orleans, La., 13, 65, 71
New Smyrna, Fla., 85–86
Newsweek, 10
New York University, 51
New York Burning: Liberty, Slavery, and Conspiracy in Eighteenth-Century Manhattan (Lepore), 131
New York City, N.Y., 13, 123, 127
New York Times, 10, 180, 181
New York Tribune, 172, 186
Nimitz, Chester, 222
Nissan, 237
Nixon, Richard M., 69
Non Sum Qualis Eram Bonae sub Regno Cynarae (Dowson), 27
North: eating in, 34–35; Louisiana Purchase and, 111, 115–17; population of, 11–12; race relations in, 31, 37–39; religion and, 11, 21; slavery and, 101, 104–6, 123–24, 125–28; Southern opinion of, 10–11; unfriendliness in, 12–13; universities in, 51
North Carolina, 138; barbecue tradition in, 36; colonization of, 77; Constitution, U.S. and, 107; Regulator War of 1771 and, 87, 89–90; secession and, 18, 135
North Carolina, University of, Chapel Hill, 51, 52
Northwest Territories, 112–14

O

O'Connor, Flannery, 42, 57, 182
The Official Records of the War of the Rebellion, 154
Old South: erasing public memory of, 1, 3–4; symbols of, 28–29
Ole Miss, 56

Olive Branch Petition, 91
Olmsted, Frederick Law, 132
1001 Things Everyone Should Know about the South (Reed and Reed), 29
Orbison, Roy, 56
Ordinance of Secession, 136–37
The Outlaw Josey Wales, 69
Overmountain Men, 26, 95

P

Parks, Rosa, 67
Paterson, William, 105
patriotism, Southern, 59, 97–99, 221, 234–35
Patton, George S., Jr., 217, 222, 226–28
Patton, Tazewell, 226
Paul W. Bryant Museum, Ala., 68–69
Pearson, David, 41
Peckinpah, Sam, 109
Pember, Phoebe Yates, 197
Percy, Walker, 182
Percy, William Alexander, 121
Perkins, Carl, 56
Pershing, John J., 210, 217–19, 223
Petty, Richard, 41
Philadelphia, Pa., 13
Pickering, Chip, 19
Pickering, Thomas, 116
Piedmont Airlines, 17
Pinckney, Charles, 104, 105, 109
Pius IX, 63, 192–93
Poe, Edgar Allan, 182
The Politically Incorrect Guide™ to English and American Literature (Kantor), 40
Polk, James K., 121
Polk, Leonidas, 193–94, 233
Pollard, Edward, 185
Ponce de León, Juan, 78–79
Post, Emily, 14
Preservation Hall, 65
Presley, Elvis, 56, 69
Princeton University, 15

Pulitzer, Joseph, 209
Puller, Lewis "Chesty," 221

R

race relations, 31, 37–39, 236
racism: Davis, Jefferson and, 187–89;
  Reconstruction and, 232; South and,
  11
Radcliff, 51
Radical Republicans, 164; Reconstruc-
  tion and, 204–7
Rains, Gabriel, 158
Rains, George Washington, 20
Raleigh, Sir Walter, 79–80
Randolph, George, 158
Randolph, John, 89
Rangel, Charles, 19
Ransom, Roger, 200
Reconstruction: black education and,
  206; Confederate treason and, 199,
  201–2; education, Southern and, 206;
  Johnson, Andrew and, 202, 203–4;
  KKK and, 38; Lincoln, Abraham and,
  199–201, 202; racism and, 232; Radi-
  cal Republicans and, 204–5, 206, 207;
  segregation and, 206–7, 232; slavery
  and, 204; South, rebuilding and,
  202–6; vote, right to and, 205–6
Reed, Dale Volberg, 29
Reed, John Shelton, 29
Reed, Walter, 211
Regulator War of 1771, 87, 89–90
religion: North and, 11, 21; South and,
  3, 236–37
The Religious Instruction of Negroes,
  129–30
Republicans, Radical, 164
Requiem for a Nun (Faulkner), 61
Revenue Act, 89
Revolutionary War. *See* American Rev-
  olution
Rhett, Robert Barnwell, 185
Rice University, 52

Richard, Little, 57
Richardson, J. P. "The Big Bopper," 56
Richmond, Va., 138–39
Richmond Examiner, 185
Rickenbacker, Eddie, 218
Ride with the Devil, 94
Ridgeway, Matthew, 228
Rio Grande, 109
River Road Recipes (Junior League of
  Baton Rouge), 44
Robert E. Lee on Leadership (Crocker
  III), 153
Robert E. Lee (Tate), 166
Robertson, John, 195
Robertson Hospital, 195–97
Rockefeller, John D., Jr., 63
Roosevelt, Theodore, 139, 209, 211;
  Confederate symbols and, 212–14
Rosenburg, R. B., 184
Rough Riders, 209, 210, 211
Ryan, Abram, 194

S

Salem College, N.C., 51
Saturn, 237
Savannah, Ga., 70
Saxton, Rufus, 170–71
Schecter, Barnet, 192
Schimmelfennig, Alexander, 176
Scott, Robert Lee, 220
Scott, Winfield, 45, 118, 121, 150
SEC. *See* Southeastern Conference
secession: Confederacy and, 138; Con-
  stitution, U.S. and, 136–37, 199,
  201–2; Declaration of Independence
  and, 136; as economic issue, 139–43;
  Lincoln, Abraham and, 135, 138; rea-
  sons for, 135–47; War for Southern
  Independence and, 18–19, 135–47.
  See also Confederacy; War for South-
  ern Independence
Second American Revolution. *See* War
  for Southern Independence

Index

Segars, J. H., 184
segregation: of armed forces, 199; Reconstruction and, 206–7, 232; in South, 38, 199
Seranne, Ann, 44
Seward, William, 143
Shaara, Jeff, 154
Shaara, Michael, 154
Shadows-on the Teche, La., 73
Shays, Daniel, 103
Sheridan, Philip, 155
Sherman, John, 147
Sherman, Roger, 105
Sherman, William Tecumseh, 28, 147, 149, 153, 155–57, 163, 166–68, 170–71, 200
She Wore a Yellow Ribbon, 109
Shiloh, Tenn., 65
Sigel, Franz, 176
slavery: colonial era and, 81–84; colonization of freed slaves and, 169, 181–83; compensated emancipation and, 141–42; Constitution, U.S. and, 104–6, 119, 139–40, 144, 199; Declaration of Independence and, 93; education, Southern and, 131–32; Emancipation Proclamation and, 169, 199; Lincoln, Abraham and, 146, 169; North and, 101, 104–6, 123–24; Reconstruction and, 204; slave trade and, 123, 125–28; slave treatment and, 123, 128–33; in South, 101, 104–6, 123–34, 232; War for Southern Independence and, 135, 135–36, 139–45, 169–70
Smalls, Robert, 206
Smith, Fred, 238
Snowden, Ben and Lou, 50
Song of the South, 117, 234
Soodalter, Ron, 131
South: American Revolution and, 1, 87, 231; climate of, 9, 12, 29; colonial history and, 77–86; common ancestry in, 1–2, 9; creative atmosphere in, 237–38; defining characteristics of, 1, 2, 31–47; economic growth in, 1, 2, 237; as elitist, 39–40; generosity of, 11; government, U.S. and, 101–9; heroes of, 44–47; historic locations in, 60–70; Jewish communities in, 176–78; language in, 31, 32–34; men of, 9, 14–15, 29, 238; mentality of, 10, 13, 41, 43, 210; movie-making in, 49, 57–58; music in, 40–41, 56–57, 65, 69–70, 71, 237–38; Northern opinion of, 9–11, 59–60; patriotism in, 59, 97–99, 221, 234–35; population of, 1, 2–3, 11–12, 23; race relations in, 31, 37–39, 236; Reconstruction and, 2, 199–207, 232; religion and, 3, 236–37; segregation in, 38, 199, 206–7; slavery in, 81–84, 101, 104–6, 123–34, 232; sports in, 23–26, 41–43, 71–73; things you don't know about, 49–58; universities in, 50–56; U.S. history in, 77–86; westward expansion and, 111–14, 115–17, 120–22; women of, 9, 14–15, 25, 29, 238–39; World War I and, 217, 218–19; World War II and, 217, 219–29. *See also* culture, Southern; education, Southern; War for Southern Independence
South, University of, Tenn., 233
South Carolina: barbecue tradition in, 36; colonization of, 77; Constitution, U.S. and, 107
Southeastern Conference (SEC), 53
Southern by the Grace of God (Grizzard), 29
The Southern Junior League Cookbook (Seranne), 44
Southern Ladies and Gentlemen (King), 21
Southern Living magazine, 44
"A Southern Mode of the Imagination" (Tate), 41

"The Southern Quality" (McLuhan), 191

The Southern Tradition at Bay: A History of Postbellum Thought (Weaver), 67, 129

A Southern Woman's Story (Yates), 197

Spanish-American War, 209–11, 211–12, 217, 218

sports: college, 23–24; culture, Southern and, 23–26; golf, 72–73; hockey, 24; horse racing, 72; stock car racing, 24, 26, 41–43, 71–72

Sprague, William, 181

Spruance, Raymond, 222

Stagville Plantation, N.C., 28

Stamp Act of 1765, 87

Stanton, Edwin, 155, 156–57, 164, 167–68, 181, 190

state sovereignty, 102

states' rights, 138, 145–47

St. Augustine, Fla., 85–86

Stephens, Alexander, 199

Stevens, Thaddeus, 203

Stilwell, Joseph W., 220

stock car racing, 24, 26, 41–43, 71–72

Stone Mountain, Ga., 59, 68

Stonewall Jackson: The Black Man's Friend (Williams Jr.), 155

Stonewall Jackson: The Good Soldier (Tate), 173

Stowe, Harriet Beecher, 138, 142–43

Stratford Hall Plantation, 63

Stuart, James Ewell Brown "Jeb," 60, 221; as Southern hero, 44, 45, 46–47

Suffolk Resolves of 1774, 90–91

symbols: Confederate flag, 3, 56, 59, 212–14, 233; of culture, Southern, 28–29; of Old South, 28–29

T

Taft, William Howard, 214

Taney, Roger B., 184

Tariff of Abominations, 147

Tarleton, Banastre, 96–97

Tate, Allen, 41, 166, 173

Taylor, John M., 161

Taylor, Maxwell, 228

Taylor, Richard, 121, 204

Taylor, Zachary, 121

Tennessee, 36, 135, 138

Texas: barbecue tradition in, 36, 37; secession and, 18, 140–41; War for Southern Independence and, 180–81

Texas, University of, Austin, 52

Texas v. *White*, 201–2

Thirteenth Amendment, 144, 199, 204, 205

Time magazine, 9, 32–34

Tippin, Aaron, 41

Tobacco: A Cultural History of How an Exotic Plant Seduced Civilization (Gately), 113

Tomb of the Unknown Soldier, 61

Tompkins, Sally, 195–97

Toole, John Kennedy, 182

Toyota, 237

Treaty of Paris (1784), 101, 136

Truman, Harry S., 206

Trump, Donald, 16

Tryon, William, 89

Tulane University, 52

Turchin, John, 157

Turnbull, Andrew, 84–86

Turner, Curtis, 41

Turner, Nat, 131, 144–45

Tuskegee Institute, Alabama, 18, 206

Twain, Mark, 13, 45, 73, 141, 182

U

UDC. *See* United Daughters of the Confederacy

Uncle Tom's Cabin (Stowe), 138, 142–43

The Undefeated, 109

Underground Railroad, 21